A Garland of Jewels

༄༅། །ཤ་ལ་མ་ཆི་བ་མ་ཚད་ལྗི་ཀོ་གར་ཁོ་ཅེ་ཁེ་ཇུ་མི་ལ་ཁ།

A GARLAND *of* JEWELS
The Eight Great Bodhisattvas

by Jamgön Mipham
translated by Yeshe Gyamtso

KTD Publications

Published by:
KTD Publications
335 Meads Mountain Road
Woodstock, NY 12498, USA
www.KTDPublications.org

Distributed by:
www.NamseBangdzo.com

ISBN 978-1-934608-03-6
Printed in the United States on acid-free paper.

Contents

Foreword

Khenpo Karthar Rinpoche

This account of the Buddha's great regents, the eight bodhisattvas, the eight great heart-sons, was composed by Jamgön Mipham Rinpoche. He was Manjushri appearing in our decadent age as a human spiritual friend. Lama Yeshe has translated it into English, and my devoted disciple Maureen McNicholas and others have worked together to publish it. I rejoice in this from the depths of my heart. May all who read this book achieve liberation and omniscience.

Written with respect by Karthar, who is called "Khenpo."

Jamgön Mipham Rinpoche

Introduction

Yeshe Gyamtso

This book is a translation of a collection of stories about the eight great bodhisattvas. These stories are all taken from sutras and tantras taught by the buddha, such as the *Avatamsaka Sutra* and the *Lotus Sutra*. They were collected and edited by the great Buddhist teacher Mipham Namgyal.

Mipham was born to a noble family in 1846 in eastern Tibet. From early childhood he demonstrated extraordinary intelligence, and wrote a number of treatises before the age of ten. At twelve, he became a monk at a branch monastery of the great Nyingma seat Shechen.

At fifteen, he began an eighteen-month retreat, during which he meditated on and accomplished the bodhisattva Manjushri. After completing this retreat, he had the ability to understand any sutra, tantra, or shastra just by reading it once. He continued to meditate on the many forms of Manjushri throughout the rest of his life, and composed many liturgies to support such meditations.

Mipham embodied the nonsectarian movement of the nineteenth century, and studied with masters of all schools of Tibetan Buddhism. His root guru was the nonsectarian master Jamyang Khyentse Wangpo. His other teachers included both Jamgön Lodrö Thaye and Dza Paltrul Rinpoche.

Mipham was one of the greatest teachers of his time, and is

considered to have been an emanation of Manjushri. His writings remain the basis for much of the study conducted by his own tradition, the Nyingma school of Buddhism, and by other traditions such as the Karma Kagyu. He passed away in 1912.[1]

In writing his book, Mipham combined edited extracts from his sources with his own writing about his subject. He wove the two together so skillfully that it is often not immediately obvious where the extract ends and his comments begin. Often he summarized long passages. He also omitted some of the sutras' didactic material in order to emphasize the stories he wanted to tell. Although we typically think of Buddhist sutras as teachings accompanied by sparing narrative, we discover in this book that the great sutras of the mahayana are repositories of extraordinary accounts of miracles and great deeds performed by buddhas and bodhisattvas.

In his afterword Mipham wrote that his purpose in writing his book was to provide inspiration. The purpose of these stories is to inspire us to emulate these great bodhisattvas and give us confidence in the effectiveness of the mahayana path. The reader is asked to open his or her mind to the vastness and profundity of the mahayana. The miracles described here are often outrageous in their transgression of what we regard as laws of nature. This is very much to the point. It seems that there is no way to enter the mahayana without being open to the inconceivable.

We have translated and published this book so that readers who might otherwise never have the opportunity to experience the tremendous richness of the mahayana sutras will have the opportunity to do so. In order to make this translation accessible to readers, many of the less-known proper names have been translated into English. Names well known to English-speaking Buddhists have been given in Sanskrit.

We often meditate on and pray to these bodhisattvas without much understanding of who and what they are. Although

1. An excellent biography of Mipham by his disciple Khenpo Kunpal has been translated by John Pettit and included in his *Mipham's Beacon of Certainty* (Wisdom Publications, 1999).

to fully understand bodhisattvas you have to be one, the stories in this book do communicate the particular activity and deeds for which these eight bodhisattvas are renowned, allowing us a glimpse into their world: a world of freedom, compassion, and wisdom far beyond ordinary experience.

Yeshe Gyamtso

His Holiness the Seventeenth Karmapa, Ogyen Trinley Dorje,
Karma Triyana Dharmachakra, May 2008

This translation is dedicated to Ogyen Trinley Dorje,
the Seventeenth Gyalwang Karmapa.

"May I and all others become just like
The eight great heart-sons in their bodhichitta,
Deeds, aspirations, wisdom, love, capability,
And unsurpassable miracles of primordial wisdom."

— *Jamgön Mipham Rinpoche*

THE EIGHT GREAT BODHISATTVAS

ཨོཾ། ཁམས་གསུམ་སེམས་ཅན་ཐམས་ཅད་ཀྱི་དོན་དུ་རྟོགས་ཏེ་ཆོས་ཉིད་དུ་ལྷུན་གྱིས་གྲུབ་ལ།

THE YOUTHFUL MANJUSHRI

འཇམ་དཔལ་གཞོན་ནུ།

I PROSTRATE TO THE YOUTHFUL MANJUSHRI,[2] THE BODHISATTVA MAHASATTVA! I VENERATE YOU! I TAKE REFUGE IN YOU!

This protector, this lord of wisdom, is the single body of the utterly nonconceptual primordial awareness of all buddhas of the three times. He will abide in the form of a bodhisattva for as long as space and the dharmadhatu remain. To some, he appears as a buddha, all of whose qualities are complete. To some, he appears as the foremost son of the victors. To some, he appears as a trainee on the path whose qualities are incomplete. To some, he appears as an ordinary being. Through various deeds he performs all the functions of all victors and all their children, and enters all the realms of beings. His deeds are inconceivable.

Therefore in the *Sutra of Heroic Samadhi* it is taught that he has already achieved buddhahood. In the *Sutra for the Benefit of Angulimala* it is taught that he is living as a buddha now. In the *Sutra of the Array of Manjushri's Realm* it is taught that innumerable kalpas from now he will demonstrate buddhahood as the protector All-Seeing. Although he demonstrates the various deeds of both a buddha and a bodhisattva, he is without decrease or increase. With a wisdom body that is like

2. Manjushri has many names, some of which are explained later in this chapter. *Manjushri* means "gentle splendor." *Manjughosha*, another of his names, means "gentle melody." Manjushri is said to be called "youthful" because he first appeared to the sangha in the form of a youth, and because he embodies timeless and therefore ever-youthful primordial awareness.

space, he engages in a variety of deeds equal to the number of beings.

From the *Secret Tantra of Manjushri*

> I appeared in the past.
> I appeared before all buddhas.
> I will appear in the future.
> I appear in the present.

And:

> My body appears in the three times.
> When all the teachings have vanished
> My teachings will appear.

> All that is peaceful
> Is my peaceful body.
> All that is wrathful
> Is my wrathful body.

I will therefore summarize and clarify some of the deeds of the youthful Manjushri as they are found in the perfect words of the tathagata.

From the *Mahayana Sutra of the Noble Source of the Three Jewels*

The bodhisattva All-Overpowering asked, "Bhagavat, the youthful Manjushri abides within the dharmadhatu and teaches dharma without attachment. How much time has passed since the youthful Manjushri first entered the dharmadhatu?"[3]

The bhagavat replied, "Billions and billions of buddhas who have passed into parinirvana were established in unsurpassed awakening by the youthful Manjushri. All of them have passed into parinirvana in utterly pure realms.

3. The epithet *bhagavat* is used in this book as a form of address referring to buddhas. It may be translated as "blessed conqueror" indicating that buddhas have overcome all that is to be overcome and attained all that is to be attained. Here it is used to refer to the historical buddha, Buddha Shakyamuni.

"Once, a number of kalpas ago that is immeasurable, innumerable, inconceivable, incomparable, and indescribable, there appeared in the world a buddha called Glorious Wisdom.

"Long before that appeared a tathagata called Source of Wisdom.

"Long before that appeared a tathagata called Highest Wisdom.

"Long before that appeared a tathagata called Sight of Wisdom.

"Long before that appeared a tathagata called Conduct of Wisdom.

"Long before that appeared a tathagata called Treasury of Wisdom.

"Long before that appeared a tathagata called Source of Wisdom.

"Long before that appeared a tathagata called Glorious Wisdom.

"Long before that appeared a tathagata called Lion's Roar.

"Long before that appeared a tathagata called All-Controlling Lion.

"Long before that appeared a tathagata called Intelligent Lion.

"Long before that appeared a tathagata called Conquering Power.

"Long before that appeared a tathagata called Holder of Strength.

"Long before that appeared a tathagata called Piled Essence of Splendor.

"Long before that appeared a tathagata called Complete Conquest.

"Long before that appeared a tathagata called King of Supreme Joy.

"Long before that appeared a tathagata called All-Surpassing Strength.

"Long before that appeared a tathagata called Conduct
of Utter Peace.

"Long before that appeared a tathagata called King
of Peaks of Peaceful Light-Rays.

"Long before that appeared a tathagata called
Boundless Intelligence.

"Long before that appeared a tathagata called Boundless
Taming.

"Long before that appeared a tathagata called Lotus Peak.

"Long before that appeared a tathagata called Immaculate
Countenance.

"Long before that appeared a tathagata called Moonlight.

"Long before that appeared a tathagata called Immaculate
Light-Rays.

"Long before that appeared a tathagata called Excellent
Conqueror of All Fears.

"Long before that appeared a tathagata called Radiant.

"Long before that appeared a tathagata called
Overpowers All.

"Long before that appeared a tathagata called Bearer
of Amrita.

"Long before that appeared a tathagata called
Famous Amrita.

"Long before that appeared a tathagata called
Immaculate Eyes.

"Long before that appeared a tathagata called Irreversible.

"Long before that appeared a tathagata called
Immaculate Vision.

"Long before that appeared a tathagata called King
of Supreme Fragrance.

"Long before that appeared a tathagata called Glorious
Supreme Fragrance.

"Long before that appeared a tathagata called King
of Fragrance.

"Long before that appeared a tathagata called Incense
of Intelligence.

"Long before that appeared a tathagata called Utpala Eyes.[4]

"Long before that appeared a tathagata called Eyes
 of Boundless Light.

"Long before that appeared a tathagata called Tames
 All Enemies.

"Long before that appeared a tathagata called Manifestly
 Superior Ornamental King of Mountains.

"Long before that appeared a tathagata called
 Brahma Peak.

"Long before that appeared a tathagata called Protected
 by Brahma.

"Long before that there appeared in a single kalpa and world sixty thousand buddhas. The first of them was called Light. The last of them was the tathagata Famous Light.

"Long before that forty million buddhas appeared in the world. The first of them was the tathagata Dipankara. The last was the tathagata Eyes of Awareness.

"Long before that ninety million buddhas appeared in a single kalpa. The first of them was the tathagata Blissful Eyes. The last was the tathagata Discerns with Discernment.

"Long before that the tathagata Supreme Joy appeared in the world. In that buddha's realm he was accompanied by the great bodhisattvas Given Fame, Heroic Skill, Eye of Brahma, Sandalwood, Utterly Beautiful, Lion Holder, All-Beautiful, Boundless Confidence, Considerable Intelligence, Certainty, and Easy Company. All eleven of them possessed millions of pleasant qualities and abided in chastity.

"At that time lived a brahmin called Given by the Sun, who was as upright as a great sal-tree. He was learned, sharp minded, and intelligent. Accompanied by about five hundred other brahmins, he came out of the town called Jewel and went to a park called Various Delights. He observed the eleven bodhisattvas seated there and regarded them with awe.

4. An utpala is a type of lotus flower that blooms every hundred years.

"The holy being Given Fame looked upon the demeanor of the rishi Given by the Sun and thought, 'This holy being is a vessel for unsurpassable awakening!' He said to the other ten holy beings, 'Venerable ones! This Given by the Sun has the bearing of a son of the buddhas. He will become a vessel for the unsurpassable buddhadharmas. If he receives kind instruction, he will benefit many beings and be a source of illumination. Think well about this!'

"The brahmin Given by the Sun approached the eleven holy beings and prostrated to them as teachers. He remained standing to one side in an attitude of immense respect and joy. The son of family Given Fame taught Given by the Sun about the rarity of buddhas in the world and the difficulty of realizing their profound dharma, which transcends all worlds.[5] He taught him their dharma, the inexpressible, unborn, and unceasing nature of all dharmas. Like a drawing in space, dharmas have never arisen; do not arise; and will never arise. All the brahmins were delighted and perfected the profound buddhadharmas.[6]

"The brahmin Given by the Sun and the eleven holy beings entered the presence of the tathagata Supreme Joy. They prostrated to him and remained at one side. They heard from that tathagata the dharma of the common characteristic of all dharmas, which is their lack of characteristics. The brahmin Given by the Sun gained the power of virtue. He rose to the height of seven palm trees in the sky and saw innumerable worlds in the realms of the ten directions. He saw innumerable bodhisattvas in them perfectly engaged in various skillful means. He also saw innumerable bodhisattvas appear to pass away in Tushita, enter the womb, achieve buddhahood, and pass into nirvana.[7]

"With a mind filled with the utmost delight, the brahmin Given by the Sun praised the buddha Supreme Joy in meaningful verse. The virtue of his doing so ensured that for innumerable kalpas he would never become insane or stupid; that wherever he was born he would remain a great being; that he would never fall into perversity; never need to depend on others; never need to depend on pleasing others; and never fail to fully ripen beings even during the duration of a finger snap.

"The son of family Given Fame is now the son of family Guardian of Goodness. The brahmin Given by the Sun is the youthful Manjushri. In that way, if a bodhisattva wants to never need to depend on others, never need to be led by others, and never need to depend on pleasing others, that bodhisattva should rely upon, consider, and serve spiritual friends in order to fully enter into the dharmadhatu. In order to hear profound dharma, bodhisattvas should be thoroughly inquisitive."

From the *Mahayana Sutra of Heroic Samadhi*

Amidst the buddha's retinue were two hundred adherents of the bodhisattvayana who became discouraged, thinking, "Omniscience is hard to attain. We shall pass into parinirvana through the pratyekabuddhayana."[8]

In order to subdue them, the youthful Manjushri said to the bhagavat, "In the past occurred the kalpa called Complete Radiance. During that kalpa I passed into parinirvana three hundred and sixty sextillion times through the pratyekabuddhayana."[9]

That retinue doubted this. Shariputra asked the bhagavat, "Since there is no continuation after nirvana, how could this be possible?"

The tathagata replied, "Ask Manjushri. He will tell you."

Shariputra asked Manjushri, "How are we to understand what you said?"

---

system of one billion worlds or more. A buddha realm is the field of activity of any one buddha; it may coincide with one world realm, but may also be far more extensive.

8. There are three vehicles or spiritual approaches in the Buddhism of the sutras. These are the shravakayana, the vehicle of the hearers; the pratyekabuddhayana, the vehicle of the solitary awakened ones; and the bodhisattvayana, the vehicle of the bodhisattvas or "heroes of awakening." According to the sutras of the bodhisattvayana (often called "mahayana" or "great vehicle"), only the bodhisattvayana leads to full buddhahood, often referred to in this book as "omniscience."

9. As used in the U.S. and in the international scientific community, a sextillion is 1,000,000,000,000,000,000,000. As large numbers such as this occur frequently in this book, they will be defined in subsequent notes by their number of zeros. For example, a sextillion has twenty-one zeros.

Manjushri replied, "The omniscient tathagata is my witness. Were I to declare otherwise I would be lying to the tathagata. During the kalpa of Complete Radiance a sambuddha called Victor appeared.[10] He passed into parinirvana, but his holy dharma lasted for a hundred thousand years. After its disappearance, the beings there came under the power of conditions and could only be tamed by the demeanor of a pratyekabuddha. Even had a hundred or a thousand buddhas taught them they would have been uninterested; they were only interested in pratyekabuddhas. At the time there were no pratyekabuddhas to receive their offerings, so I declared myself to be a pratyekabuddha in order to ripen those beings. Wherever I went — villages, palaces, and towns — I was perceived as a pratyekabuddha. I displayed the appearance and demeanor of a pratyekabuddha. Those beings respected, served, and supported me. As they gradually became vessels, I taught them dharma. I rose into the sky like the king of geese. They gained faith and made the aspiration to pursue the path leading to such miracles. In such ways I fully ripened the virtues of many beings.

"When I felt that those beings had become tired of supporting me, I caused the words, 'It is time for me to enter nirvana' to be heard. Those beings came to me, carrying various offerings. I entered an absorption in which all perception and sensation ceased, and passed into parinirvana through the force of aspiration. They cremated my body and placed my ashes in a stupa built for that purpose. They venerated my remains and believed that I had passed into nirvana.

"In such a way I passed into parinirvana through the pratyekabuddhayana three hundred and sixty sextillion times during that intermediate kalpa, at the royal palace and elsewhere. By doing so I tamed thirty-six million beings by means of the pratyekabuddhayana. Although I passed into parinirvana through the pratyekabuddhayana, I never passed into complete parinirvana."

10. The terms *sambuddha*, "pefect buddha"; *samyaksambuddha*, "completely perfect buddha"; *tathagata*, "thus-gone"; *sugata*, "blissfully gone"; *jina*, or "victor"; and *buddha*, or "awakened one" are synonyms in this book.

Note however that pratyekabuddhas are not buddhas; they are *arhats* or "foe destroyers" and have achieved liberation but not omniscience.

When Manjushri said this, the great earth shook six times and became filled with a great light. The devas cast down a rain of flowers in order to venerate him. They also proclaimed the wondrousness of dharma. Those devas exclaimed, "By seeing the tathagata and the youthful Manjushri, and by hearing of his heroic samadhi, we have attained that which is well attained!"

They then asked the bhagavat, "If Manjushri possesses such inconceivably wondrous dharmas, through what samadhi does he display them?"

The bhagavat replied, "He displays such wondrous dharmas while abiding in the heroic samadhi. While abiding in this samadhi, he has conformed to others' faith. He has been an arhat and a pratyekabuddha, and has displayed all their deeds up to parinirvana, but he does not abide in parinirvana, and continues to display various births."

The great elder Mahakashyapa then said to the buddha, "According to my understanding of what the tathagata has said, I think that this youthful Manjushri has performed the deeds of a buddha in the past, has shown the heart of awakening, has turned the dharmachakra, and has demonstrated parinirvana."

The buddha replied, "It is so. In the past, innumerable, more than innumerable, immeasurable, and more than immeasurable kalpas ago, to the south of this buddha realm, three thousand buddha realms distant, was a world called Equality. It was even and smooth, without mountains, rocks, or precipices. In that world appeared the bhagavat tathagata Supreme Family of Nagas. He lived for forty thousand years and ripened seventy million beings through the bodhisattvayana; eighty million through the shravakayana; and one hundred million, ninety-six thousand through the pratyekabuddhayana. Eventually, the sangha of the shravakas of that tathagata became immeasurable. Having benefited the worlds of devas and humans, he passed into parinirvana. His relics increased. The stupas containing them were thirty-six million. Beings there venerated them, and his dharma lasted for a hundred thousand years.

"That tathagata predicted, 'After my passing, the bodhisattva Wisdom Light will become a buddha. He will become the tathagata Wisdom Light.'

"That tathagata Supreme Family of Nagas is now the youthful Manjushri. Look at the power of his heroic samadhi! Although he demonstrated the deeds of a buddha, from entering the womb up to buddhahood and nirvana, he never cast aside the nature of a bodhisattva and never completely passed into parinirvana."

Mahakashyapa then said to Manjushri, "It must be difficult for you to demonstrate such inconceivable deeds!"

Manjushri replied, "All dharmas are fabricated by causes and conditions, and are without self. Therefore one can accomplish whatever one wants to. For someone who has seen the truth, there is no difficulty in this whatsoever."

From the *Sutra for the Benefit of Angulimala*

To the south of our realm is a world called Adorned by All Jewels. In that realm presently lives the tathagata arhat samyaksambuddha Delightful to See for All the World, Superior Great Vigor. He was Angulimala.[11] All the beings in that buddha's realm are free from aging, sickness, and all other discomfort. Their life span and splendor are immeasurable.

To the north of our realm is a world called Always Utter Joy, Delight, and Enthusiasm. In that realm presently lives the tathagata arhat samyaksambuddha Heart of Enthusiastic

11. Angulimala was a famous disciple of Buddha Shakyamuni. Before meeting the buddha, Angulimala had killed nine hundred and ninety-nine people and wore a finger from each of his victims on a necklace. His name means "finger garland." In spite of his previous wrongdoing, Angulimala achieved liberation and, according to the sutra quoted here, went on to achieve buddhahood.

Utter Delight, King of Piled Jewels, who is teaching dharma now. He is the youthful Manjushri. In that buddha's realm there are no shravakas or pratyekabuddhas. There is no suffering, such as that of aging and sickness. All the beings there possess all manner of happiness. Their life span and splendor are immeasurable.

Whoever hears or continually prostrates to the names of Angulimala or Manjushri will see the world Delight in their own home. The door to the four bad rebirths will be closed.[12] The door to the four bad rebirths will be closed for anyone who hears their names, even if they are an outsider, a defeated person, or someone who has performed actions of uninterrupted consequence, and even if they denigrate those names, disregard them, forget them, or merely repeat them after others or for the sake of gain or praise.

Any son or daughter of family who is guarded by these two names will be protected from all danger even in the wilderness. They will not be assailed by devas, nagas, yakshas, carnivores, or any predator.

From the *Compassionate White Lotus*

Assembly of the Powerful, the third son of King Nemi, said to the tathagata Ratnagarbha, "I will create a pure realm, and will not quickly attain buddhahood. For as long as I engage in the deeds of a bodhisattva, may I see all of the buddhas of the infinite worlds in the ten directions. May I first cause all beings to generate bodhichitta, and then establish them in the paramitas. May I witness their individual attainment of buddhahood, as numerous as the particles in all the infinite realms.

"May I perform the deeds of a buddha. May all the beings born in my pure realm be like devas of Brahma's realm. May my realm maintain an array of qualities equal to those of as

12. The four bad rebirths are rebirth as a hell being, a preta (hungry ghost), an animal, or an asura (jealous god). The five actions of immediate consequence are matricide, patricide, to kill an arhat, to draw blood from the body of a buddha with malicious intent, and to cause a fundamental schism in the sangha. These actions gain their collective name from the fact that their severity causes the person who commits any of them to be reborn in the worst of hells immediately after this life.

many buddha realms as there are grains of sand in the Ganges rivers of a billion worlds. May the wall around my realm reach the peak of existence. May it be made of jewels and adorned by jewels. May the ground of my realm be made entirely of beryl, and be free from dust and other pollution. May there be no eight leisureless states, no suffering, no imposition of discipline, and no need to arise from downfall in my realm. May there be not even the names of shravakas, pratyekabuddhas, or beings with kleshas there. May there be no need for food there; may all possess the food of joy and the food of dharma. May my realm be populated only by miraculously born bodhisattvas in their final life who abide in utter chastity and have pure intentions. May they all cut their hair and beards, and wear saffron dharma robes. From birth, may their bodies emit great radiance.

"May they hold precious begging bowls filled with delicious food of many flavors. Although we who live there do not eat food, may we offer it to buddhas and their retinues in other worlds and donate it to beings. As soon as we think of doing so, may we achieve samadhis of inconceivable deeds, and go without impediment to infinite realms in the ten directions. May we delightedly offer that food to buddhas, shravakas, and beings. May we talk of dharma, and then return that same morning to our own buddha realm. May we do the same thing with precious robes. May the bodhisattvas of my realm share all their possessions with buddhas, shravakas, and other beings, and only thereafter use them themselves.

"May that realm be decorated by millions of luminous jewels. May it possess features unseen and unheard of anywhere throughout the ten directions. May merely saying the name of something cause it to appear and remain in that realm without exhaustion for a million years. May any substance, such as gold, silver, crystal, or beryl, appear upon being wanted. May these appear only to those who wish for them. In that way, may any possession or article of use appear according to one's wish.

"Although there will be no sun or moon in my realm, may its bodhisattvas radiate such light that they be able to illuminate ten sextillion buddha realms. Other than the opening and closing of lotuses, may there be not even the name of day and night in that realm. Other than when the bodhisattvas of my realm pass away in Tushita in order to achieve buddhahood in other realms, may there be no passing out of my realm and rebirth in another realm. May there be no heat, cold, sickness, aging, dying, or death. May all in that realm pass into the parinirvana of unsurpassable awakening in the sky, like the tathagatas. From the sky's midst may the sound of a million cymbals resonate with the sound of the paramitas, the three jewels, and the bodhisattvapitaka. May only the sounds wished for arise. May sounds that cause attachment never be heard.

"May there be no supreme mountain, no perimeter, no mountains of particles, no great oceans, and no ordinary trees in my realm. May it contain various trees far surpassing those of devas. May it be filled with mandarava and great mandarava flowers like those of devas. May their fragrance never decay, but fill that realm with a vast variety of fine scents.

"May all the arrays of qualities of infinite, innumerable buddha realms in the ten directions, and all their adornments, characteristics, wonders, and aspirations, be present in mine, excepting the arrays of shravakas, pratyekabuddhas, and five-fold degeneration.[13]

"When, having accomplished the deeds of a bodhisattva, I create my realm, may all those bodhisattvas established by me in the initial generation of bodhichitta and in the paramitas be born there. May this buddha realm here be included within mine. May all suffering here be pacified.

13. Fivefold degeneration is the degeneration of beings' life span, emotions, physical bodies, views, and times (in the sense of "the times we live in").

"May I attain buddhahood in that realm in front of a tree of awakening called Lustrous. May it be composed of seven types of jewels. May its trunk's thickness be that of ten thousand four-continent worlds. May its branches cover an area equal to ten billion worlds. May its fragrance and light fill all buddha realms. In front of that tree may there be a vajra seat adorned by various jewels and called Perfect Immersion in the Shade That Reveals the Wisdom of Utter Peace. May that seat cover an area equal to five four-continent worlds. May its height be four hundred thousand yojanas.[14] Having crossed my legs on that seat, may I immediately achieve buddhahood. May I remain on that seat, without uncrossing my legs or arising, until my parinirvana. Remaining there, may I emanate buddhas and bodhisattvas throughout innumerable buddha realms. May each of those buddhas place innumerable beings in unsurpassable awakening every morning. May those emanated bodhisattvas perform the deeds of a bodhisattva. May my body appear in innumerable realms in the ten directions. May all who see it be certain to achieve unsurpassable awakening. May all those beings be inseparable from buddhas until they achieve unsurpassable awakening and nirvana. May they always possess complete faculties.

"May any bodhisattva who wishes to see me be able to do so immediately upon giving rise to that wish no matter where they are. As soon as they see me seated in front of my tree of awakening, may they become free from any doubt about dharma. May they seek what has not yet been taught.

"May the number and life span of the beings in my realm be immeasurable. May they be beyond the estimation of anyone other than those with omniscient wisdom. From the time of my buddhahood until my parinirvana may none of the beings in my realm have long hair or wear white clothing. May they all cut their hair, wear saffron robes, and possess the complexion and demeanor of renunciates."

14. According to the abhidharma, a yojana is approximately five miles.

In response to his aspiration, the tathagata Ratnagarbha said, "Holy being, excellent! You are wise and lucid. You possess qualities and wisdom. Your aspiration for beings' benefit is excellent. It is auspicious with the supremacy of your intellect. May you, who have undertaken the supreme qualities of all buddha realms, be known as Manjushri. Manjushri, in the future, after twice as many innumerable kalpas as there are grains of sand in the Ganges River, and at the beginning of a third series, you will become the tathagata arhat samyaksambuddha All-Seeing in the southern realm Perfect Accumulation Without Particles, which will include this world of Saha.[15]

"All of the aspirations you have made as a bodhisattva will be achieved. You will therefore possess the virtues of billions of buddhas. You will be like medicine for beings. Your wishes will be fulfilled. You will conquer all kleshas and spread all virtues."

From the "Array of the Qualities of Manjushri's Realm," the fifteenth chapter of the *Ratnakutasutra*

The bhagavat said, "A very long time ago, as many kalpas ago as there are grains of sand in seven hundred thousand decillion Ganges Rivers, there was to the east of here a world called Good Elements.[16] In that realm, the tathagata King of Thunder's Melody attained buddhahood and taught dharma. At that time, Manjushri was the chakravartin called Sky.[17] He, his children, his wives, and his retinue served that tathagata and his retinue of shravakas and bodhisattvas for eighty-four thousand years, offering them excellent food and other necessities. Then King Sky went into solitude and thought, 'To what end should I dedicate my roots of virtue? To the state of Brahma, or that of Indra, or that of a chakravartin, or that of a shravaka, or that of a pratyekabuddha?'

"From the sky came the voices of devas, saying, 'Great king,

15. Saha is the name of the billion-world system of which our world is a part. The name *Saha* means "endurance" and refers to the great suffering that beings in our world realm endure.

16. A decillion has thirty-three zeros.

17. A chakravartin is a monarch ruling an entire world.

give rise to no such base aspiration! Use your vast roots of virtue to generate the intention to attain unsurpassable awakening!'

"Delighted, the chakravartin thought, 'I shall not turn back from awakening!'

"Accompanied by eight hundred sextillion other beings, he entered the presence of the tathagata King of Thunder's Melody. With joined palms, the chakravartin described his thoughts.

"That tathagata said,
'All dharmas are conditioned.
They fully depend on intentions.
You will attain the result
Of whatever aspiration you've made.'

"With those and other stanzas, that tathagata taught the king to generate bodhichitta. The king generated the intention to attain unsurpassable awakening and described how he would attain it, saying, 'From now on, until awakening, I call the buddhas of the ten directions to witness! I will not give rise to kleshas. I will abandon all wrongdoing. I will emulate the buddhas through the immaculate morality of chastity. I do not wish to attain buddhahood quickly. Until the end of time, I will engage in deeds for the benefit of every sentient being. I will purify immeasurable and innumerable buddha realms. May my name be heard and proclaimed throughout the ten directions.'

"Twenty million of the beings accompanying the king generated bodhichitta as well.

"As many kalpas as there are grains of sand in seven hundred thousand decillion Ganges Rivers have passed since the youthful Manjushri generated bodhichitta. As many kalpas as there are grains of sand in sixty-four Ganges Rivers have passed since he attained patience with unborn dharmas. Since then he has achieved the complete ten strengths of a tathagata. He has completed the ten stages of a bodhisattva and has fully achieved the level of a buddha.[18] Although he has perfected all buddhadharmas, he has never even once thought, 'Shall I or shall I not manifest the awakening of perfect buddhahood?'

"All of the twenty million other beings who generated bodhichitta at the same time as King Sky have achieved buddhahood, benefited innumerable beings, and have all, with one exception, passed into parinirvana. All of them were established in the six paramitas by this youthful Manjushri. He also venerated all of them and held their dharma.

"The only one of them who has not passed into parinirvana is the tathagata Earth God. He is now living in the world Earth Melody, which is beneath us, as many realms distant as there are grains of sand in forty-four thousand Ganges Rivers. That tathagata has a sangha of innumerable bodhisattvas. His life span is immeasurable."

The bodhisattva Lion's Power then loudly exclaimed, "Manjushri, if you have in that way completed the bodhisattva stages and achieved all buddhadharmas, why have you not achieved buddhahood?"

Manjushri replied, "If all buddhadharmas are perfectly complete, there is no subsequent achievement of awakening, since it has been present from the beginning. Since the nature of all dharmas is the same as those dharmas, just as they are, there is no origination and no cessation. If there is no origination and no cessation, there is no awakening."

The bhagavat then said, "Manjushri, reveal your aspirations for the array of your realm's qualities."

Manjushri, with the intention of revealing his aspirations,

18. Patience with unborn dharmas is a level of realization of emptiness that is often equated with the eighth bodhisattva level. The ten strengths of a buddha are: 1. the strength of knowing what is and what is not possible; 2. the strength of knowing the ripening of karma; 3. the strength of knowing beings' various interests; 4. the strength of knowing beings' diverse dispositions; 5. the strength of knowing beings' individual degree of intelligence; 6. the strength of knowing the path that applies to all beings; 7. the strength of knowing all meditative states; 8. the strength of knowing all past events; 9. the strength of knowing beings' death and rebirth; 10. the strength of knowing the exhaustion of defilement. The ten bodhisattva levels are the ten stages or bhumis that bodhisattvas pass through before achieving buddhahood.

planted his right knee on the ground, joined his palms, and bowed to the bhagavat. As many worlds as there are grains of sand in the Ganges River shook six times.

19. A tredecillion has forty-two zeros.

Then Manjushri said, "Bhagavat, these have been my aspirations for ten tredecillion kalpas:[19] May I gaze with the unobscured eyes of a buddha at the infinite worlds in the ten directions, and see that all buddhas, all bhagavats, have been placed in awakening, in bodhichitta, and in the paramitas, and have been encouraged and taught, by me. Until I see that, I will not achieve the buddhahood of unsurpassable awakening. When I no longer see a single tathagata in any of the ten directions that was not placed in buddhahood by me, I will achieve the manifest buddhahood of unsurpassable awakening."

The bodhisattvas in that assembly thought, "This Manjushri will see all the buddhas, all the bhagavats, that there are!"

The bhagavat, knowing their thought, said, "Children of family, it is like this: If someone ground these billion worlds into their smallest particles, even a skilled mathematician would be unable to count those particles by hundreds, thousands, or hundred thousands. The youthful Manjushri, when he looks with unobscured eyes, will see that many buddhas in each of the ten directions."

Manjushri then said to the bhagavat, "My single realm will be vaster than as many buddha realms as there are grains of sand in many Ganges Rivers. It will be decorated by hundreds and thousands of jewels. It will equal the peak of existence. Its tree of awakening will be the size of ten billion worlds. That tree's light will fill that entire buddha realm. Although I will remain seated in front of that tree, without arising, from buddhahood until nirvana, my emanations will teach dharma to beings in innumerable realms to the ten directions.

"In that realm there will not even be the names of shravakas or pratyekabuddhas. There will be no gender or birth. That realm will be populated entirely by bodhisattvas who will appear miraculously, wearing saffron robes and with crossed legs, without the faults of anger, rigidity, or deceptiveness. Their conduct will be utterly pure.

"As for the food in that realm, it will surpass even the delightful food of Sukhavati.[20] In my realm, whenever the wish for food arises, one's right hand will hold a vessel filled with food of a hundred delicious flavors. First, one will offer it to the buddhas and shravakas of the ten directions. Then one will distribute it in an instant, with the miraculous ability of the five supercognitions, to all impoverished and hungry beings, such as those born as pretas.[21] Only after satisfying those beings and teaching them dharma will one partake of the food. One will do the same thing with one's clothing, which will be fit for a renunciate yet made of various precious materials. All the possessions and utensils used by the bodhisattvas in my realm will arise and be used in this way.

"In that realm even the names of the eight leisureless states,[22] wrongdoing, suffering, faults, and unpleasant forms will be absent. That realm will be filled with sextillions of precious jewels previously unseen and nonexistent in any world in the ten directions. Merely by saying the name of any of those jewels, they will appear and last for a hundred billion years.

"For all born in that realm there will be no pain of heat and cold, and not even the names of sickness, aging, or death. Those bodhisattvas who wish to achieve buddhahood will pass into other realms, finishing their lives in Tushita and then achieving buddhahood.

"If bodhisattvas in my realm wish to see things made of gold, may those things appear to them according to their wish. Other than the radiance of that realm's bodhisattvas and tree of awakening, there will appear no light, such as that of the

20. Sukhavati is the pure realm of the buddha Amitabha.

21. The five supercognitions are: miraculous abilities, the eye of the devas, the ear of the devas, recollection of the past, and knowledge of others' minds.

22. The eight leisureless states are the states of hell beings, pretas, animals, absorbed devas, barbarians, those born in a world without buddhas, those with wrong views, and those with incomplete faculties.

sun, moon, stars, or lightning. May day and night be absent even in name, other than as distinguished by the opening and closing of lotuses. May the light of that realm fill a hundred sextillion buddha realms.

23. A quintillion has eighteen zeros.

"The sound of a hundred quintillion invisible cymbals will continuously resound from the sky above.[23] That sound will be the sound of the dharma — the paramitas, the three jewels, the bodhisattvapitaka — and the sound of whatever dharma is wanted by the bodhisattvas.

"Whenever anyone in that realm wants to see a buddha, they will immediately see the tathagata seated at the foot of the tree of awakening. They will be freed from doubt. They will understand the meaning without the need for teaching.

"This single realm will contain and include all the qualities, arrays, ornamentation, aspirations, and characteristics of all the infinite sextillion decillion buddha realms in the ten directions, except for the arrays of shravakas and those who attain buddhahood in worlds of fivefold degeneration.

"If one were to describe that buddha realm's splendid array for as many kalpas as there are grains of sand in the Ganges River, one could not finish doing so. It is encompassed only by the unimpeded wisdom of a tathagata."

The buddha said, "Manjushri, it will be so! The tathagata knows it!"

Then Manjushri said, "When an illusion is emanated, the emanated illusion does not exist. Similarly, although all dharmas appear to arise and cease, there is no arising and no cessation. This is sameness." On that same occasion, other majestic bodhisattvas such as Higher Wisdom displayed their confidence, thereby benefiting many beings.

Then the bhagavat, knowing the thoughts of the bodhisattvas

in that assembly, said, "The name of the realm will be Perfectly Complete and Purely Gathered without Particles. It will arise in the south, and will be within this world of Saha. When the youthful Manjushri attains buddhahood his name will be the tathagata All-Seeing. He will see the buddhas, the bhagavats, of sextillion novemdecillion worlds in the ten directions.[24] All the beings who see that tathagata are certain to attain unsurpassable awakening. Whoever hears that tathagata's name will enter the unchanging state. Aside from those with little interest, all such beings will achieve the unsurpassable awakening of buddhahood. That is why he will bear this name."

24. A novemdecillion has sixty zeros.

Sextillions of bodhisattvas among that assembly then declared with one voice, "He will befit his name, All-Seeing. If beings who merely hear that name will gain that which is worthy to be gained, what shall we say about those born in his realm? We consider those who will hear this dharma of prophecy and the name of the youthful Manjushri to be like those who directly see a buddha."

The bhagavat replied, "Children of family, it is so! It is just as you have said! Whoever recites the name of the youthful Manjushri generates merit far greater than that of someone who recites the names of sextillion buddhas. What need is there for me to speak of the recitation of the name of the tathagata All-Seeing? If you ask why, it is because the youthful Manjushri, during each and every kalpa, accomplishes an amount of benefit for beings that surpasses that accomplished by sextillion buddhas."

Millions of devas and others within that assembly then exclaimed, "I prostrate to the youthful Manjushri and the tathagata All-Seeing!" Eighty-four sextillion beings generated the intention to achieve unsurpassable awakening. Innumerable beings ripened their roots of virtue and achieved irreversibility from unsurpassable awakening.

Then some of the bodhisattvas within that assembly thought, "Manjushri's realm and Sukhavati are similar in feature and array."

The bhagavat knew their thought and said, "If someone divided the tip of a hair into hundredths and used one of them to take a single drop out of a vast ocean, view that extracted drop as like the features and array of the realm of Sukhavati, and all the water remaining in the vast ocean as like the features and array of the tathagata All-Seeing's realm."

The bodhisattva Lion's Power then asked in a loud voice, "Has this realm no equal?"

The buddha replied, "In the east is a world called Manifestly Exalted through Consecration by Aspirations. In that realm there lives at present the tathagata King of Ubiquitous Light-Rays and Oceans of Permanent Qualities. His life span is immeasurable. His realm and that of All-Seeing are equal.

"There are also four bodhisattvas adorned with the raiment of the inconceivable who abide in conduct like Manjushri's. Their realms will be like his. Those bodhisattvas are called Peak of Light, Higher Wisdom, Peaceful Power, and Intelligent Aspiration."

Then the bodhisattva Lion's Power asked in a loud voice, "Manjushri, when will you attain buddhahood?"

Manjushri replied, "When space becomes form, I will attain buddhahood. When people created by magicians attain buddhahood, I will attain buddhahood. Manjushri is awakening. Awakening is Manjushri. Emptiness is awakening."

Then the bhagavat said, "Children of family, although the tathagata Amitabha's assembly of bodhisattvas and shravakas is inconceivably vast, it is like this: A single sesame seed extracted from among all the sesame seeds in Magadha is like the assembly in the realm of Sukhavati. All the remaining sesame seeds are like the assembly in the realm of the tathagata All-Seeing. They are that different.

"The life span of the tathagata All-Seeing is like this: If these billion worlds were divided into their smallest particles, kalpas equal in number to those particles could not be said to be even a hundredth or even a thousandth of it. Know that 'the life span of that tathagata is beyond number and immeasurable."

Then the buddha spoke of the amount of time until the youthful Manjushri's buddhahood, saying, "If a few people reduced these billion worlds to their particles, and one of those people took one of those smallest particles and placed it in the east, as many billionfold worlds distant from here as there are smallest particles in these billion worlds, and then continued to transport one particle after another, each an equal distance from the last, they could eventually use up all the smallest particles in these billion worlds.

"If, at the same time, a second person placed an equal number of particles to the south, and eight other people did the same thing in the remaining eight of the ten directions, one would be unable to count the number of worlds in the ten directions across which the particles were extended, even in hundreds, thousands, or hundred thousands.

"If all those worlds on which those particles were placed and all the worlds between them were reduced to their smallest particles, even a skilled mathematician would be unable to count those particles in hundreds, thousands, or millions. Any sentient being who tried to count them would go mad. The tathagata, however, knows how many hundreds of such smallest particles there would be, how many thousands, and how many of any greater number."

The bodhisattva Maitreya said, "Bhagavat, for the sake of such great wisdom this bodhisattva would be willing to burn in hell until the end of time! I will never give up such great wisdom!"

The buddha replied, "Just so! Just so! What sentient being, other than a very lazy one with little interest or diligence, would not want such wisdom?

"The youthful Manjushri will engage in the deeds of awakening for a number of kalpas exceeding the number of particles in all the worlds in the ten directions on which particles were placed in the example I spoke of, and all the worlds between them. His perfect aspirations are inconceivable. Therefore his life span and sangha of bodhisattvas at the time of his awakening will be inconceivably vast."

The bodhisattva Lion's Power then addressed the bhagavat in a loud voice, exclaiming, "It is wondrous that this Manjushri will continue his great involvement for so many kalpas without fatigue! His great conduct is wondrous!"

The youthful Manjushri responded, "Space does not think 'This many kalpas have passed!' In the same way, bodhisattvas do not enter into the perception of anything whatsoever. They are therefore without fatigue, birth, and death."

Then the bhagavat said, "Children of family, if a bodhisattva gazed upon all the buddha realms throughout the ten directions with the unobscured eyes of a tathagata and, filling those realms with the seven jewels, offered them to each tathagata; and if that bodhisattva also undertook and kept all moral vows, motivated by impartiality toward all beings, and bestowed generosity upon all beings until the end of time, that bodhisattva would not accumulate even a hundredth of the merit accumulated by a bodhisattva who retained this dharma and thinking, 'I shall emulate the youthful Manjushri,' walked

seven paces. The merit of the former would not withstand comparison to that of the latter!"

Then the youthful Manjushri entered a samadhi called Illusory Origination of All Appearances. As soon as he did so, all the bodhisattvas in that assembly saw all the buddhas in the innumerable worlds to the ten directions. In front of each of those buddhas was a youthful Manjushri, describing the qualities and array of the realm of his buddhahood. Seeing this, all the bodhisattvas in that assembly thought, "The appearance of Manjushri in so many worlds at once is a great wonder! His aspirations, samadhis, and wisdom are extraordinary!" They were amazed.

From the *Sutra on the Dispelling of Ajatashatru's Guilt*

While the bhagavat was residing on Vulture Peak Mountain along with all his retinue, Manjushri was speaking of dharma on the steps of Mount Meru to a great assembly that included twenty-five holy beings and four devas from Tushita. At the same time, tathagatas emanated by Manjushri were ripening many beings by teaching dharma and so on. When the bhagavat summoned Manjushri, he and his retinue entered the buddha's presence and spoke with him of various aspects of dharma.

Within that assembly were two hundred devas who had previously possessed the conduct but had subsequently lost bodhichitta by thinking, "I am unable to accomplish unsurpassable awakening! I will pass into nirvana as a shravaka or pratyekabuddha!"

In order to place them in unsurpassable awakening, the bhagavat emanated a householder outside that assembly. That householder offered a begging bowl filled with food of a hundred flavors to the buddha, who accepted it.

Manjushri said to the bhagavat, "If you eat that food without giving me any, you will have demonstrated ingratitude!"

Shariputra wondered, "What did Manjushri do for the bhagavat in the past to allow for ingratitude now?"

Knowing Shariputra's thought, the buddha said, "Shariputra, the tathagata knows the right time. I will tell you. Wait!"

He then cast the begging bowl into the vast earth. Instantaneously, the bowl passed through as many buddha realms below this one as there are grains of sand in the Ganges River, and was observed by the buddhas in those realms. It reached a world called Illuminated, in which resided the tathagata King of Light Rays. The bowl remained in the sky of that realm.

When the retinues of all those buddhas asked about the begging bowl, the buddhas answered, "The tathagata Shakyamuni cast it down from the realm called Saha that is above us in order to tame some bodhisattvas."

Then the bhagavat said to Shariputra, "Find that begging bowl."

Shariputra entered ten thousand samadhis. Even though he used the strength of his own discernment and the power of the buddha to go to ten thousand buddha realms, he did not see the begging bowl, and returned to the buddha's presence. In the same way Maudgalyayana, Subhuti, and about five hundred other great shravakas searched for the begging bowl using miraculous abilities and the divine eye, but were unable to find it.

Subhuti said to the bodhisattva Maitreya, "Find that begging bowl."

Maitreya answered, "Although the tathagata has predicted

that only one birth remains for me until unsurpassable awakening, and that when I attain awakening I will become a tathagata whose very footsteps are unknowable to bodhisattvas like Manjushri, I do not know even the name of the samadhis that the youthful Manjushri enters. Ask Manjushri to recover the bowl. He can do so."

Subhuti asked Manjushri to recover the bowl. The bhagavat, as well, said, "Do it."

The youthful Manjushri entered a samadhi called All-Reaching. Without moving from his seat, and while remaining visible to that assembly, he extended his right arm. His hand saluted the buddhas in all the buddha realms below us, and gave forth the sound of greeting. From each pore in the skin of his arm emerged one hundred billion light rays. On the tip of each of them was a tathagata seated in the center of a lotus. All those tathagatas proclaimed praises of the tathagata Shakyamuni. Each buddha realm the hand passed through shook six times, was filled with bright light, and became decorated by parasols and victory banners.

Manjushri's right hand passed through as many buddha realms as there are grains of sand in seventy-two Ganges Rivers. It reached Illuminated, the realm of the tathagata King of Light Rays. The hand greeted him and performed the miracle of the light rays. A bodhisattva named Glorious Light, an attendant of that buddha, asked, "Whose is this miraculous, delightful, beautiful hand?" The tathagata told him how the hand came from Saha above them. The bodhisattva asked to see the realm of Saha, its bodhisattvas, the tathagata Shakyamuni, and the youthful Manjushri.

The tathagata King of Light Rays sent forth light from his forehead. All the beings it touched attained the bliss of chakravartins. All the yogins it touched attained fruition. All the bodhisattvas it touched attained a samadhi as brilliant as the sun. The beings of that realm saw our realm of Saha.

Seeing it, the bodhisattva Glorious Light wept and exclaimed, "Like priceless jewels cast into the mud are the bhagavat and mahabodhisattvas who live in that realm of Saha!"

The buddha King of Light Rays said, "Don't say such things! It is more meritorious to meditate on love for one morning in the realm of Saha than to remain in meditation for ten kalpas in this realm! The mahabodhisattvas who guard holy dharma in Saha will purify all karmic obscurations and kleshas by doing so!"

The light sent forth by the buddha King of Light Rays was seen by beings in this realm of Saha. The bhagavat explained it to the assembly.

Then the bhagavat performed the miracle of sending forth light rays that allowed beings of our realm to see the realm Illuminated far beneath us. All the bodhisattvas touched by those light rays attained a samadhi called Beacon like Mount Meru, and were able to see that buddha realm beneath us.

The youthful Manjushri picked up the begging bowl in that realm with his right hand. His hand returned to our realm, accompanied by sextillions of bodhisattvas. As his hand returned through each realm between Illuminated and Saha, the light radiated by his arm disappeared from that realm. Finally, he cast the begging bowl into the sky before the bhagavat Shakyamuni. Prostrating to the bhagavat's feet, Manjushri said, "Please accept this begging bowl!" The buddha did so.

Then the bodhisattvas who had accompanied the youthful Manjushri's hand on its return to our realm prostrated to the bhagavat, greeted him, and took their seats.

Finally, the bhagavat told Shariputra of past events, saying

"More than sextillion novemdecillion kalpas ago, there was a world called Undenigrated. In that realm appeared a tathagata called Unbeatable Victory Banner. He taught dharma based on the three vehicles. In that realm lived a bhikshu and dharma teacher called Wisdom Victory Banner, who got dressed one day and went to the great royal palace to beg for alms. He was given food of a hundred flavors and left with it. The bhikshu was observed doing this by a merchant's son named Stainless Host, who was seated in his mother's lap. Stainless Host arose from his mother's lap, rushed over to the bhikshu, and asked him for food. The bhikshu gave him some, and then the boy followed the bhikshu back into the presence of the tathagata Unbeatable Victory Banner.

"The bhikshu gave the boy all the alms that he had received. The boy offered the food to the tathagata, saying, 'Eat this.' Although the boy offered the entire begging bowl to the tathagata, it did not become empty. He then fed eighty thousand shravakas and twelve thousand bodhisattvas from the same bowl. The boy continued to feed that buddha and his retinue for a week without using up the begging bowl's contents. He was delighted by this and spoke words of praise. The bhikshu gave the boy the vow of taking refuge in the three jewels. He also caused him to confess wrongdoing, rejoice in virtue, pray, and generate the intention to achieve unsurpassable awakening. When the boy's parents came looking for him and entered the tathagata's presence, they too and many other beings generated the intention to achieve unsurpassable awakening and renounced the world.

"That bhikshu and dharma teacher Wisdom Victory Banner is now the youthful Manjushri. I, Shakyamuni, was that merchant's son, Stainless Host. Wisdom Victory Banner gave me alms and caused my generation of bodhichitta. That was the first time I ever generated bodhichitta. Therefore all the greatness of my buddhahood as a tathagata, such as the ten strengths, my fearlessness, and all buddhadharmas, have

come from the youthful Manjushri's causing me to generate bodhichitta. There are innumerable buddhas in the ten directions who, like me, are called Shakyamuni. I have also seen buddhas called Tisha, Jina, Crown, Light, and by other names. All of these were established in awakening by the youthful Manjushri. I could not proclaim all the names of all the buddhas currently turning the dharmachakra whom Manjushri established in awakening even if I did so for longer than a kalpa. What need is there to say that there are countless others who are now engaged in the conduct of a bodhisattva, or abiding in Tushita and so forth, or entering the site of their awakening?

"For those reasons, I declare to you all that the perfect protector of all bodhisattvas, their progenitor, their compassionate caregiver, their inspiration and guide, is the youthful Manjushri."

Hearing this, the two hundred devas thought, "All dharmas follow their causes and depend on conditions. They are rooted in intentions and steered by aspirations. If even the bhagavat was caused to generate bodhichitta by another, it is unfitting for us to generate an inferior intention in this tathagata's presence." With the best intentions, they generated the intention to achieve unsurpassable awakening. Because of the miracle of the extended arm, innumerable beings in this realm and in those beneath it also generated bodhichitta.

In order to venerate Manjushri and serve him in dharma there appeared from innumerable buddha realms in the ten directions the buddhas of those realms, in the form of bodhisattvas holding precious parasols with which they covered this world. From those parasols came the words, "Just as Shakyamuni said, we too were placed in awakening by the youthful Manjushri."

Then King Ajatashatru and his court entered the bhagavat's

presence. The king asked the buddha, "Give me the means to free myself from my unbounded wrongdoing — the murder of my father — and remove my guilt and anxiety!"

The bhagavat thought, "This King Ajatashatru, while passionate, has faith in profound dharma. No one other than the youthful Manjushri is capable of removing all of his anxiety!"

Through the buddha's power Shariputra said to King Ajatashatru, "Invite Manjushri to dine tomorrow. He will remove your anxiety and benefit many others as well."

The king made the invitation. The bhagavat told Manjushri, "Go to Ajatashatru's to dine. It will help him and many others."

That night, during the first watch, Manjushri went instantaneously to a world called Always Sound, which was eight million buddha realms to the east of our realm. In that world lived the tathagata Glorious Sound. Manjushri entered his presence and, prostrating to him, asked, "Please command the mahabodhisattvas of this realm to attend the banquet that will be given tomorrow in Saha by King Ajatashatru."

The tathagata Glorious Sound said to the bodhisattvas surrounding him, "All of you accompany Manjushri on his return to Saha!"

Eighty-two thousand bodhisattvas from that tathagata's retinue accompanied Manjushri to Saha. Manjushri taught them the dharma of retention. Five hundred of the bodhisattvas attained retention. Then in the middle watch of the night, he extensively taught those five hundred bodhisattvas the dharma of the bodhisattvapitaka. During the last watch he extensively taught them the vajra words of the irreversible wheel. Some of those bodhisattvas attained the samadhi called Flowers of Light Rays.

At sunrise Ajatashatru sent messengers to escort his guests. The shravaka Mahakashyapa, accompanied by five hundred bhikshus, came to Manjushri. Manjushri said, "Kashyapa, why are you leaving so early?"

Kashyapa replied, "I'm going begging."

Manjushri said, "Mahakashyapa, please come with your retinue to my banquet."

Kashyapa replied, "I seek dharma, not material dharmas. However, I will accompany you. In case you are wondering why, it is because I will hear you teach dharma that I could never hear from anyone else."

Then the youthful Manjushri entered the samadhi that emanates all miracles. This realm of Saha became as flat and smooth as the palm of a hand. All its billion worlds were filled with bright light. All its inferior states and kleshas ceased. Everyone within it abided in love. The great earth shook six times. With the sound of cymbals, a rain of flowers fell. The devas made earnest offerings. The nagas made all roads even and adorned them with inconceivable arrays of wondrous and amazing offerings.

Then the youthful Manjushri arrived at King Ajatashatru's palace, accompanied by the eighty-two thousand bodhisattvas and about five hundred great shravakas. Previously, Manjushri had told the king that he would be accompanied by about five hundred others. There was therefore only enough food prepared for five hundred. The king thought, "This is no good!"

Son of Rest and other bodhisattvas consoled the king, saying, "Great king, be not displeased! Manjushri has great wisdom and miraculous blessing. If he wanted to, he could feed all the beings of these billion worlds with a single morsel of food. What need be said about this gathering? His skill in giving is inexhaustible!" Ajatashatru was relieved.

Then Manjushri said to All-Seeing and other bodhisattvas gathered there, "Arrange seats for this gathering."

They miraculously created sufficient space and seats and then sat down on them. King Ajatashatru and his court prepared to serve them. Brahma, Indra, and many other devas and nagas also came to serve Manjushri and his retinue.

Then however, King Ajatashatru thought, "These bodhisattvas have no begging bowls. Out of what will they eat?"

Suddenly their begging bowls appeared from their realm and fell from the sky. They rinsed themselves in the eight-branched water of Lake Manasarovar and alighted on lotus flowers held by eight thousand naginis, who offered them to the bodhisattvas.[25] The king then served the food, which became inexhaustible. Amazed, he asked Manjushri about this.

25. Eight-branched water is clean water with eight qualities: it is sweet, cool, soft, light, transparent, clean, pleasant to the throat, and beneficial to the stomach.

Manjushri said, "It is inexhaustible, just like your guilt."

The bodhisattvas in that assembly, having eaten, threw their begging bowls into the sky. They remained in the sky, unsupported. The king asked Manjushri, "What is supporting them?"

Manjushri answered, "The same thing that is supporting your guilt. Although nothing is supporting them, they do not fall. In the same way, all dharmas are unfixed and unsupported and yet never fall."

Then the king knelt down in front of Manjushri and begged him, "Remove my guilt!"

Manjushri replied, "Even as many buddhas as there are grains of sand in the Ganges River would be unable to remove your guilt!"

Knowing that he was without a protector, Ajatashatru fell to the ground. The elder Mahakashyapa said to him, "Great king, don't fear! Manjushri is skilled in considered speech. Ask him what he meant." The king got up and asked.

Manjushri said, "Just as the buddhas, the bhagavats, are unborn; and just as space can never be disturbed; when there is nothing to remove, even buddhas can't remove it."

Hearing this, King Ajatashatru achieved patience concordant with emptiness. His guilt was removed.

Then Ajatashatru brought priceless fabric and attempted to adorn Manjushri's body with it. Manjushri's body, however, disappeared. The sound arose, "Look at guilt and all dharmas in this way. Offer what you are holding to someone whose body is visible."

Ajatashatru attempted to offer the fabric to Glorious Wisdom Victory Banner, a bodhisattva seated in front of Manjushri, and then to each of the bodhisattvas in turn, and finally to the arhat Mahakashyapa. They each, however, demonstrated the dharma of nonacceptance. All their bodies disappeared. Then the five hundred bhikshus also disappeared. Ajatashatru thought, "I will give this fabric to the queen!"

When he attempted to do so, however, he could not see her. He could not see any of the women of his court, or any of his servants. In that samadhi, he saw nothing other than his own body. He heard the sound, "Offer it to whomever you can see."

He thought, "I will place it on myself," but then he could no longer see even his own body. He perceived no form whatsoever.

He heard the words, "Great king, you see no form at all. Look in that way at your guilt. However you see your guilt, look in that way at all dharmas."

As soon as Ajatashatru arose from that samadhi devoid of perception and thought, he saw his own body and everything else as before. He asked Manjushri, "Where was everything when I couldn't see it?"

Manjushri said, "It all went wherever your guilt has gone."

Based on that and other remarks of Manjushri's, the king attained concordant patience for dharmas. Thirty-two thousand women of his court generated the intention to achieve unsurpassable awakening upon seeing Manjushri's miracles. Five hundred men of the court attained the pure eye of dharma.

Thousands of people came to the palace gates from the town of Rajgir in order to venerate Manjushri. He touched the earth with his toe, and the great earth was transformed into beryl, in which could be seen the reflections of the youthful Manjushri and his retinue. All those beings generated bodhichitta. Manjushri taught them the dharma that brings the pure eye of dharma. Then he left the palace. On the road he met a man who had killed his mother and was weeping in front of a tree, saying, "I will go to hell because of my wrongdoing!"

Because he was someone Manjushri could tame, Manjushri emanated another man along with that emanation's parents. They quarreled about which road to take, and the emanation killed both his parents. Then the emanation who had killed both his parents walked over to the matricide.

The matricide thought, "He and I are similar. I will go wherever he goes."

The emanation, weeping, said, "I am going to see

Shakyamuni. He protects those without a protector."

The emanation and the matricide went there together. The emanation said to the buddha, "I have killed my parents. Please protect me! What shall I do?"

The buddha said, "It is good that you have told the truth. However, a mind can not be killed by anything."

The emanation realized the dharma taught by the buddha. He renounced the world and passed into parinirvana in the sky. Seeing this, the matricide thought, "If someone who has killed both his parents can attain nirvana, why could not I, who have only killed my mother?"

He bowed to the bhagavat and said to him, "I have killed my mother!" The bhagavat repeated what he had said before. Then from every pore on that man's skin emerged the fires of hell. He was burning and without a protector. He exclaimed, "I take refuge in the bhagavat!"

26. These are the truth of suffering, of its cause, of its cessation, and of the path.

The bhagavat touched his golden fingers to the top of the man's head. Immediately, all of his pain ceased and he was at ease. With great respect for the tathagata, he asked to renounce the world. The buddha gave his consent, and taught him the four truths.[26] The man saw the truth, and by meditating on the path, became an arhat. Saying, "Bhagavat, I shall pass into nirvana," he rose into the sky and cremated his body with his own fire element. Thousands of devas bowed to him as he did this.

Seeing the taming of such a person, Shariputra was amazed and said to the buddha, "This taming of someone of unbounded wrongdoing is amazing! Other than you, the buddha, the bhagavat Shakyamuni; the youthful Manjushri; and other mahabodhisattvas who wear the same armor, no one knows the various faculties of beings. They are unknown even by shravakas and pratyekabuddhas!"

The bhagavat replied, "It is so. Shariputra, the youthful Manjushri first caused Ajatashatru to generate bodhichitta during a kalpa called Stainless, through the teachings of a tathagata called Good Hand. Three million buddhas appeared during the kalpa called Stainless. All of them were requested to turn the dharmachakra and to live long by Manjushri.

"As Ajatashatru has a bit of remaining karma — like a fragment of a mustard seed — he will fall into hell, but only in the way that devas from Thirty-Three descend to Jambudvipa and then return home.[27] Like a pundarika flower, his body will be untouched by suffering. He will then be born in a world called Decorated in the presence of the tathagata Pile of Jewels. That world is above ours, at a distance of four thousand buddha realms. Immediately after his birth there, Ajatashatru will see Manjushri and hear profound dharma. He will attain patience with unborn dharmas.

27. Thirty-Three is the second level of the desire realm devas. It is named after the thirty-three great devas who rule it.

"When Maitreya attains buddhahood, Ajatashatru will become the bodhisattva Unmoving. He will again see the youthful Manjushri and will recollect the dharma he heard in the past. He will then ripen beings and engage in the conduct for eight hundred vigintillion kalpas.[28] The beings ripened by him will become free from karma and kleshas. They will have acute faculties, and will be free from guilt and doubt. After eight hundred vigintillion kalpas, Ajatashatru will attain buddhahood. During the kalpa called Delight to See, in the world called Unsullied by Mud, he will become the tathagata Utterly Pure Objects. No one in his realm will die in a state of guilt or go to bad rebirths after death."

28. A vigintillion has sixty-three zeros.

Then all the bodhisattvas from other realms who had come to this one with Manjushri declared, "Bhagavat, anywhere Manjushri abides is not empty of tathagatas! Bhagavat, please do not think otherwise! Why? Because beings ripened by Manjushri are without bad rebirths, states without leisure, the actions of Mara, and the danger of kleshas!"

The buddha replied, "Children of family, it is just as you have said."

The bodhisattvas gathered there from the ten directions cast enough flowers to fill the world at the tathagata and Manjushri, exclaiming, "May the beacon of the great sage's dharma blaze long! Bhagavat, if we cannot serve the youthful Manjushri with our flesh and blood, by what else shall we venerate him?"

Saying that and similar things, they circumambulated the bhagavat three times, venerated Manjushri also, and then returned to their own buddha realms, where they used the dharma they had heard here to establish innumerable beings in certain, perfect awakening.

From the *Prajnaparamitasutra of Seven Hundred Stanzas*

"Bhagavat, this Manjushri is inconceivably glorious! If you ask why, it is because his confidence is inconceivable!"

The buddha replied, "It is so."

From the *Ratnatalasutra*

Shariputra said to Manjushri, "Son of family, it is like this. Just as even a little vajra can destroy a great mountain, the wisdom that abides in any one of your pores does not exist within as many beings such as me as there are smallest particles."

From the Sutra Requested by the Naga King Manasarovar

While the bhagavat was teaching dharma at the invitation of the naga king, Lake Manasarovar became covered by a beautiful web of precious flowers the size of chariot wheels, with hundreds or thousands of petals and a delicious fragrance. One of the flowers was a particularly beautiful lotus, pleasing to the eye and blazing like a jewel. Ananda saw it and asked the bhagavat, "Whose coming does this herald?"

The buddha answered, "Wait a bit. You'll see."

Not long afterward the youthful Manjushri appeared, surrounded by sixty thousand other bodhisattvas. They came from a world called Array of Jewels, the realm of the buddha Precious Peak. That realm is far beneath ours, as many realms distant as there are sand grains in sixty Ganges Rivers. Manjushri came here to listen to the chapter called the "Dharma Gate to the Pure Path," which the buddha was about to teach to the naga king Manasarovar.

Manjushri sat down with crossed legs on the lotus flower. That entire assembly, amazed, bowed to those bodhisattvas. The youthful Manjushri then rose into the sky and was prostrated to by Brahma, Indra, and other devas holding precious parasols. Manjushri and the other bodhisattvas, remaining in the sky at a height of seven palm trees, cast a rain of flowers the like of which was previously unseen and unheard of, in order to venerate the bhagavat. From those flowers came the sound of the buddha Precious Peak greeting the bhagavat. Then the bodhisattvas descended, bowed to the bhagavat, and sat down on their individual lotus flowers.

The elder Kashyapa then asked the bhagavat, "Where is the realm of the tathagata Precious Peak?"

Manjushri answered, "It is so far away that if you who possess abundant miraculous powers were to try to go there, your life would end and you would attain parinirvana before getting there."

The elder Kashyapa and Manjushri then discussed the mind's liberation. Finally, Kashyapa said, "Manjushri, be confident! I am unable to answer you!"

The bodhisattva Piled Wisdom asked Manjushri, "Why is the elder Kashyapa so humble?"

Manjushri replied, "He is a shravaka, and not fearless."

29. The three gates of liberation are emptiness, absence of attributes, and freedom from aspiration.

Piled Wisdom asked, "Why did he regard the three gates of liberation as unimportant?"[29]

Manjushri replied, "The tathagata skillfully benefited Kashyapa by allowing him to regard the three gates of liberation, which are inestimable, as unimportant."

Then Manasarovar and Manjushri said, "View all dharmas, such as form, as the tathagata. Although the tathagata is invisible to the fleshly eye, to enter without thought into the meaning of natural peace — not composite, equal to the unequalled — is to view the tathagata."

All the bodhisattvas gathered there praised them.

From the *Sutra Taught by Manjushri*

30. The Jetavana was a residence built for and offered to the buddha and his sangha during the buddha's lifetime.

At one time the bhagavat was residing in the Jetavana, surrounded by a retinue of shravakas and bodhisattvas.[30] During that time, the youthful Manjushri approached the bhagavat while holding a precious parasol with a diameter of ten yojanas. Manjushri stood there, holding the parasol over the bhagavat's head. A deva named Good Border exclaimed, "Manjushri, are you still unsatisfied by your service to the bhagavat?"

Manjushri replied, "Deva, just as a great ocean is never filled by any amount of rainfall, a mahabodhisattva who seeks the wisdom of omniscience, which is like an immeasurably deep ocean, must never be content with their service to the tathagata."

The deva asked, "Manjushri, with what in mind do you venerate the tathagata?"

Manjushri replied, "Deva, I venerate the tathagata with four things in mind: bodhichitta, the full liberation of all beings, the unbroken succession of the three jewels, and the purification of all buddha realms. With those four things in mind, I venerate the tathagata."

That whole assembly rejoiced.

From the *Sutra of Fourfold Accomplishment*

On another occasion, Manjushri taught the dharma of accomplishing those very four things. The deva Good Glory delightedly rejoiced in this, and, together with his retinue, cast divine flowers such as mandaravas in veneration of Manjushri. Immediately, through the buddha's power, there appeared in the sky beautiful and fragrant lotus flowers the size of chariot wheels. In the center of each lotus was a bodhisattva bearing the thirty-two marks.[31]

The bhagavat smiled. From his mouth issued light of various colors that illuminated the whole world and then returned to his mouth.

The deva Good Glory asked, "What is the meaning of this?"

The buddha answered, "All these bodhisattvas gathered from the ten directions into the sky above us, seated on lion thrones and lotuses, were ripened by the youthful Manjushri. They have assembled here to listen to dharma. They all have only one life remaining, and will attain buddhahood in various realms in the ten directions."

Shariputra remarked, "Bhagavat, I could cheerfully count the stars above these billion worlds, but I could not count the number of these bodhisattvas, even in a hundred years."

The buddha replied, "Shariputra, you could count the smallest particles in Jambudvipa, but you could not count these bodhisattvas."

31. The thirty-two marks and eighty signs are signs of perfection that are fully present on the body of a buddha and may be partially present on the bodies of bodhisattvas and chakravartins.

Shariputra remarked, "The existence of a number of prospective realms of buddhahood corresponding to this many bodhisattvas is unlikely."

The buddha replied, "The tathagata sees innumerable realms without buddhas."

That entire assembly exclaimed, "We are fortunate that our teacher possesses the sight of great wisdom."

Then the deva Good Glory said to Manjushri, "Manjushri, the deeds through which you have ripened innumerable beings to awakening are excellent, excellent! Any place you inhabit and any place this dharma is practiced should be viewed as a place where a buddha has appeared and a place where the dharmachakra has been turned!"

The bhagavat concurred, saying, "It is so."

From the *Sutra of the Presentation of the Noble Relative and Absolute Truths*

When the bhagavat was living on Vulture Peak Mountain near Rajgir, surrounded by shravakas, bodhisattvas, and devas, a deva named Lord of Utter Peace and Complete Calm asked the bhagavat, "Bhagavat, where is the youthful Manjushri now? I and this entire assembly desire to hear that holy person's dharma teaching!"

The buddha replied, "He is in the presence of the tathagata Precious Peak in the world Endowed with Jewels, which is eighteen thousand buddha realms distant from our realm, to the east."

The deva said, "Bhagavat, please make the youthful Manjushri come here. Why? Because one does not hear from shravakas, pratyekabuddhas, or conceptual bodhisattvas what one hears from Manjushri. No one other than the tathagata is able to teach such dharma! Bhagavat, whenever Manjushri teaches dharma the abode of maras is darkened.[32] No mara finds opportunity. All attacks are eradicated. Those with concepts become free from concepts. The holy dharma is caused to remain for a long time. The tathagatas rejoice and give their support."

The tathagata, understanding the deva's prayer, emitted from between his eyebrows light rays that illuminated this world. They filled the world Endowed with Jewels and alerted the youthful Manjushri. Together with ten thousand other bodhisattvas, he entered the bhagavat's presence in the time it would take for someone to stretch out and withdraw their arm. The youthful Manjushri and the other bodhisattvas remained invisible, but caused such a rain of flowers to descend from the sky that these billion worlds were knee-deep in flowers. Everyone in that assembly was amazed, and asked, "What is the reason for this?" The bhagavat said, "It is through the power of Manjushri and other bodhisattvas."

Everyone in that assembly then wanted to view Manjushri and the other bodhisattvas. Manjushri and his retinue descended from the sky, bowed to the bhagavat, and took their seats. The bhagavat gave his permission, and the deva questioned Manjushri. Manjushri said, "Absolute truth is unborn. Its character is inexpressible." Through his teaching on that occasion, innumerable mahabodhisattvas achieved patience with unborn dharmas. Manjushri benefited many beings there.

Then the bodhisattvas who had accompanied Manjushri here declared their wish to return to their own realm. The youthful Manjushri blessed this world so that it became identical to Endowed with Jewels, the realm of the tathagata Precious Peak. All those bodhisattvas perceived it as being that realm. When, however, they looked at this world within samadhi, they realized that they had not left this realm of Saha.

32. Maras are beings or other things that prevent awakening. Often they are listed as four: the aggregates, the kleshas, the child of the devas, and death. The child of the devas, devaputra-mara, is both our addiction to pleasure and the malevolent interference of external beings, such as devas, in our pursuit of awakening. When the word *mara* is used as a proper name and therefore capitalized, it usually refers to the ruler of Control of Others' Emanations, the sixth and highest level of the desire realm devas.

They praised Manjushri's blessing and aspired to emulate it.

Then, while sitting on his seat, the youthful Manjushri rested in samadhi. From the top of his head emerged a light ray called Dispeller of All Beings' Concepts and Ignorance. It illuminated all the buddha realms in the ten directions. Then Manjushri, acting as though he had never heard it before, listened to the bhagavat Shakyamuni's dharma teaching of the two truths. In order to venerate the buddhas and bodhisattvas of the infinite realms in the ten directions, Manjushri filled all those realms with offering clouds that rained down an abundance of all dharmas that bestow supremely great bliss, such as divine flowers and incense. He then arose from samadhi and circumambulated, without conceptualization, the bhagavat Shakyamuni hundreds and thousands of times. Manjushri then departed from this realm of Saha.

From the *Noble Sutra on the Absence of Origin of All Dharmas*

Once the bhagavat and Manjushri taught that because all dharmas are unborn they are equal. They taught this with vajra words, words of those who have reached the levels, penetrating words. From the sky above them ten thousand devas cast divine flowers such as utpalas at the tathagata and Manjushri. Those devas bowed to them and cried, "This bhagavat is splendor without attachment. That is Gentle Splendor. This bhagavat is nonabiding splendor. That is Gentle Splendor. This bhagavat is splendor without substance. That is Gentle Splendor. This bhagavat is splendor without kleshas. That is Gentle Splendor. This bhagavat is the splendor of that-itself. That is Gentle Splendor. This bhagavat is the unmistaken splendor of that-itself. That is Gentle Splendor. This bhagavat is the splendor of the dharmadhatu. That is Gentle Splendor. This bhagavat is the splendor of the perfect end. That is Gentle Splendor. This bhagavat is holy splendor. That is Gentle Splendor. This bhagavat is supreme splendor.

That is Gentle Splendor. This bhagavat is the ultimate splendor. That is Gentle Splendor. This bhagavat is unsurpassable splendor. That is Gentle Splendor."[33]

The youthful Manjushri said to them, "Devas, do not conceptualize me! I have never actually seen anything holy, supreme, or ultimate. Devas, I am the splendor of desire. Therefore I am Gentle Splendor. I am the splendor of anger. Therefore I am Gentle Splendor. I am the splendor of stupidity. Therefore I am Gentle Splendor. I am not beyond desire and the rest. Childish, ordinary beings seek to transcend them, but bodhisattvas do not change, depart from, or transcend anything. All dharmas, like illusions, are beyond transcendence."

Because of what Manjushri said to them, those ten thousand devas attained patience with unborn dharmas.

From the Sutra Requested by the Devi Vimalaprabha

The buddha said, "In the future, in the land of Li, there will appear a renunciate called Pure Moon who will liberate wild people from samsara.[34] This will be the bodhisattva Manjushri, who is the father of all buddhas of the past. Manjushri also preserves the remains of all buddhas in this fortunate kalpa.

"When the bhagavat passes into nirvana, Manjushri will become a Buddhist brahmin called Gotra. When kings quarrel over my remains, that brahmin will place them in several vases and conceal them.

"At a time when few bodhisattvas will appear in the land of Li, and when there will no longer be stupas, images of the buddha, or monasteries in that land, Manjushri will appear as a woman of family. What will Manjushri do? He will display a variety of desirable forms, including those of bodhisattvas, kings, queens, renunciates, and brahmins. He will enter into

33. Manjushri means "gentle splendor." Manjughosha, another of his names, means "gentle melody."

34. Li is said to be in western China.

all the forms of beings in the realm of desire. He will be as versatile as a skilled musician. Especially, he will appear to beings of a passionate disposition.

"Why will Manjushri take female form? Because women are especially passionate, Manjushri will appear often as a woman. Because there are women who engage in the conduct of awakening, he will appear as a woman. Having been born female, Manjushri will have great compassion. Manjushri will inspire other women to be cautious, to realize samsara's defects, and to become independent of men."

From the Sutra Requested by Upali

The youthful Manjushri said to Upali, "Upali, all dharmas are utterly tame. In order to tame the mind, I teach taming. All dharmas are without affliction. Since there is no self, I teach the taming of regret."

Upali asked the bhagavat, "Bhagavat, everything that the youthful Manjushri teaches is based on the inconceivable!"

The buddha replied, "Upali, the youthful Manjushri's dharma teaching is a cause of liberation. There can be no liberation without relying upon the inconceivable. The youthful Manjushri is free from any thought. He teaches dharma in order to dispel the arrogance of thought."

From the Sutra of the Irreversible Wheel

One day at dawn, while Shariputra was within the youthful Manjushri's dwelling, Manjushri, with crossed legs, passed through Shariputra, his dwelling, and as many realms to the east as there are sand grains in the Ganges River. He reached the world called Irreversible Expanse. From the tathagata Blooming Lotus Body Covered by Light Rays he heard the irreversible dharmachakra. He passed through an equal number of realms in the other nine directions and heard the same dharma nine more times. He then returned to this realm of Saha while it was still dawn.

In the Jetavana, Ananda noticed that all the water had become clear and was covered by lotuses and emitting bright light and the sound of music. He bowed to the bhagavat and asked him about this. The bhagavat said,

"Manjushri is fearless.
Why?
His wisdom is unpolluted.
It is the unsurpassable wisdom of buddhahood."

In that way the buddha declared the events to be signs of profound dharma teaching. Manjushri then taught the equality of all dharmas in being unborn. Hundreds and thousands of beings transcended doubt.

The bhagavat then said, "These beings were all previously ripened into awakening by Manjushri. They are now irreversible from awakening through the guidance of the youthful Manjushri, their spiritual friend."

When Manjushri taught that dharma, he bound Mara with his blessing, making Mara incapable of doing anything. When Manjushri withdrew his blessing, Mara the Wrongdoer approached the buddha and said, "When I heard the sound of the irreversible wheel and the name of the bhagavat Shakyamuni, I, Mara, became old and feeble and afraid."

From the *Saddharma Pundarika*

The bhagavat said to the bodhisattva Piled Wisdom, "Son of family, stay for a while. Discuss dharma with my bodhisattva the youthful Manjushri. Travel through my buddha realm later."

The youthful Manjushri came from the palace of the naga king in the ocean. He rose into the sky, seated on a thousand-petal lotus the size of a chariot wheel, surrounded by many other bodhisattvas, and landed on Vulture Peak Mountain in front of the bhagavat. He bowed to the feet of the bhagavat Shakyamuni and the tathagata Many Jewels, sat down, and conversed pleasantly with the bodhisattva Piled Wisdom.

The bodhisattva Piled Wisdom asked Manjushri, "While you were in the ocean, how many beings did you tame?"

Manjushri replied, "I tamed so many that words could not describe them, that the mind could not conceive of them. Stay here for a moment. You will see!"

As soon as Manjushri said that, thousands of lotuses flew out of the ocean into the sky. Seated on them were thousands of beings, all of them bodhisattvas. They all flew into the sky above Vulture Peak Mountain. All of them had been tamed into unsurpassable awakening by Manjushri alone. Those among them who had begun the path by entering the mahayana praised the paramitas. Those among them who had begun the path as shravakas taught the shravakayana. However, they all had realized the emptiness of all dharmas and accomplished the mahayana supercognitions. Manjushri had tamed them by teaching the dharma of the *Pundarika*.

Piled Wisdom said, "This sutra is profound, subtle, and hard to understand. If there exist no other sutras like it, will beings be able to understand this sutra and attain manifest, perfect buddhahood?"

Manjushri replied, "They will. When the daughter of the naga king Samudra was eight years of age she already possessed great intelligence, acute faculties, wisdom, retention, samadhi, and great aspirations. She was always smiling with a bright countenance, had a loving mind, and spoke pleasantly. She was able to attain buddhahood."

Piled Wisdom said, "The tathagata Shakyamuni exerted himself for many kalpas for the sake of unsurpassable awakening. There is not even a mustard-seed-sized space in any direction where he did not give up his life for the sake of awakening. Only after such an accumulation of merit did he attain buddhahood. Who could believe that she attained unsurpassable awakening so quickly?"

At that time, that very girl was present. She bowed to the bhagavat and praised him in verse. She said to him, "I shall attain buddhahood equal to yours!"

Shariputra said to her, "You have irreversible bodhichitta and immeasurable wisdom, but perfect buddhahood is hard to attain. There are those who have perfected the paramitas over many kalpas and still not attained buddhahood. As a woman, there are five things you cannot attain. What are the five? They are the states of Brahma, Indra, the four great kings, a chakravartin, and an irreversible bodhisattva."[35]

35. The four great kings are the rulers of the first level of desire realm devas.

That girl possessed a jewel so valuable that it could have paid for the purchase of these billion worlds. She offered it to the buddha, who kindly accepted it. Then that nagini said to Piled Wisdom and Shariputra, "The bhagavat quickly accepted the jewel I offered him, but I shall miraculously attain buddhahood even more quickly."

It appeared to Shariputra and all in the world that her female organs disappeared, and that male ones took their place. She went to the world called Stainless in the south. There, as a bodhisattva, she sat down in front of a tree composed of seven jewels and attained buddhahood. The light of her body, adorned with marks and signs, filled the ten directions. As she taught dharma, her light was seen by beings of our realm of Saha. All the beings taught dharma by that tathagata attained irreversibility from unsurpassable awakening.

From the "Great Lion's Roar of Maitreya," a part of the
Ratnakuta

The elder Mahakashyapa asked the bhagavat, "Bhagavat, in
the future, during the last five hundred years, what hypocrisy
shall arise among bodhisattvas?"[36]

36. The last five
hundred years
are the last five
hundred of the
predicted five thou-
sand years during
which Buddha
Shakyamuni's
teachings will
remain in
this world.

The buddha replied, "Kashyapa, there will be many bodhisattvas who, influenced by evil companions and weak in
benevolence, will seek food and clothing. They will diligently
venerate, through the offering of flowers and so forth, the
relics of the tathagata. Kashyapa, I have only taught the presentation of offerings so that the unintelligent may accomplish
virtue. But they will say, 'Bhikshus, defer the pursuit of peace
and tranquility! Brahmins and householders with faith, venerate the buddha's relics.'

"Those who abandon yoga, meditation, study, and recitation
for the making of offerings are foolish. Kashyapa, if a bodhisattva filled this realm of a billion worlds from the depths of
its oceans up to the world of Brahma with oil, lit a wick in it
the size of the supreme mountain, and offered this as a lamp
to the tathagata, they would accumulate far less merit than a
bodhisattva with excellent benevolence and moral discipline
who received the transmission of one four-line stanza from an
abbot or master and recited it while walking seven paces.
Kashyapa, a bodhisattva who filled this realm of a billion
worlds with flowers, incense, powder, and fragrance and
offered it to the tathagata three times every day and three
times every night for a hundred thousand years would accumulate far less merit than a bodhisattva who, fearing distracting conversation and the three realms, and desiring the benefit
of all beings, walked seven paces toward a hermitage.

"Kashyapa, what do you think of this? Are you thinking, 'The
tathagata has said this in jest or for the sake of conversation'?

If you are, do not view it in that way! Why? Because I am not like that!

"Kashyapa, in the past, innumerable and more than innumerable kalpas ago, an immeasurable and inconceivable number of kalpas ago, there appeared in the world a tathagata called Various Flowers. His life span was eight kalpas, and his dharma remained for another kalpa after his passing. In his time there was a chakravartin with sovereignty over four continents called Nemi. He had a thousand and two sons, of whom the last two were miraculously born. Their names were Dharma and Sudharma. King Nemi supported the tathagata Various Flowers and his sangha of bhikshus for eighty-four thousand years. During that time, the king thought of nothing but the service of that tathagata and his sangha, and offered them robes, food, and all manner of fine dharmas.

"At the end of those years, on the last day of their patronage, after offering food to the tathagata, the two princes Dharma and Sudharma, accompanied by four servants, bowed to the tathagata and mentally asked him, 'Bhagavat, is there any virtue that surpasses the tremendous virtue generated by King Nemi through his long service?' Asking this in their minds, they prostrated. Immediately afterward, the whole earth shook.

"That tathagata had an attendant named Hard to Beat. He asked the tathagata why the earth was shaking. The tathagata replied, 'Son of family, what good will asking do you? If the benevolence of these two boys, their patience with the profound, their meditation, their great compassion, and their degree of reliance on the tathagata were explained, the world with its gods would go mad!'

"Then that tathagata said to Son of Dispassion, his disciple with the best miraculous abilities, 'Arise and pick up these two boys! Display your miraculous powers!'

"Son of Dispassion tried to pick up the two boys with his hands and lift them, but was unable to do so. He then exerted his great strength and miraculous power and attempted again to lift them, but was unable to so much as move the tip of one of their hairs. He shook all those billion worlds, but could not lift those two boys.

"Then that tathagata took hold of that great shravaka's mind and bestowed further miraculous power upon him. Son of Dispassion was then able to shake as many buddha realms beneath theirs as the Ganges River's sand grains. He was able to turn them all upside down. He was still unable, however, to move even part of the tip of a hair on either boy's head.

"Son of Dispassion said to that tathagata, 'It seems my miraculous powers have diminished! Why do I say so? Because I am unable to lift two boys so young they are practically newborns!'

"That tathagata replied, 'Son of Dispassion, your miraculous powers have not diminished. The blessings of bodhisattvas are inconceivable. It is difficult for shravakas or pratyekabuddhas to move them or even understand them. If every being in this realm of a billion worlds achieved miraculous powers like yours and then performed various miracles for a million kalpas, they would still be unable to lift or even move these two boys.'

"When that tathagata said this, forty-two thousand beings in that assembly generated supreme bodhichitta, thinking, 'Even if bodhisattvas have not achieved omniscient wisdom, they are superior to great shravakas. Their miraculous abilities are wondrous! We must achieve such blessings and the wisdom of buddhahood!'

"Present at that assembly was a bodhisattva called Sumati. He asked that tathagata to lift up the two boys and to reveal what question they had asked. That tathagata snapped his fingers. The sound of it was heard throughout as many realms in the ten directions as there are sand grains in the Ganges River. All those realms shook and were filled with light. When the two boys heard that sound, they arose from before the feet of that tathagata. All the musical instruments of devas and humans in those billion worlds gave forth their sounds without anyone playing them. A rain of flowers fell.

"After arising, the two boys bowed to the feet of that tathagata and circumambulated him. Then they stood before him with palms joined, gazing at his face. Then that tathagata told Sumati what question the two boys had asked mentally when first meeting him.

"The bodhisattva Sumati then asked the tathagata Various Flowers to answer, for the benefit of many beings, the question that the two boys had asked.

"That tathagata replied, 'Son of family, know that far, far greater than the merit of King Nemi's generosity is the massive merit of a bodhisattva who abides in solitude, in isolation, in the wilderness, and for even the duration of a finger snap thinks with patience, "All dharmas are unborn." Never mind the merit of King Nemi! If every being in this realm of a billion worlds performed the same generosity as King Nemi, the merit of them all would be less than a hundred thousandth of the merit of a single benevolent bodhisattva on the perfect path who could tolerate for the duration of a finger snap the thought, "All dharmas are empty and without coming or going." Never mind the aggregate of the merit of all beings of these billion worlds! If every being in as many realms of a billion worlds as there are grains of sand in the Ganges River simultaneously, during each unit of time with the duration of a finger snap, performed the same generosity as King Nemi, and continued to amass such virtue for as many kalpas as there are grains of sand in the Ganges River, they would not

collectively gather so much as a hundredth of the merit gathered by these two boys simply touching the tathagata's feet and prostrating to me!'

"Eighty-four thousand bhikshus from that assembly then declared their rejoicing at such wisdom and bodhichitta. The buddha Various Flowers then continued, 'If your minds are not yet fully liberated, your virtue will cause you to be reborn as chakravartins as many times as there are grains of sand in the Ganges River. You will then attain perfect buddhahood.'

"The two boys then praised what the tathagata had said about devotion to emptiness, living in solitude, and the giving of dharma. The two of them then ascended to a height of seven palm trees in the sky and began to teach profound dharma in verse. As a result, eighty-four thousand beings generated the intention to achieve unsurpassable awakening, and innumerable beings accomplished various roots of virtue. The two boys then descended from the sky and explained the bodhichitta of equality. Twenty thousand bodhisattvas achieved patience with unborn dharmas. King Nemi, his thousand other sons, and five thousand other kings all generated the intention to achieve unsurpassable awakening.

"Then the two boys became renunciates. King Nemi placed his eldest son on the throne and, along with all his other sons, eighty-four thousand women, five thousand kings, and a million other beings, he too became a renunciate.

"Seven days after his coronation, the eldest son went into solitude. He disliked being a king, and wanted renunciation. On the day of the full moon, he declared his intention to renounce the world in verse while touring the four continents of his world. In all those four continents, there was not a single person who liked home life; every single person wanted renunciation. That tathagata knew this and dispatched emanations, accompanied by sanghas of bhikshus, to each village and town. Everyone in that world became a renunciate.

"A harvest of salu grain appeared in that world without being plowed or planted in order to feed all those renunciates. Fine cotton robes fell from the wish-fulfilling tree, and the devas dressed all those beings in them.

"After renunciation, the two boys were diligent. They did not fall asleep or allow their minds to become torpid for sixty-three million years. Other than when eating, they never rested. With their every step and movement they recollected their intention to attain omniscience. They were free of vanity. They achieved the samadhis called Ubiquitous and Endowed with Vajra Character. Thereafter, any place where they crossed their legs became made of vajra. The two boys heard, retained, and taught widely the dharma teaching of six quintillion buddhas of the ten directions.

"Not even one of the inhabitants of those four continents who followed the shravakayana died as an ordinary being. Even the laziest among them became a nonreturner at death and was born in the pure abodes.[37] All the followers of the pratyekabuddhayana were reborn after their deaths in wealthy homes in realms without buddhas. They all subsequently became renunciates through the force of their previous virtue and attained pratyekabuddhahood within seven days. They all benefited innumerable beings and passed into nirvana. All the bodhisattvayana followers achieved the five supercognitions, the four abodes of Brahma, unassailable confidence, and retention.[38]

"I, your teacher Shakyamuni, was King Nemi at that time. The bodhisattva Maitreya was the eldest prince. The tathagata Kashyapa was the bodhisattva Sumati. The youthful Manjushri was the boy Dharma. The bodhisattva Suryagarbha was the boy Sudharma.

37. Nonreturners have achieved the third of the four stages of the shravakayana. The four stages are: stream-enterer, once-returner, non-returner, and arhat. The five pure abodes are the five highest levels of the realm of form. Although they are part of the three realms of samsara, it is taught that the five pure abodes are inhabited exclusively by those engaged in completing a Buddhist path.

38. In this context, the four abodes of Brahma are the four immeasurables: boundless love, compassion, empathetic joy, and impartiality.

"As I said, the two bhikshus Dharma and Sudharma abided in the diligent pursuit of their aim and remained free from many activities. They therefore did not present offerings to the relics of the tathagata Various Flowers and did not visit his stupa. Millions of devas and new bhikshus began to say, 'These two bhikshus do not present offerings to the tathagata's relics and do not circumambulate his stupa. They are faithless and disrespectful!'

"The two bhikshus responded, 'Friends! When in order to serve the tathagata you offer dharmas to his relics, which have no mind, do you think those relics receive the offerings?'

"The bhikshus and devas answered, 'These relics are distinguished by the aggregates of morality and the rest. They are therefore worthy of service.'

"The two bhikshus replied, 'Morality, samadhi, wisdom, liberation, and liberated wisdom are indeed worthy of service. In comparison, are not relics unworthy of service?'

"The bhikshus and devas answered, 'It is so.'

"The two bhikshus continued, 'Friends! In that case, what is the character of morality and the rest?'

"The devas and bhikshus answered, 'Their character is the absence of manifest formation.'

"The two bhikshus asked, 'Can that which is without manifest formation be served through manifest formation?'

"The bhikshus and devas answered, 'It cannot.'

"The two bhikshus continued, 'Then friends, be without the manifest formation of the self. That will be service of the tathagata. When you conceptualize the buddha, you do not see the buddha. What need is there to speak of presenting offerings? It is useless! If you wish to serve the tathagata, serve yourselves.'

"The bhikshus and devas asked, 'Why should those wishing to serve the tathagata serve themselves?'

"The bhikshus Dharma and Sudharma replied, 'Friends! Serve yourselves because the tathagata saw all beings to be worthy of service. Cultivate what was cultivated by the tathagata. Be without vanity! Utterly discern the nature of dharmas, and become free from the thought of anything whatsoever. When you have served yourselves in that way, you will have served the tathagata. You will have become worthy of service. Those wishing to serve the tathagata's relics should serve themselves as the tathagata has served them by achieving the qualities that make those relics worthy of service. By doing so, they serve the tathagata. Whoever does not give rise to the conceptual perception of characteristics and is without the thought and concept of the self, of permanence and termination, of coming and going, and of any characteristic is serving the tathagata. Since the tathagata's body is unborn, noncomposite, and nondual in character, it is hard to serve it through what is born, composite, and dual.'

"Through the teaching of this dharma, forty-two thousand bodhisattvas in that assembly achieved patience with unborn dharmas. Eighty-four thousand beings generated wisdom and insight, and achieved the passionless state of a nonreturner. Twenty-three thousand beings who had not yet generated bodhichitta gave rise to the intention to attain unsurpassable awakening. All the bhikshus and devas present there were thereafter diligent in the accomplishment of their own benefit. They engaged in few activities and did not present offerings to the stupa and so forth. They thereby perfectly entered unsurpassable, profound dharma.

The bhagavat concluded, "Kashyapa, emulate such holy beings' skill and patience with the profound."[39]

39. Patience with the profound is a tolerance for the inconceivable nature of things. Patience is required because this nature cannot be realized by a conceptual mind.

From the *Dharani of the Hundred Thousand Ornaments of the Heart of Awakening*

Once, the youthful Manjushri took up a begging bowl and, placing within it the entire dharmadhatu spoken of by the bhagavat, offered it to the bhagavat. The bhagavat extended his golden hand and took hold of the bowl. He then cast it into the sky before him. The begging bowl became innumerable tathagatas filling all the sky in this realm of a billion worlds. They all said to the bhagavat Shakyamuni, "Excellent!" Before each of those tathagatas there appeared a bhagavat Shakyamuni with his retinue. In front of each of those Shakyamunis appeared a Manjushri offering a begging bowl.

Then the mahabodhisattva Vajrapani asked the youthful Manjushri, "Manjushri, for whose benefit has this wondrous, excellent, great miracle — this sudden assembly and display of all tathagatas — appeared? What are its causes and conditions? Why has this miracle of effusive light-rays been displayed?"

Manjushri replied, "What! Vajrapani, do you not know the causes and conditions of this appearance of light and miracles?"

Vajrapani responded, "Manjushri, I do not know them. I have never up to now seen or heard of as great a miracle as this assembly and display of all tathagatas. Today is my first time!"

Then Vajrapani brandished his vajra, circumambulated the bhagavat three times, and asked the bhagavat, "What dharma are you about to teach that you have displayed this wondrous, excellent miracle, the like of which I've never seen or heard of before now?"

The bhagavat replied, "Vajrapani, wait a bit. In a moment, it will become apparent."

As soon as the buddha said that, a stupa made of the seven precious materials suddenly appeared. It was seven thousand yojanas in height and five thousand yojanas in breadth, and was adorned by fine and abundant decoration. From the sky appeared devas, venerating and prostrating to the stupa. The bhagavat then asked Vajrapani to open the stupa's door. With his right hand Vajrapani did so. Inside the stupa was a throne made from the gold of the Jambu River, adorned by the seven jewels, and covered by divine fabric. Seated on the throne in meditation was the bhagavat tathagata arhat samyaksambuddha Expansive Golden Countenance Supremely Heroic Light-Rays Victory Banner Peak.

Then that tathagata said to the bhagavat Shakyamuni, "This miracle of yours is wondrous! You have assembled and displayed all tathagatas! While, in absolute truth, all dharmas have never possessed assembly and dispersal, no previous buddha has ever displayed so wondrous a miracle in this world! Please now teach the king of realizations, the dharani of the hundred thousand ornaments of awakening!"

In response to his encouragement, the bhagavat taught it. When the Lord of Secrets, Vajrapani, then asked the bhagavat about the dharani's benefits, the bhagavat replied, "Ask Manjushri."

Vajrapani did so. All present in that assembly who heard Manjushri's words of explanation of the dharani's benefits achieved irreversibility from unsurpassable awakening. Some of them also received prophecy of their unsurpassable awakening.

From the *Mahayana Sutra of the Container of the Noble Three Jewels*

Shariputra once said, "I want to hear dharma from the youthful Manjushri. I do not want to teach. Why? Because I have

seen Manjushri teach dharma in the presence of many buddhas in the past, leaving even the greatest shravakas speechless. To the east, past hundreds and thousands of buddha realms, is a world called Wonderment. Living there now is the tathagata called Light Peak. His mahashravaka with the greatest wisdom is called Wisdom Beacon. When Manjushri and I went there together, Manjushri was followed by thousands of bodhisattvas and devas. The youthful Manjushri stayed among the Clear Light devas of that realm. Once, he cleared his throat. The sound was heard throughout those billion worlds. All the abodes of Mara were disturbed. The mahashravaka Wisdom Beacon, unable to withstand the sound of Manjushri clearing his throat, fell to the ground shaking like a bird in a tornado and was amazed. He asked the tathagata Light Peak, 'Who made that sound?'

"The tathagata replied, 'It was made by the power of the youthful Manjushri.'

"Manjushri came there, bowed to that tathagata, and discussed dharma with him. When Manjushri spoke of dharma to the mahashravaka Wisdom Beacon, all the devas in that assembly cast flowers of various colors at Manjushri and said, 'Wherever the youthful Manjushri appears, a tathagata is directly seen! Any place where the youthful Manjushri abides becomes a stupa! Wherever Manjushri teaches dharma, all the beings that know or will know his teaching come to possess all merit!'

"Then Manjushri asked the mahashravaka Wisdom Beacon, 'It is said that you have the greatest wisdom. Is your wisdom composite or noncomposite?' By asking that question, Manjushri rendered the shravaka speechless.

"Then having received the permission of that tathagata, Manjushri taught that assembly the isolation of all dharmas.

Eight hundred bodhisattvas achieved patience with unborn dharmas.

"In that way, no shravaka or pratyekabuddha can impede Manjushri's confidence. Therefore unless asked, someone like me is unable to speak in Manjushri's presence."

The venerable Subhuti asked, "Shariputra, when you accompanied the youthful Manjushri to buddha realms what miracles did you see?"

Shariputra replied, "When I went to buddha realms with Manjushri, he filled realms that were burning with the water of lotuses. The fire became as soft to the touch as snakeheart sandalwood and kachalidi cotton. If a realm was empty space, he filled it with bodhisattvas meditating in the palace of Brahma. He caused realms that were arising to appear to be in the midst of destruction, realms filled with bad rebirths to be devoid of bad rebirths, and the beings in all those realms to achieve love born from the seven factors of awakening.[40] How? While meditating on the seven factors, Manjushri taught dharma to beings afflicted by attachment and other kleshas so that they could abandon them.

"At the time I thought that Manjushri's miraculous abilities and mine were equal. Manjushri knew my thought and, when an entire realm of a billion worlds was on fire, he remained between worlds and asked me, 'Shariputra, shall we escape through your power or through mine?'

"I answered, 'We shall escape through my power.' I then quickly demonstrated my miraculous abilities by pacifying the fire in an area the size of an arm span and remaining within its shelter with Manjushri for seven days.

"At another time an even larger world was burning. While we were between worlds Manjushri asked me, 'Shariputra,

40. The seven factors of awakening are: recollection, discernment, diligence, joy, pliancy, equanimity, and samadhi.

through whose miraculous power shall we escape this time?'

"I said to him, 'We shall escape through your power.'

"With a single moment of bodhichitta, he covered that entire world with a web of lotuses and we escaped. He then said to me, 'Which of us is quicker?'

"I answered, 'The difference between my miraculous speed and yours is far greater than the difference between the speed in flight of a languli bird and that of a garuda, the king of birds. As shravakas have not eradicated habits, even though our miraculous powers are unequal I thought they were equal.'

"Manjushri said to me, 'There once lived at the shore of an ocean a rishi named Dharma Desire, who had achieved the five supercognitions, and a rishi named All-Given, who could fly through the power of awareness-mantra. All-Given believed that their miraculous powers were equal. He once flew over the ocean to an island of rakshasis.[41] Hearing the rakshasis' lovely voices and seeing their beauty, All-Given fell to the ground; his power of awareness-mantra was impaired. Dharma Desire compassionately took him by the hand and rescued him. At the time, I was Dharma Desire. You were All-Given. At that time also, although we were unequal, you thought we were equals.'

41. Rakshasas are nonhuman beings that eat human flesh. Rakshasis are female rakshasas.

"Another time Manjushri and I, Shariputra, went to buddha realms to the south. We passed through billions and billions of buddha realms and reached a world called Decorated With All Ornaments. This is the realm of the tathagata Precious Life-Tree. When we arrived there Manjushri asked me, 'Noble Shariputra, how do you see the realms through which we have passed?'

"I replied, 'Some of them are filled with fire. Some are filled with water. Some are just space. Some are affluent and vast. Some are just arising. Some are being destroyed. Some are filled with bad rebirths. Some are without bad rebirths.'

"He then asked me, 'How are they to be viewed?'

"I replied, 'Those filled with fire are to be viewed as filled with fire, and so on. Manjushri, how do you see them?'

"He said, 'I see all those realms as space. Their appearance of being filled with fire or water and so on is inauthentic. It comes from temporary conditions. It arises and is destroyed. Space does not come from conditions; it abides naturally. In the same way, although temporary kleshas afflict the mind, the mind's nature is never afflicted. For example, even though there have occurred as many kalpas of burning as there are sand grains in the Ganges River, space has never been burnt. In the same way, although each being has done as many unvirtuous actions as there are sand grains in the Ganges River, the nature of their minds has never become afflicted. That nature is utterly pure. It is the dharmadhatu. It does not change. It is not obscured. It is without even the slightest formation or transformation. This is the dharma gate of no transformation. Bodhisattvas who abide in this have entered the utterly pure nature of all dharmas. They will never become obscured by any fault.'

"That is my direct, although partial, experience of Manjushri's miraculous abilities."

The venerable Ananda said to Shariputra, "I too have experienced such things. Once, when the bhagavat was residing at the Jetavana, an unseasonably great cloud appeared over Shravasti and sent down heavy rain for seven days. Those bhikshus who had achieved meditation passed their time in samadhi. Those who had not achieved it were cut off from food and became desperate. They were also unable to move about in order to see the bhagavat. When I informed the bhagavat of the bhikshus' hardship, he said, 'Tell Manjushri about this.'

42. Lokapalas are devas who guard the world.

43. A gandi is a wooden concussive instrument used to summon the sangha.

"I went to Manjushri, who was teaching dharma to Brahma, Indra, and other lokapalas, and told him.[42] He said, 'Ananda, lay out the seats. When it is time to eat, beat the gandi.'[43] I went to do so. The youthful Manjushri entered the samadhi called Utter Destruction of the Body's Appearance. While an emanation continued teaching dharma to Indra and the rest of them, Manjushri arose and went to beg in Shravasti. I, of course, did not see this.

"Mara the Wrongdoer cast a spell so that no one in the whole town could see Manjushri, in order to prevent them from offering him alms. Knowing this, Manjushri said, 'By the truth of my words, by the truth of the statement that there is more merit and wisdom in any single pore of my skin than in all the Mara the Wrongdoers in as many worlds as there are sand grains in the Ganges River, may this spell of Mara's cease. May Mara the Wrongdoer be compelled to appear at every corner and intersection in this town in order to offer alms to Manjushri. May he proclaim, "The benefit of offering as much food as would fit on the tip of a fingernail to the youthful Manjushri is far greater than the benefit of respectfully serving all the sentient beings in a realm of a billion worlds with all manner of pleasant things for a hundred thousand years."'

"Immediately this occurred. Mara was forced to carefully place a pleasing variety of foodstuffs in Manjushri's begging bowl. Manjushri blessed the bowl so that it could contain enough food for five hundred bhikshus and twelve thousand bodhisattvas. When it did, Manjushri placed it on the ground outside the town of Shravasti. He then said to Mara the Wrongdoer, 'Carry this begging bowl and walk before me.'

"Mara tried to pick up the begging bowl, but could not move it. When he told Manjushri this, Manjushri said, 'Mara, if you are powerful, lift it with miraculous strength.'

"Mara displayed all his miraculous abilities but was still unable to raise the bowl by even the width of a hair. He became embarrassed, and said, 'If I wanted to, I could pick up Mount Plow-Shaft in the palm of my hand and toss it into the sky. I cannot, however, lift this little begging bowl off the ground. Why?'

"Manjushri replied, 'You cannot lift it because I have placed within it the weight of the heaviest and largest beings.'

"Then Manjushri picked up the begging bowl and said, 'Wrongdoer, carry this and walk before me.' Mara therefore walked ahead of Manjushri and, as though his disciple, carried his begging bowl. Twelve thousand powerful devas bowed to Manjushri and asked him, 'Why is the wrongdoer walking before you like a servant?'

"Through Manjushri's power, Mara replied, 'Mara's power is the power of stupidity. The power of bodhisattvas is the power of wisdom.' As a result, five hundred devas within that assembly generated the intention to achieve unsurpassable awakening, and two hundred bodhisattvas achieved patience with unborn dharmas.

"Then Manjushri and Mara the Wrongdoer placed the begging bowl in the courtyard of the sangha's residence and left together. I neither saw nor heard them. It was then time for the sangha's meal. As I did not see Manjushri anywhere, either within or without the residence, I wondered, 'Has Manjushri deceived the sangha of bhikshus?' I conveyed my concern to the bhagavat.

"He replied, 'Do you see anything in the courtyard?'

"I answered, 'There is a begging bowl filled with food there.'

"He said, 'Beat the gandi and summon the sangha.'

"I asked, 'How will we make do with a single begging bowl?'

"He said, 'Even if all the beings in these billion worlds were fed from that one begging bowl, it would not be emptied. It has been blessed by the youthful Manjushri, whose perfection of generosity is a source of inexhaustible merit.'

"I therefore beat the gandi. When I did so, Manjushri emerged from his dwelling into the courtyard, accompanied by many devas and bodhisattvas. All the many bhikshus and bodhisattvas were fed and satisfied with the fine and flavorful food that we found in the begging bowl, which was still not empty.

"Then Mara the Wrongdoer emanated forty thousand unpleasant bhikshus in order to obstruct Manjushri. They wore their skirts and other robes askew, were deformed, were greedy, had incomplete faculties, and were of extreme variations in height. They too were fed, and the food was not used up, even though Mara had cast a spell so that each of them could and did eat ten Magadha pounds of cooked rice.[44] The servers became exhausted because the emanated bhikshus were insatiable.

44. About 10.5 pounds.

"Then Manjushri blessed the bhikshus emanated by Mara so that each of them held in one hand a begging bowl filled with food, in the other hand still more food, and in their mouths a mouthful of food that they could not swallow. They all simultaneously fell to the ground, grabbing at their throats, with their eyes rolled back into their heads. Manjushri said to Mara, 'Wrongdoer, why are your bhikshus not eating?'

"Mara replied, 'Manjushri, if my bhikshus are dying it is because you have mixed poison into their food.'

"Manjushri answered, 'Whatever is poisonous produces poison. How could something without poison produce it?

Wrongdoer, poison is desire, anger, and stupidity. These do not exist within the dharma, the vinaya, which has been well taught. The buddha's teaching is the teaching of amrita, the teaching of bliss, and the teaching of simplicity.'

"Because of what Manjushri said, five hundred devas in Mara's company generated the intention to achieve unsurpassable awakening and made aspirations.

"At that time the bhagavat said, 'In the future, during the final five-hundred years, when the holy dharma is being destroyed, most bhikshus will be like these. They will wear their robes askew. They will be inattentive. Their behavior will be ugly. They will be deformed. They will suffer from various ailments. They will have renunciation not for the sake of dharma but for the sake of acquisition and service. They will be busy with various doings. Mara will be delighted, and his activity will appear. Through diligence in dharma, eradicate Mara and uphold holy dharma!'

"Because of what the buddha said, thirty-two thousand bodhisattvas achieved patience with unborn dharmas."

Then Mahakashyapa said, "Some of Manjushri's miracles have been revealed to me too. Not long after the bhagavat attained buddhahood, and not long after I became a renunciate, the youthful Manjushri appeared among us. He came to this world from the buddha realm of the tathagata Precious Life-Tree in order to see, prostrate to, and serve the bhagavat. At that time, the bhagavat had promised to remain for the summer within the enclosure built by Anathapindada, the Jetavana. Manjushri also promised to stay for the three months of summer. However, we never saw him again during those three months. He did not appear in the buddha's presence, within the sangha, or at the renewal and purification ceremonies.

"When the three months were over, at the concluding ceremony of renewal, purification, and the removal of restrictions, I saw Manjushri. I asked him, 'Manjushri, where have you been for these three months of summer?'

"He replied, 'Noble one, I have been in this town of Shravasti, in the palace of King Prasenajit's queens.'

"When I heard that I thought, 'It is wrong for a being guilty of such downfalls to join this pure sangha at the removal of restrictions!' I strode out to the courtyard and began to beat the gandi in order to expel Manjushri.

"The bhagavat said to Manjushri, 'Mahakashyapa is beating the gandi. In order that he not be without faith in you, reveal the purity of your behavior. Please these great shravakas!'

"Manjushri entered the samadhi called Perfect Display of All Buddha Realms. In as many buddha realms in the ten directions as there are sand grains in the Ganges River appeared disciplined bhikshus like me, Mahakashyapa. All of them were beating their gandis in order to expel the youthful Manjushri.

"The bhagavat asked me, 'Kashyapa, why are you beating the gandi?'

"In reply, I told him why. Light emerged from all parts of the bhagavat's body. He then said to me, 'Kashyapa, look at what is appearing in the ten directions.' So I looked, and I saw what I have described to you. The bhagavat then asked me, 'Which Manjushri are you going to expel, the one before us, or all the ones present before all the buddhas of the ten directions?'

"Embarrassed, I wanted to throw the gandi to the ground. I was unable to do so, however, and it kept making its clacking sound uninterruptedly. Furthermore, the gandis in the realms of all buddhas were doing the same thing as our gandi in the Jetavana.

"I then bowed to the bhagavat's feet and said, 'My wisdom is only partial. I beat the gandi in ignorance of the immeasurable conduct of bodhisattvas. I apologize to the youthful Manjushri!'

"The buddha said, 'Kashyapa, all the Manjushris who appear in all buddha realms have spent the three months of summer in householders' homes in order to ripen beings. Manjushri promised to remain for the summer in the queens' palace here in Shravasti. Among the retinue of the queens of King Prasenajit, five hundred women, five hundred men, five hundred boys, five hundred girls, and five hundred prostitutes have been ripened by him into irreversibility from unsurpassable awakening. He has tamed many other beings with the shravakayana, ensuring their migration to higher states.'

"I asked the bhagavat, 'Through what dharma teaching has Manjushri ripened them?'

"The buddha replied, 'Ask Manjushri. He will tell you.'

"I asked Manjushri, who replied, 'Noble Mahakashyapa, such beings cannot be ripened through dharma teaching. Some beings are ripened through delightful play, some by remaining in the palace, some by argument, some by generosity, some by poverty, some by great displays, some by various miracles, some by my taking the form of Brahma or other gods, some by criticism, some by harsh words, some by gentle speech, and some by being helped. As beings' lifestyles vary, so must the means of ripening them. Once ripened, they are all finally tamed by the teaching of dharma.'

"I asked him, 'Manjushri, how many beings have you ripened through such deeds?'

"He replied, 'As many as there are in the dharmadhatu. The dharmadhatu, the extent of space, and the extent of beings are not different things.' Manjushri then explained the thirty-two armors of a bodhisattva. As a result, twelve thousand devas generated the intention to achieve unsurpassable awakening."

After Kashyapa finished speaking, the venerable Purna, Maitri's son, said, "I too have witnessed some of the miracles of the youthful Manjushri. Once, the bhagavat was staying, along with a great sangha of bhikshus, in a mansion in a large park in the town of Shravasti. At that time Truthful, an adherent of the Naked Ones, was living in Shravasti, where he was venerated as their guru by sixty thousand disciples. When I entered samadhi and viewed the virtue of the tirthikas, I saw that there were many tirthika disciples.[45] I went among them and taught dharma, but they paid me no respect. They covered their ears, did not listen, and reviled me with harsh words. For three months I was unable to ripen a single being. Disappointed, I returned to the sangha.

45. Tirthikas are adherents of non-Buddhist Indian religious traditions.

"The youthful Manjushri then emanated five hundred tirthikas. He appointed me to teach the sangha in his absence, and he and his emanations went to where Truthful the Naked One was living. Manjushri and his emanations bowed to Truthful's feet, sat before him, and said, 'We have heard of your fame, noble one, and are here to request that you be our teacher and guide us. Please make sure that we never see the bhikshu Gautama or his shravakas, and that we never hear his discordant teaching.'[46]

46. Gautama was Buddha Shakyamuni's family name.

"Truthful replied, 'Excellent, you with faith! You will quickly come to understand my teaching!' He then instructed his disciples, 'Practice together with these five hundred brahmin youths. Live with them in joy and harmony! Keep well in your hearts whatever they say to you!'

"So Manjushri and his five hundred emanations began to live

with those tirthikas. They continuously surpassed them in austerity and the other features of their conduct. They also, from time to time, praised the three jewels. At other times they praised the virtuous qualities of the Naked One, Truthful. Everything they said was believed by the other disciples.

"On one occasion, the youthful Manjushri said to the tirthika disciples, 'Venerable ones, in all our shastras, mantras, vedas, and other scriptures, there are praises of the bhikshu Gautama. Why? Because he was born in the flawless family of a chakravartin and was taken up by Brahma and Indra.'

"Manjushri told them about the buddha's life — how he received prophecy from brahmins, how he became a renunciate and attained buddhahood, how he taught dharma of triple virtue and fourfold chastity, and so on. Through Manjushri's praise of the buddha, five hundred tirthikas achieved the pure eye of dharma. Thousands of other tirthikas generated the intention to achieve unsurpassable awakening.

"Then the five hundred emanations touched their five limbs to the ground while saying, 'I prostrate to the buddha.' In imitation of them, all the tirthikas in that assembly began to bow to the buddha.

"The deva Indra then gave them mandarava flowers, saying, 'Offer these to the bhagavat.' The youthful Manjushri and his large retinue went to the park surrounded by bamboo where the bhagavat was staying. They all bowed to the buddha, and the tirthikas offered the mandarava flowers they had been given. They circumambulated three times and then sat down as a group.

"Then Manjushri's five hundred emanations said, 'Bhagavat, the tathagata is the dharmakaya. We do not seek to see the buddha. Bhagavat, dharma is inexpressible. We do not seek to hear dharma from the bhagavat.' In that way they explained

47. *Freedom from acceptance* refers here and elsewhere in this book to freedom from rebirth. Acceptance is the acceptance of craving, which compels one to be reborn.

the aspect of dharma that shows that, since dharma is without any essential nature, it is not to be sought. Two hundred bhikshus achieved freedom from acceptance, the liberation of their minds from defilements.[47]

"There were, however, two hundred other bhikshus there who were proud because they had achieved the four meditative stabilities. They said, 'The dharma they have taught contradicts everything in the world.' Saying that, they arose from their seats and walked off.

"Then I, Purna, said to Manjushri, 'Those two hundred bhikshus have left out of disrespect!'

"Manjushri replied, 'Noble Purna, some dharma teaching does contradict the entire world. The world is fixated on the aggregates and so forth, and seeks nirvana through the abandonment of them. This is contradicted by the fact that samsara does not exist in itself, and that there is therefore no nirvana to be achieved. The equality and nonduality of samsara and nirvana are beyond contradiction.' Manjushri taught such dharma on that occasion.

"The bhikshus who had left saw that wherever they went became filled with fire. When they attempted to miraculously fly over it they found that the sky was covered by an iron net. When they looked beneath the fire they saw an impassably large body of water. They became terrified. When in their desperation they looked back toward the Jetavana, they saw that the path back to it was covered with lotus and utpala flowers that were being cast on the ground by many people who wanted to hear dharma from the bhagavat. The bhikshus therefore turned back and returned to the Jetavana and its courtyard surrounded by bamboo, where the bhagavat was staying. Having reached it, they all prostrated to the bhagavat, circumambulated him three times, and sat down as a group.

"Then I, Purna, asked them, 'Where did you go? From where have you returned?'

"They replied, 'We are arhats who have exhausted defilements, achieved meditative stability, and perfected the bases of miracles. When we heard the youthful Manjushri teach contradictory dharma, we arose from our seats and left. We saw, however, that this realm was filled with fire, and we were unable to get past it.'

"I asked the bhagavat, 'What is the level of an arhat who has exhausted defilements?'

"He replied, 'Purna, it is impossible for those engaged in the fire of desire, anger, and stupidity to pass beyond that mass of fire. It is impossible for those obscured by the net of views to cut through that iron net. It is impossible for those immersed in the water of existence to cross that body of water. That mass of fire, that net, and that water did not come from anywhere and have not gone anywhere. They appeared through the blessing of Manjushri. Since, in the same way, desire and the rest do not come and go, they are no more than the incorrect thought that is the superimposition of a self where there is no self. Therefore yogins who accomplish one-pointed tranquility of mind and meditative stability should be without vanity and craving. A mind that has been made workable through meditation should discern the individual causes and conditions of all dharmas, and thereby ascertain the progressive and reversed twelve links of interdependence. They will thereby realize absolute truth, the unborn nature of all dharmas.'

"By saying that, the buddha caused those bhikshus' minds to be utterly freed from all defilements.

"Then because his retinue had become so reduced, Truthful the Naked One came into the bhagavat's presence along with five hundred attendants. He said to the buddha, 'I had heard that

you, the bhikshu Gautama, steal others' followers through deception. Now I have actually seen it! Manjushri has divided my followers and offered them to you, Gautama. You have accepted them, and they no longer come to me!'

"When Truthful had spoken the ubiquitous Jinamati, who was present there, said to Truthful, 'Do not disbelieve in the bhagavat, his shravakas, and Manjushri! You will suffer unnecessarily for a long time! The supposedly wondrous meditation of you outsiders is as pointless as trying to make butter by churning water! The dharma, the vinaya, of the bhagavat is meaningful, like making butter by churning milk. Those who have set aside your teaching and taken up that of the tathagata are like those who set aside a clay vessel and take up one of precious metal. They are not deceived; they are like people who have left the wrong road for the right one! So take your remaining followers, Naked One, and go!'

"Truthful the Naked One left with twelve thousand of his followers. Those who remained achieved supercognition. The bhagavat caused them to become renunciates with the words, 'Come here!'

"At that time the bhagavat said to Jinamati, 'Because the twelve thousand naked ones who left with Truthful heard this profound dharma, they will be among the first of Maitreya's disciples. Truthful will be the disciple of Maitreya with the greatest wisdom, like Shariputra now. They actually respect me even now, but are unable to give up their views because of their great pride.'

"Then Manjushri and the bhagavat taught Jinamati dharma based on the absence of pride and the cultivation of diligence and attention. He generated bodhichitta, achieved patience with unborn dharmas, and was prophesied to become the tathagata Heap of Wisdom."

After Purna said this, they continued to recount what they had witnessed of Manjushri's demonstration of miracles in the bhagavat's presence and his demonstration of miracles while teaching dharma.

From the *Avatamsakasutra*

The youthful Manjushri had no fixed residence. He was attended and served by bodhisattvas of similar fortune; his constant follower Vajrapani; devas of the family of body; devas who walked on their feet; the goddess of the earth; the rulers of nagas, yakshas, and ghandharvas; Indra; and Brahma.[48] One day, adorned with the impressive finery of a bodhisattva, he emerged from his dwelling, circumambulated the bhagavat hundreds of times, presented many different offerings, and then left, heading south.

48. Yakshas are powerful non-humans associated with wealth. Ghandharvas are beings nourished by smells.

Through the buddha's blessing, Shariputra saw the youthful Manjushri, adorned by the abundant splendor of a bodhi-sattva, leave the Jetavana for the south. Shariputra thought, "I shall accompany the youthful Manjushri as he wanders through various lands." Together with about sixty bhikshus, he left his dwelling, went into the bhagavat's presence, prostrated to him, received his permission, and left with Manjushri.

Among the bhikshus accompanying Shariputra were Sagaramati, Mahasudatta, and Punyaprabha. They were all new bhikshus, having recently become renunciates. They had all attended previous victors, were interested in the profound, had regard for the tathagata's qualities and the essence of dharma, were devoted to great deeds, and were capable of helping others. They had all been tamed by the youthful Manjushri's dharma teaching.

When the venerable Shariputra set out on his journey he looked at all the bhikshus accompanying him and said to the

bhikshu Sagaramati, "Sagaramati, the body of the bodhi-sattva Manjushri is fully adorned by excellent marks and signs. It is utterly pure. It is inconceivable to devas and humans. The mandala of its light is utterly pure and generates joy in the hearts of innumerable beings. Manjushri's ornamental web of light rays pacifies the suffering of innumerable beings. All those in his excellent retinue are endowed with virtue from the past. Whenever he travels, his path is ornamented like a checkerboard. It is ornamented in such a way that he can traverse it easily, and so that he can view the horizon in all directions. It is ornamented by his merit so that great treasure appears to his right and his left. In accordance with the virtue of his service to previous buddhas, ornaments appear among the leaves of every tree he passes. All the rulers of the world bow to him and send down rains of gifts from clouds of offering. The tathagatas of the ten directions emit mandalas of webs of light rays that proclaim all buddha-dharmas and gather above his head. Look!"

In that way, the venerable Shariputra fully described the immeasurable, ornamental qualities that arise whenever the youthful Manjushri sets out on a journey. As Shariputra revealed Manjushri's qualities, the bhikshus' minds became more and more pure and filled with wonder. They became faultless and free from any obscuration. They became devoted to the buddha and the dharma. Their bodhisattva faculties became utterly pure. Their faith and compassion intensified. They reached the mandala of the paramitas. The entire ocean of the buddhas of the ten directions appeared to them. Having achieved a powerful resolve to attain omniscience, they said to Shariputra, "Preceptor, please bring us into the presence of that holy being!"

So Shariputra brought those bhikshus to Manjushri and said to him, "Manjushri, these bhikshus would like to see you."

The youthful Manjushri regarded those bhikshus and the

entire mandala of his retinue in that place with the majestic gaze of an elephant. The bhikshus bowed the crowns of their heads to Manjushri's two feet. They joined their palms and said, "Holy being, through the virtue of seeing you and of prostrating to you; and through all the virtue known to you, known to our preceptor, and directly seen by the tathagata Shakyamuni, may we become just like you. May we have bodies, voices, names, and miraculous abilities like yours."

Manjushri said to them, "Bhikshus, a son or daughter of family who has entered the mahayana and whose bodhichitta is endowed with ten types of tirelessness will not only achieve the bodhisattva levels, they will reach the level of a tathagata. What are the ten? They are: bodhichitta that never tires of viewing the tathagatas and venerating them; bodhichitta that never tires of the accumulation of virtue; bodhichitta that never tires of the search for dharma; bodhichitta that never tires of the application of the paramitas of a bodhisattva; bodhichitta that never tires of the accomplishment of samadhi; bodhichitta that never tires of passing through all time; bodhichitta that never tires of the purification of oceans of realms; bodhichitta that never tires of the ripening of all beings; bodhichitta that never tires of the accomplishment of a bodhisattva's deeds in all realms and all kalpas; and bodhichitta that never tires of the one-pointed accomplishment of the strength of the tathagatas by ripening all beings, one by one, through as many applications of the paramitas as there are fine particles in all realms. Through the possession of these ten, all virtues will be accomplished. They will rise above the whole continuum of samsara. They will surpass all shravakas and pratyekabuddhas. They will join the family and continuum of tathagatas. Their bodhisattva training will become utterly pure. They will achieve the strength of a tathagata. They will subdue Mara and aggression. They will pass through the bodhisattva levels and will closely approach the level of a tathagata."

When the bhikshus heard this, they achieved the samadhi called Seeing All Buddhas Without Impediment. They saw, through its power, the tathagatas of all the innumerable realms in the ten directions. They saw all the beings born in those realms and knew their suffering in even its most subtle aspects. They heard the oceans of euphony of those tathagatas' voices, and fully understood the words of their dharma teaching. They knew the minds, faculties, and thoughts of each being in all those realms. They recollected the ten most recent lives and foresaw the ten next lives of each of those beings. They became learned in the terms of ten dharmachakras turned by each of those tathagatas. Each of the bhikshus achieved ten miraculous abilities. Each of them accomplished ten aspects of the teaching and mastered ten terms used in teaching. Each of them achieved ten varieties of perfect awareness. As soon as they achieved that samadhi, they perfected a myriad of bodhisattva qualities, a myriad of samadhis, and a myriad of aspects of the paramitas. Through the power of that mandala's appearance — great, radiant wisdom — they achieved ten varieties of a bodhisattva's supercognition.

Because, although their bodhichitta was stable, the seedling of their supercognition was young and slender, Manjushri established them in the conduct of Samantabhadra. They entered the ocean of vast aspirations and fulfilled them.

Having established those bhikshus in unsurpassable awakening, the youthful Manjushri journeyed to the south. He came to a large town called Source of Happiness. To the town's east was a large forest called Adorned by Victory Banners of Various Sal Trees. In that forest was a stupa of the tathagatas where devas, nagas, yakshas, and others regularly gathered. Manjushri taught there a sutra called *Full Appearance of the Dharmadhatu*. This sutra is the source of one hundred sextillion sutras. Hearing that sutra, sextillions of nagas from the great ocean became so devoted to the tathagata that they were transformed from nagas into devas and humans. Ten thousand of those nagas achieved irreversibility from unsurpassable awakening. By teaching this dharma, Manjushri gradually tamed innumerable beings through the three vehicles.

When the people of the town Source of Happiness heard that Manjushri was living in the forest Adorned by Various Sal Trees, a number of them came there. Among them were the upasaka merchant Mahaprajna and the upasaka Sudatta, who were accompanied by five hundred other upasakas; the upasika Mahaprajna and the upasika Suprabha, who were accompanied by five hundred other upasikas; Sudhana the merchant's son and the merchant's son Sushila, accompanied by five hundred other merchants' sons; and Suvarna — the daughter of the householder Mahaprajna — and five hundred other women such as Bhadri.[49] They all prostrated to Manjushri's feet, circumambulated him three times, and sat down as a group.

49. An upasaka is a Buddhist lay disciple. An upasika is a female upasaka.

Manjushri then subdued that assembly with his splendor and satisfied them with his love. He taught them dharma with compassion. He distinguished between wisdom mind and thought, and taught dharma with great perfect awareness. Pleased, he gazed upon Sudhana the merchant's son, who had served victors of the past and generated virtue, and possessed the utmost qualities, such as great devotion. Gazing upon Sudhana and speaking pleasantly, Manjushri taught them about the all-inclusive qualities of buddhahood. Sudhana and everyone in that great assembly generated the intention to achieve unsurpassable awakening. They recollected their previous virtues. Then the gathering dispersed.

Having now heard of the victor's qualities and greatness, Sudhana the merchant's son became devoted to the pursuit of perfect awakening. He followed Manjushri and requested from him, while praising him in verse, instruction on the conduct of a bodhisattva.

Manjushri replied, "Son of family, you have generated the intention to achieve unsurpassable awakening and follow spiritual friends. You want to complete the path of a bodhisattva and therefore are thinking about a bodhisattva's conduct. Excellent! Excellent! Son of family, reliance on spiritual friends and asking them to teach you is the basis of the achievement of omniscience. Therefore never tire of serving spiritual friends!"

Sudhana said, "How shall I cultivate the conduct of a bodhisattva? What shall I emphasize?"

Manjushri praised him further and instructed him to seek and attend spiritual friends. He said, "In this southern region there is a district called Supremely Excellent Women. In it is a mountain called Fine Throat. Living there is a bhikshu called Glorious Cloud. Go to him and ask him how to cultivate a bodhisattva's conduct. He will show you the mandala of Samantabhadra's conduct."

As instructed by Manjushri, Sudhana the merchant's son went to the bhikshu Glorious Cloud and to other bodhisattvas, tirelessly seeking instruction on the conduct of a bodhisattva. He witnessed the miracles of bodhisattvas that are rarely seen by beings. Each of the bodhisattvas he attended sent him to another one. Each of them ripened and blessed him in a different way, all of them demonstrating distinct and inconceivable gates of liberation. Sudhana achieved vast qualities unknown to other bodhisattvas even though they accompany bodhisattvas for a hundred quadrillion kalpas.[50] Finally, as instructed by the boy Shrikara and the girl Shrimati, he entered the presence of the bodhisattva Maitreya.

Maitreya praised bodhichitta, displayed within his dwelling

50. A quadrillion has fifteen zeros.

an ocean of miracles of buddhas and bodhisattvas, and blessed Sudhana, causing him to achieve vast qualities such as retention and samadhi. Then Maitreya said, "Son of family, return to the youthful Manjushri and ask him how a bodhisattva should train. He is the spiritual friend who will teach you. Why? Because the youthful Manjushri has perfected the conduct. Aspirations like his are not found even among sextillion bodhisattvas. His accomplished aspirations and his complete bodhisattva qualities are immeasurable. The youthful Manjushri is like the mother of sextillion buddhas. He is the teacher of sextillion bodhisattvas. He is supremely diligent in ripening and taming all realms of beings. The wheel of his name is utterly victorious in all the worlds in the ten directions. He is the subject of conversation in all the mandalas of the retinues of all tathagatas. He is praised by all tathagatas. He possesses profound wisdom that sees all dharmas perfectly, just as they are. He perfectly possesses all types of liberation. He has achieved the bodhisattva training of Samantabhadra.

"Son of family, he is the spiritual friend who will give birth to you in the family of the tathagatas. He will increase all your virtues. He will cause you to accomplish the many accumulations of a bodhisattva. He will be a perfect spiritual friend. He will perfectly encourage you to develop all qualities. He will lead you into the web of all great aspirations. He will bring you to the manifest accomplishment of all aspirations. You will hear from him the secrets of all bodhisattvas. He will perfectly reveal to you all that is inconceivable about bodhisattvas. He will cause you to continue the conduct you began in previous lives.

"Son of family, go therefore and sit at Manjushri's feet. In order to receive all wondrous instructions, be without fatigue and laziness. Why? Sudhana, all the spiritual friends you have seen, all the wondrous conduct of which you have heard, all

the miracles you have witnessed, and all the aspirations you have learned are due to the power and blessing of the youthful Manjushri. The youthful Manjushri has achieved all the supreme paramitas."

Sudhana the merchant's son bowed his head to Maitreya's feet, circumambulated him hundreds and thousands of times, and departed while gazing at him repeatedly. Sudhana journeyed through a hundred and ten towns, anticipating with delight his next encounter with the youthful Manjushri, who was staying in the town Manifest Happiness. As Sudhana approached the town, the youthful Manjushri extended his arm for a distance of a hundred and ten yojanas and placed his hand on Sudhana's head.

Manjushri said, "Son of family, excellent! Excellent! Those who lack the faculty of faith, who become discouraged, who are timid, who turn away from diligence, who are complacent with the slightest qualities, who fixate on only a single virtue, who lack skill, who are without a spiritual friend, and who are not considered by buddhas are unable to fully understand dharmata. They are unable to comprehend, believe in, or achieve such conduct as this!"

Manjushri spoke to Sudhana of perfect dharma, encouraged him, and delighted him. Sudhana achieved the great appearance of boundless wisdom that is endowed with innumerable dharma gates. Manjushri blessed him with a bodhisattva's retention, samadhi, confidence, supercognition, and boundless wisdom. He placed him in the mandala of Samantabhadra's conduct. Having established Sudhana the merchant's son in a state like his own, Manjushri left.

Then Sudhana the merchant's son saw the utterly pure body of the bodhisattva Samantabhadra, who was in the presence of the tathagata Vairochana. Sudhana saw that within any one part of Samantabhadra's body was an inconceivable

ocean of miracles, enough to fill the dharmadhatu. Through the blessing of seeing that, Sudhana achieved a state equal to Samantabhadra's. Sudhana sang in verse an aspiration to engage in excellent conduct just like that of the supremely noble Samantabhadra. In it, he sang:

"I fully dedicate all this virtue
To becoming as wise and heroic as Manjushri
And just like Samantabhadra.
May I emulate them!"

From the "Sutra Presenting the Inconceivability of Buddhahood," part of the *Aryaratnakutasutra*

Manjushri benefited innumerable beings by teaching the equality and inconceivability of buddhahood. Then the deva Shribhadra said to him, "Manjushri, shall you continue to teach dharma in Jambudvipa? I pray that you come to Tushita and teach dharma to the devas there. There are devas in Tushita who have served victors of the past and have generated roots of virtue. However, because of the magnificence of the environment they have become careless and have failed to listen to dharma from the bhagavat or you. If those devas hear dharma from you their roots of virtue will increase."

It then seemed to the deva Shribhadra and the rest of that assembly that they traveled to Tushita. Manjushri miraculously caused them to see a wondrous array including beautiful gardens and palaces. The deva Shribhadra saw his own dwelling with all its ornamentation and even his servants. He said to Manjushri, "It is wondrous how quickly you have transported us to Tushita! I see the gardens and palaces and even my own dwelling and servants!"

The venerable Subhuti said to the deva Shribhadra, "Deva, you have not moved from this same place of gathering. We have not traveled to Tushita. The perception of everyone in this assembly that they have traveled to Tushita is due to the miraculous power and blessing of the youthful Manjushri."

The deva Shribhadra said to the bhagavat, "Bhagavat, the youthful Manjushri's miraculous power and the blessing of his samadhi are inconceivable! None of us in this assembly have moved from this place, and yet we all thought we had traveled to Tushita! How amazing!"

The buddha replied, "Deva, I know the extent of the youthful Manjushri's miracles. You only know of some of them. Deva, if the youthful Manjushri wanted to, he could perfectly display in a single realm all the features of as many buddha realms as there are sand grains in the Ganges River. He could support on the top of his head as many realms as the sand grains of the Ganges River and place them all in the sky. He could pour all the water of all the oceans in all those realms into any one pore on his skin without harming a single being. The beings of those oceans would all perceive themselves as remaining in their respective oceans. He could bless all the Mount Merus of all those realms and combine them into a single mountain. He could place that mountain inside a mustard seed. None of the devas living on those mountains would be harmed. They would all perceive themselves as still living on their respective mountains. He could hold all the beings of the five types born in all those realms in the palm of his hand and cause them all to experience the happiness of a world adorned by all manners of pleasure.[51] He could bless enough fire to burn up as many realms as there are sand grains in the Ganges River and turn it into the single flame of a lamp and make it perform a lamp's function. With the light emerging from any one of his pores he could outshine the light of all the suns and moons that exist in as many buddha realms as the sand grains of the Ganges River. Deva, I could teach about the youthful Manjushri's miracles for kalpas! His miracles and the power of his blessing are inconceivable!"

51. The five types of beings are hell beings, pretas, animals, humans, and devas. Beings of a sixth type, the asuras, are sometimes considered a separate realm and sometimes divided into two groups: greater asuras, considered part of the deva realm; and lesser asuras, considered part of the animal realm.

Mara the Wrongdoer was present at that assembly. He transformed his form into that of a bhikshu and said to the bhagavat, "Bhagavat, I wish to see the youthful Manjushri's miracles. The bhagavat has described them in words, but what good is that? Show them to me!"

The bhagavat knew that the apparent bhikshu was Mara the Wrongdoer, but in order to increase the roots of virtue of innumerable beings he said to Manjushri, "Manjushri, I exhort you! Display to this assembly your miraculous power. The roots of virtue of innumerable beings will increase!"

Aware of the bhagavat's exhortation, the youthful Manjushri entered the samadhi called Display of the Mind's Mastery of All Dharmas. As soon as he did so, everyone in that assembly saw that Manjushri's miraculous abilities were exactly as the bhagavat had said. They all became amazed and exclaimed, "The appearance of the buddha is excellent, excellent! The appearance of the buddha is of great benefit to beings! Because of the buddha's appearance, holy beings such as this also appear in the world and illuminate it with inconceivable miracles like this!"

Mara the Wrongdoer saw those great miracles and was so amazed that he joined his palms, bowed to the youthful Manjushri, and said, "The youthful Manjushri's miracles are inconceivable and wondrous! I think that any being who hears of them will be amazed! Bhagavat, I, Mara the Wrongdoer, will never succeed in obstructing any being devoted to Manjushri even if my forces are as numerous as the River Ganges' sand grains! Bhagavat, I, Mara the Wrongdoer, am constantly searching for opportunities to harm the tathagata. I exist in order to harm beings — especially their minds — and in order to obstruct the virtue of the diligent. However, I promise that from now on I will not come or look within a hundred yojanas of any place where this particular dharma is practiced. I will treat anyone who teaches this dharma with

the same respect I treat you, the teacher. Nevertheless within my retinue are some who may still try to obstruct the tathagata's teaching and distract the diligent. In order to prevent them from doing so, I offer you this secret mantra."

Then Mara recited the mantra. The bhagavat said, "Excellent! Because you have taught this secret mantra here, as many worlds as the sand grains in the Ganges River have shaken six times. You should also know that all of the confidence that enabled you to teach this mantra came from the blessing of the youthful Manjushri."

Then the deva Shribhadra, the youthful Manjushri, and all the bodhisattvas and shravakas with them actually went to Tushita. All the devas from all the realms starting with Four Great Kings and up to Akanishtha gathered in Tushita. Manjushri taught dharma there and benefited innumerable beings.

Then at the request of the deva Shribhadra, the youthful Manjushri entered the samadhi called Stainless Light. Above our realm, as many buddha realms distant as there are sand grains in twelve Ganges Rivers, appeared the world Light of All Qualities. Residing there was the tathagata Samantabhadra. All the realms between our realm and that one became filled with light. When those gathered around Manjushri asked why this was occurring, he explained that because of prophecies made by the tathagata Samantabhadra, the bodhisattvas of his realm had asked to view our realm of Saha, the buddha Shakyamuni, and the youthful Manjushri. The tathagata Samantabhadra emitted light from the soles of his feet. This light filled our realm, allowing the bodhisattvas of our realm and his to see one another.

The tathagata Samantabhadra then said to his bodhisattvas, "Children of family, great dharma teaching is about to occur in that realm of Saha. Who among you wishes to go there?"

A mahabodhisattva named Wisdom Lamp Holder, accompanied by ten million other bodhisattvas, came into Manjushri's presence in the time it would take someone to extend and withdraw their arm. Wisdom Lamp Holder bowed to Manjushri and said, "We have been sent here by the tathagata Samantabhadra."

Everyone in that assembly expressed their amazement at the miracles of bodhisattvas. Then Manjushri taught dharma to that vast gathering and subsequently disappeared from Tushita with the speed of thought. The bodhisattva Wisdom Lamp Holder and his retinue went into the bhagavat's presence, prostrated to him, and took their respective seats. The bhagavat said to those gathered there, "Friends, look at these holy beings, and the youthful Manjushri, and the bodhisattva Wisdom Lamp Holder! Consider their miracles, their blessing, their ripening of beings, their skill, their awareness, their wisdom, and their confidence! Friends, these bodhisattvas have been helping beings through buddha activity for innumerable kalpas. It must be said that any being who encounters these holy beings through any of the six faculties will never again be subject to the attacks of Mara!"

From the "Teaching on the Indivisibility of the Dharmadhatu" in the *Ratnakutasutra*

The youthful Manjushri taught that all dharmas are the dharmadhatu in nature. He taught the profound point that they are beyond either affliction or awakening from affliction, and beyond bondage or liberation. Two hundred bhikshus present within that assembly became discouraged, thinking, "If no one is ever liberated, what point is there in our renunciation and diligently traversing the path?" They left the gathering. On their way they encountered a bhikshu whom Manjushri had emanated. He said to them, "I do not like the youthful Manjushri's teaching! I do not believe him!

I am leaving!" They told him that they felt the same way.

The emanated bhikshu asked them, "Have you merely fled out of dislike for his teaching, or have you also renounced and disparaged it?"

They replied, "We have merely fled out of dislike for it. We have not renounced or disparaged it."

The emanated bhikshu said, "Venerable ones, the absence of disputation is the greatest virtue of a renunciate. Do not denigrate Manjushri's teaching. Do not dispute it. Simply distance yourselves from it for a while. Venerable ones, is the mind blue? Is it yellow, or any color? Is it real or unreal? Is it permanent or impermanent? Does it have form or no form? Examine the mind. It has no form. It cannot be displayed. It has no appearance. It is without substance. It is without location. It is invisible. Can it be said that such a mind abides within, or without, or in between?"

The bhikshus replied, "No, it cannot."

The emanation asked, "If not, then is the mind truly real?"

The bhikshus replied, "It is not."

The emanation asked, "Can something that is not truly real be liberated?"

The bhikshus replied, "It cannot."

The emanated bhikshu said, "Venerable ones, it was with that in mind that the youthful Manjushri taught that the dharmadhatu is free in its nature from affliction and awakening. Deluded, childish, ordinary beings fixate on 'I' and 'mine.' From that fixation arises the conceptual mind. Although such a mind conceives of renunciation and meditating on the path, that mind is naturally nonexistent. It is without origination,

destruction, or abiding. It is therefore beyond affliction, awakening, attainment, and realization. It was with that in mind that the youthful Manjushri taught what he did."

The two hundred bhikshus transcended acceptance. Their minds were liberated from defilements. They then returned to the youthful Manjushri's presence. They adorned him with their shawls and said, "Manjushri, you have protected us! We have not abandoned holy dharma! From now on we will not stray from the profound dharma of the vinaya!"

The elder Subhuti asked those bhikshus, "Venerable ones, what have you attained and realized that you adorn the youthful Manjushri with your shawls?"

They replied, "Noble Subhuti, we have attained and realized nothing. That is why we adorn the youthful Manjushri with our shawls. Noble Subhuti, when we had the idea of attainment we arose and left this assembly. When we no longer had the idea of attainment, we returned. Attainment is deception and vanity. Attainment and realization do not exist."

Subhuti asked them, "Who tamed you?"

They replied, "We were tamed by the nonexistence of attainment, origination, distraction, and even placement."

Subhuti asked them, "If so, then have you been tamed?"

They replied, "Ask the youthful Manjushri."

Then Ananda asked Manjushri, "Who tamed those bhikshus?"

Manjushri said, "In absolute truth they were not tamed by anyone. Relatively, they were tamed by a magical illusion."

Then the bhagavat predicted the deva Paramaratna's awakening. The sound of the prediction shook the abodes of

Mara, causing the wrongdoer and his forces to come into the bhagavat's presence.

Mara said to the buddha, "If you were to predict the achievement of arhathood by all the beings in these billion worlds I would rejoice. I do not rejoice, however, in your prediction of even a single bodhisattva. When you make such predictions, my entire realm becomes terrified! A bodhisattva like that will establish innumerable beings in the three awakenings, completely freeing them from the three realms! This is very disturbing to me!"

Manjushri said to Mara, "Wrongdoer, whether you come here or not, you are unable to obstruct a bodhisattva whose motivation is benevolent, who is skillful, and who has transcended the world through the prajnaparamita."

Through the buddha's power, Mara the Wrongdoer then asked Manjushri about benevolence, skill, and prajnaparamita. Manjushri explained them. Then the deva Paramaratna said to Manjushri, "Swallow this Mara the Wrongdoer who obstructs those who hold the dharma! Swallow him, his forces, his mount, and his realm!"

Manjushri replied, "That would not be the action of a bodhisattva. Instead, I will bless Mara the Wrongdoer, adorning his form with the marks of buddhahood and causing him to sit on a lion throne and teach dharma in emulation of the buddha."

When Mara heard those words, he wished to disappear and flee from that place, but was unable to do so. Everyone in that assembly saw Mara transformed into the form of a buddha seated on a lion throne. Manjushri then said to Mara the Wrongdoer, "Why wrongdoer, you have attained the awakening of the tathagatas! With a buddha's form, you are seated on a lion throne!"

Through the blessing of the youthful Manjushri, Mara the Wrongdoer said, "Manjushri, if even the bhagavat has not attained awakening, it is certain that I have not attained it! Why? A characteristic of awakening is that it is without the desire for attainment. Where there is no desire there is no attainment and no realization. Awakening is the attainment of the noncomposite. It has the characteristic of being beyond attainment. The nature of awakening is the three gates of liberation, the dharmadhatu, thatness, the perfect end, and selflessness. There is therefore nothing that attains manifest perfect awakening. Buddhahood is the attainment of freedom from error about the characteristic nature of all dharmas."

When Mara taught the doctrine in that way, five hundred bodhisattvas attained patience with unborn dharmas. Then Shariputra said, "Manjushri, it is amazing that through your blessing Mara the Wrongdoer has taken the form of a tathagata and taught so profoundly!"

Manjushri replied, "Shariputra, I could bless an inanimate object, such as wood, in that way. If I were to bless you, the elder Shariputra, the same thing would happen."

Shariputra thought, "If Manjushri blesses me in that way and I, a shravaka, take the form of our teacher, it will be unfitting. I had better disappear from this assembly!"

Through Manjushri's power, however, Shariputra was unable to disappear. Aware of what was in Shariputra's mind, Manjushri blessed him so that he too was seen by that assembly in the form of a buddha seated on a lion throne. Then Manjushri said to Shariputra, "Noble Shariputra, please teach dharma together with Mara just as the tathagata does."

Shariputra, in the form of a buddha, said to Mara, who was also in the form of a buddha, "Wrongdoer, by what is the awakening of the tathagatas distinguished?"

Mara replied, "Noble Shariputra, the awakening of bhagavats is distinguished by their realization of the equality of all dharmas."

After teaching that, Mara asked, "Shariputra, in what do tathagatas abide?"

Shariputra replied, "Wrongdoer, tathagatas abide in the equality of samsara and nirvana."

Through the teaching given by Shariputra and Mara, eight hundred bhikshus, without acceptance, freed their minds from defilements. Thirty-two thousand devas among those with faith in Shariputra or Mara generated unsurpassable, perfect bodhichitta. It was in order to tame those beings that the youthful Manjushri blessed Mara the Wrongdoer and the elder Shariputra, adorning them with the form and marks of a buddha and causing them to teach dharma. Afterward, Manjushri withdrew his blessing and they returned to their respective forms.

Then thousands of bodhisattvas from various buddha realms gathered there. Manjushri ripened all of them by teaching the dharma of the indivisibility of the dharmadhatu. They thereafter upheld this dharma.

The bhagavat said on that occasion, "After my passing, this dharma will spread throughout Jambudvipa."

From the "Demonstration of Great Miracles" chapter of the *Ratnakutasutra*

The buddha once said, "Innumerable kalpas ago, during the kalpa called Manifest Joy, during the teaching of the tathagata Like Mount Meru, the youthful Manjushri became the bhikshu and dharma teacher Dharmadhvaja. At that time there was a chakravartin called Virtuous Array, a dharmaraja who ruled over four continents and had a thousand sons. Dharmadhvaja taught him that the nature of awakening is emptiness without vanity. He also taught him the profound conduct of bodhisattvas. The king was utterly delighted and offered all his robes and jewelry to his dharma teacher.

"Dharmadhvaja said, 'Better than such offerings is the generation of bodhichitta and renunciation for the victors' doctrine.'

"Because of Dharmadhvaja's praise of renunciation, the king gave up the pleasures of desire and the wealth of kingship. He requested and received the permission of the tathagata Like Mount Meru to renounce home life for the vinaya that is well taught.

"The king then said to his thousand sons, 'Who among you wishes to succeed to the throne and cause beings to perfectly uphold dharma?'

"They replied, 'Father, allow us to become renunciates also.'

"The youngest of the princes, Mind of Great Compassion, said in verse to his elder brothers,

"'Renunciation brings many virtues,
    As the tathagatas have said.
    However, through compassion and for beings' good
    I will succeed to the throne.

"'I will behave purely for the rest of my life,
    And will undertake the eight branches of restoration
        and purification.[52]
    I will not wear flowers, scent, or lotions.
    I will also never taste liquor.'

"When with those and other stanzas Mind of Great Compassion expressed his nonattachment to his own benefit and his intention to ripen beings, the tathagata Like Mount

52. The eight branches of restoration and purification are the vows taken temporarily during nyungnay practice. They are also sometimes taken as lifelong vows.

Meru said, 'Excellent! Holy being, excellent! Excellent! Through the dharmic virtue of perfectly undertaking the eight branches of morality a householder bodhisattva will achieve the same virtue as one who leaves home. With your great compassion you will accomplish all the virtues of renunciation.'

"The prince Mind of Great Compassion was placed on the throne. The other nine hundred and ninety-nine princes became renunciates along with their father, the king. They all achieved the five supercognitions, retention, and the wisdom of dharma. Every full moon the prince Mind of Great Compassion taught dharma throughout the four continents of his realm. He caused nine hundred and twenty million beings to generate the intention to achieve unsurpassable awakening. They all became renunciates out of faith in that tathagata's doctrine and achieved irreversibility from unsurpassable awakening.

"The chakravartin Virtuous Array is now the deva Captain, Manjushri's disciple. His thousand sons are the thousand buddhas. I, your teacher, Shakyamuni, was the prince Mind of Great Compassion."

Then Shariputra said, "Manjushri, you and the deva Captain have engaged in chastity for a long time! You have served many buddhas and generated roots of virtue!"

Manjushri replied, "Shariputra, *chastity* is a synonym for the eightfold path of the aryas. The path is composite. I am non-composite. Therefore I have not engaged in chastity for a long time. Chastity is a type of conduct. I have no conduct. Therefore I do not engage in chastity.

"The tathagata is without form, cannot be shown, and is beyond all the senses. That-itself, the perfect end, the dharma-dhatu, equality, and the transcendence of all elaborations are his nature. It is therefore impossible to serve him.

"Roots of virtue are free from affliction, imperfect paths, and desire for the results of a shravaka or pratyekabuddha. A bodhisattva's roots of virtue include not abandoning the intention to obtain omniscience; ripening beings; holding holy dharma; and accomplishing the paramitas, retention, confidence, the ten strengths, and other qualities."

When they heard Manjushri's definitive explanation of these three points, everyone in that assembly exclaimed, "Excellent!" and cast flowers of various colors at the bhagavat and the youthful Manjushri. Everyone in that assembly exclaimed, "Any buddha realm in which the youthful Manjushri is present contains two tathagatas! Any being unafraid of this teaching of Manjushri's possesses considerable roots of virtue! They will obstruct all of Mara's activity! They will attain the illumination of the mahayana!"

Then the bhagavat, pleased by what that assembly had exclaimed, said to the deva Captain, "Deva, it is a great miracle whenever anyone hears Manjushri's teaching and is interested in it. Those beings will never be frightened by any other miracle. If you ask why, it is for the following reason. Teaching impermanence to beings who perceive permanence; teaching suffering to beings who perceive pleasure; teaching selflessness to beings who perceive a self; teaching ugliness to beings who perceive beauty; teaching insubstantiality to beings who perceive substance; teaching emptiness to beings who perceive a conceptual view; teaching the absence of characteristics to beings who perceive characteristics; teaching the absence of ambition to beings who perceive the three realms; and teaching the transcendence of all views to beings who fixatedly perceive 'I' and 'mine' are all terrifying to the world. Anyone who is not frightened by these teachings is perfectly tamed. Those who are perfectly tamed are unafraid of anything. Fear comes from fixation on 'I' and 'mine.' Those without such fixation are without fear, just

as empty space cannot be shaken, moved, added to, or diminished. Such beings have achieved perfection beyond error. They have attained a view and samadhi without obscuration. They will eventually attain all buddhadharmas.

"It is also a great miracle to teach that all dharmas are uncreated and unborn."

Then Shariputra said to Manjushri, "All buddhadharmas appear to us within the words of the youthful Manjushri."

Manjushri replied, "Shariputra, all dharmas are without a self, inexhaustible, and insubstantial. Therefore they can be established, described, and explained however one wishes. Dharmas are not taken from anywhere, carried anywhere, or accumulated and stored anywhere. Whether dharmas are explained or not, their nature never changes. The words and letters that are used to explain the nature of all beings and all buddhas do not arise solely from either the body or the mind. They arise from a combination of causes and conditions. Those letters are not indivisible. In the same way, the kleshas and the wisdom that abandons kleshas are not indivisible. To abandon the kleshas by not remaining in a state of conceptual cognition is therefore also a great miracle."

Then the deva Captain and the youthful Manjushri spoke of dharma, benefiting many beings.

From the "Sutra Requested by the Deva Stable Intellect," a section of the *Aryaratnakutasutra*

Once the youthful Manjushri was living alone in his own dwelling and perfectly absorbed in meditation. He entered the samadhi called No Kleshas, No Mind, Free from Mind. When he arose from that samadhi, innumerable buddha realms in the ten directions shook six times. The youthful Manjushri thought, "Tathagatas rarely appear in the world. It is by lis-

tening to their dharma that beings' suffering is exhausted. I shall enter the tathagata's presence and ask him to enable beings to accomplish roots of virtue; to enable bodhisattvas to achieve perfect awakening free of doubt about inconceivable buddhadharmas; and to enable the beings of this realm, whose three poisons are great, who are foolish and irreverent, who possess unvirtuous characters and are without the buddha, dharma, and sangha, to hear dharma and achieve the pure eye of dharma."

He then thought, "I shall gather the millions of bodhisattvas of the ten directions who wish to hear dharma from the tathagata and have achieved patience with the profound!"

He then entered the samadhi called Array of Stainless Radiance. At that moment, as many realms in the ten directions as the Ganges River's sand grains became filled with a great radiance of light that was soothing, gentle, stainless, and clear. Even the darkness between worlds, the interiors of mountains, and the insides of trees were illuminated.

Each of the buddhas living in those worlds in the ten directions was asked by his attendant, "What is causing this previously unseen, beautiful light? This light soothes our bodies. It has caused the desire, anger, and stupidity of beings to cease. Whose power and blessing is this?"

Those buddhas said nothing in answer. Through those buddhas' power, all the devas, nagas, yakshas, asuras, humans, birds, and animals in their worlds fell silent. All the water, wind, great oceans, musical instruments, and singing in their worlds were silenced. Without any sound whatsoever, those worlds became utterly peaceful.

Then those buddhas' attendants asked them three times, "Whose power is this light? For the good and happiness of many devas and humans, please tell us!"

All of those buddhas of the ten directions then spoke as if with one voice, and whatever was said by one tathagata was said by all of them in identical tones. Their speech filled all their realms, causing the musical instruments of devas and humans to give forth their sounds without anyone playing them. The sounds of those instruments became millions of dharma gates, proclaiming such dharmas as impermanence, suffering, self-lessness, emptiness, that-itself, and the paramitas. Vigintillions of beings achieved irreversibility from the awakenings of the three vehicles and the states of Brahma, Indra, and a chakravartin.

Those buddhas said to their attendants, "Son of family, what good will asking such a question do you? Let it go! This light is the result of the accumulation of inconceivable roots of virtue such as generosity. This is unlike anything known to any shravakas or pratyekabuddhas. If the tathagata were to praise this light fully, this world and its devas would go mad! This light is soothing because it comes from the cultivation of such virtues as love. It would be hard to praise it fully even if I spoke for longer than a kalpa. However, listen well and I will explain it!"

The attendants then asked another two or three times that the light be explained.

The buddhas replied, "Son of family, in the world called Saha abides the tathagata arhat samyaksambuddha Shakyamuni. He possesses awareness and feet.[53] That sugata knows the world. He is the unsurpassable leader and tamer of beings, the teacher of devas and humans. That buddha, that bhagavat, lives in that realm. The world in which he lives is one of five-fold degeneration. Its beings have great kleshas, are of dull faculties, are shameless and without conscience, irreverent, and engaged in the actions of the kleshas. Among such beings Shakyamuni achieved unsurpassable, perfect, complete awakening as a perfect buddha and teaches dharma.

53. *Awareness and feet* are synonymous here with wisdom and means. Sometimes it is explained that awareness and feet refer to the results of the three trainings: awareness is the result of the training of wisdom, and the two feet of means are the samadhi and morality that result from those two trainings.

"Son of family, in the realm of that bhagavat is a bodhisattva called the youthful Manjushri. He has great power, great wisdom, and great diligence. He perfectly teaches bodhisattvas. He perfectly causes them to hold dharma. He perfectly encourages them. He perfectly delights them. He serves as the father of bodhisattvas and as their mother. He is skilled in the full discernment of the ground of all dharmas. He has attained passionless prajnaparamita. He possesses unimpeded confidence. He has attained retention. He possesses the inconceivable qualities of a bodhisattva.

"He has emitted this light so that beings may accomplish roots of virtue, so that the inconceivable bodhisattvadharmas may be perfected, and so that bodhisattvas of the ten directions may gather to request and hear the dharma of the tathagata Shakyamuni. Those are the causes and conditions of this great radiance."

The attendants asked, "In what samadhi has the youthful Manjushri emitted this light?"

The buddhas replied, "The youthful Manjushri has emitted this light while abiding in the samadhi called Stainless Array of Ubiquitous Radiance."

The attendants asked, "Why do buddhas, bhagavats, not emit such brilliant, pure light as this, so utterly delightful to both body and mind?"

The buddhas replied, "Son of family, such summoning of bodhisattvas and such teaching of dharma in order to exhort bodhisattvas only occur occasionally, not constantly."

Then the innumerable billions and billions of bodhisattvas within each of those countless realms in the ten directions bowed to the buddhas of their respective realms and asked them, "Where is this brilliant light coming from? Whose light is it?"

The buddhas told them what they had told their attendants. Those bodhisattvas then asked, "May we go to Saha to see the tathagata Shakyamuni, the youthful Manjushri, and the other bodhisattvas there?"

The buddhas replied, "If you know it to be the right time to go there, you may go."

All those bodhisattvas then disappeared from their respective realms and gathered here in Saha in the time it would take a strong person to extend and withdraw their arm. Some of those bodhisattvas cast down rains of flowers while gathering in the tathagata Shakyamuni's presence. Others gathered there while casting powders, ointments, flower garlands, and rains of scent. Some played millions of cymbals. Others filled these billion worlds with melodious praises of the tathagata. In that way, they assembled with great ceremonial splendor. As soon as those bodhisattvas arrived in this realm, all of the beings in the hells, dwellings of animals, and worlds of Yama throughout this realm of a billion worlds were fully pacified.[54] No being remained afflicted by any klesha such as desire, anger, stupidity, or pride. All beings came to possess minds that were both loving and supremely joyous.

54. The worlds of Yama are the dwelling places of pretas. Yama is the lord and judge of the dead.

Then the bodhisattvas in that inconceivably vast gathering all bowed their heads to the tathagata Shakyamuni, circumambulated him three times, and then disappeared into the sky above. They all entered the samadhi called Utter Disappearance of the Body and sat down with crossed legs on the center of lotuses with millions of petals of various colors that arose from the individual aspirations of each of them.

The elder Mahakashyapa witnessed these wondrous, dharmic miracles; saw the rains of flowers, incense, and powders; heard the sound of millions of cymbals; and saw a great radiance. He saw that this world of four continents was knee-deep in flower petals and that all within that assembly who were visible to him — devas, nagas, and human monastics and male and female laity — all appeared to have become golden in color. Kashyapa arose from his seat, folded his shawl on his shoulder, faced the bhagavat, planted his right knee on the ground, joined his palms, bowed, and praised the bhagavat in verse.

Kashyapa then asked, "What are the causes and conditions of this great radiance and these great wonders?"

The bhagavat replied, "Kashyapa, what good will it do you to ask such things? Let it go! This is not caused by any shravaka or pratyekabuddha. If the tathagata explained this, the world and its gods would go mad!"

Kashyapa said, "Bhagavat, please explain this for the good, and the happiness, of many beings."

The buddha replied, "Kashyapa, the youthful Manjushri has entered a samadhi called the Stainless Array of Ubiquitous Radiance, and has emitted light rays that have summoned innumerable vigintillions of bodhisattvas. They have gathered here in Saha, have bowed their heads to my feet, circumambulated me three times, and are now sitting on lotuses that are the height of seven palm trees in the sky. This rain of flowers and these other miracles have occurred through the power of those bodhisattvas."

Kashyapa said, "Bhagavat, there are no bodhisattvas here!"

The buddha replied, "Kashyapa, they are invisible to shravakas and pratyekabuddhas. Why? Because shravakas and pratyekabuddhas do not abide in the great compassion, love, benevolence, paramitas, and conduct of bodhisattvas; and do not engage in their altruism. Kashyapa, because those bodhisattvas have entered the samadhi called Utter Disappearance of the Body they are invisible to shravakas and pratyekabuddhas. They are only visible to the tathagata. Son of family,

they are invisible even to bodhisattvas abiding on the levels and bodhisattvas who have newly entered their vehicle. What need is there to speak of shravakas and pratyekabuddhas seeing them? It is impossible!"

Mahakashyapa then asked about the causes of attaining that samadhi. The buddha said, "If you possess ten dharmas, you will achieve that samadhi. However, shravakas and pratyekabuddhas are unable to enter that samadhi. If you are ignorant even of that samadhi's name, what need is there to speak of your entering it?"

Mahakashyapa then said, "Bhagavat, I wish to see those bodhisattvas. Why? Because such holy beings are so difficult to see!"

The buddha replied, "Kashyapa, await the youthful Manjushri's arrival. Those bodhisattvas will arise from their samadhi then, and you will see them. However, Kashyapa, since you have achieved some samadhis, try now to see those bodhisattvas in their present state."

The elder Mahakashyapa listened to what the bhagavat had said. Invoking the buddha's power and his own strength, Kashyapa entered and arose from a myriad of samadhis, but did not see those bodhisattvas. He was unable to know or see their coming, going, remaining in place, or any of their deeds. He became amazed at the state of bodhisattvas, and said to the bhagavat, "How wondrous must be the wisdom of omniscience, since it is superior even to this!"

Then the elder Shariputra thought, "The tathagata has said that I have the greatest wisdom among his disciples. I shall therefore examine the conduct of those bodhisattvas." He entered three myriad samadhis, but was unable to discern the slightest dharma about those bodhisattvas.

Then the elder Subhuti, in order to view those bodhisattvas,

invoking the power of the buddha and his own strength, entered and arose from four myriad samadhis. Unable to see the bodhisattvas, he said to the bhagavat, "Bhagavat, you, the tathagata, have said that I am supreme among your disciples in freedom from kleshas. As I have achieved the samadhi of peace, even if someone were to make a drum of which the two drumheads were each made out of an entire four-continent world, and ceaselessly beat that drum in front of me for a kalpa with drumsticks the size of Mount Meru, I would not, within my samadhi of peace, hear that drum's sound. What need is there to speak of it disturbing my samadhi? It would be impossible! Yet I, who possess such stillness and such wisdom, am unable to discover those bodhisattvas even though I have entered and arisen from four myriad samadhis.

"In order to gain the wisdom of those bodhisattvas, I would be happy to burn in a great hell for as many kalpas as the Ganges' sand grains for the sake of any one being. I would never give up. Bhagavat, if my mind is not liberated without acceptance from all defilements, may I remain in samsara until the end of time. I will never abandon the mahayana!"

The bhagavat said to the elder Subhuti, "Excellent! Subhuti, your intention and words are excellent, excellent! Subhuti, if you do not pass into parinirvana with these present aggregates, your root of virtue will make you a chakravartin as many times as the Ganges' sand grains. You will attain unsurpassable, perfect awakening. You will become a buddha. Subhuti, are there many beings in a realm of a billion worlds?"

Subhuti replied, "Bhagavat, there are many."

The buddha said, "Subhuti, suppose that each of those beings possessed the same wisdom as you — the bhikshu Subhuti — and Shariputra and Mahakashyapa. If, with that wisdom, all those beings searched for those bodhisattvas for septillions of kalpas, they would be unable to see them.[55] Why? Because shravakas and pratyekabuddhas do not practice the dharma of bodhisattvas. It is unknowable to shravakas and pratyeka-buddhas."

Eighty-four thousand humans and devas, hearing the buddha, generated the intention to achieve unsurpassable awakening. Then the youthful Manjushri thought, "Having gathered this many bodhisattvas, I shall now gather millions of devas!"

He miraculously emanated eighty-four sextillion lotuses the size of chariot wheels with petals like gold, stalks like silver, hearts like jewels, and centers like beryl. He also emanated bodhisattvas with golden bodies adorned with the thirty-two signs of a great being. Splendid, majestic, colorful, and luminous, they were seated with crossed legs on the centers of the lotuses. The lotuses filled the desire and form deva abodes of these billion worlds, from Four Great Kings all the way up to Akanishtha, with euphonic sound that called and summoned all the devas of all those abodes. The bodhisattvas on the lotuses exclaimed:

"The children of the sunlike buddhas
Appear rarely in the world.
They are like the udumvara flower.
Buddhas are also extremely rare.

"Shakyamuni, the best of humans,
Has come to the world.
He teaches perfect dharma
That exhausts all suffering.

"Devas, you delight in pleasure.
No matter how long it lasts,
And no matter how good it feels,
You will still have bad rebirths.

"The longer you engage in desire,
The more your craving will increase.
There is no happiness for beings
In the three realms of samsara.

"The appearance of a buddha is so rare!
Having acquired this holy opportunity,
Whoever does not realize selflessness
Will not exhaust their suffering.

"Come now to view the buddha
And listen to holy dharma!"

In that way the emanated bodhisattvas exhorted the devas with profound dharmic verse explaining the rarity of buddhas' appearance, that when buddhas appear they teach profound emptiness, and that therefore devas should abandon heedlessness and listen. Ninety-six million desire and form devas achieved the stainless eye of dharma. Two thousand devas achieved passionlessness. Three million, two hundred thousand devas generated bodhichitta. Ten thousand devas who had already entered the mahayana achieved patience with unborn dharmas. Innumerable millions of devas instantaneously assembled in the presence of the bhagavat Shakyamuni. They bowed to him and remained in the sky as a group, casting divine flowers and incense and singing many divine songs. There was no space even the size of a staff's tip within this world of four continents that was not filled with those devas' great splendor. So many devas gathered here that this world became knee-deep in flower petals.

Then the four devas Stable Intellect, Good Border, Vimala, and Wealthy with Conscience, accompanied by ninety-six million other devas — all of whom had perfectly entered the mahayana — approached Manjushri. They circumambulated his dwelling seven times and cast such a rain of mandarava flowers that an area of ten yojanas became heaped with flowers.

Then the youthful Manjushri blessed the sky above this realm of a billion worlds so that it was filled by a web of flowers, the light of which illuminated this entire world. Manjushri then emerged from his dwelling and sat down on a seat produced by aspirations. The deva Stable Intellect and all the other devas bowed to Manjushri's feet.

Then the youthful Manjushri thought, "In whose company shall I enter the bhagavat's presence in order to ask questions and teach? Who is receptive to the explanation of what is inconceivable, profound, beyond elaboration, and inexpressible, such as the dharmadhatu? This deva Stable Intellect has attended many victors in the past. He is patient with profundity and endowed with unstoppable confidence. I shall ask my questions and teach in his company."

Manjushri asked the deva Stable Intellect, "As you are patient with profundity, would you be able to accompany me when I enter the bhagavat's presence in order to ask questions and teach?"

The deva replied, "Manjushri, if you do not speak, employ language, or listen, I will do the same."

Manjushri said, "Deva, as long as you will not listen, will not retain, will not remember, will not know, and will not teach, I will teach. Why? Because a buddha's awakening is beyond language, beyond the mind, and free of the mind. We name it, but it is unaffected by its name."

The deva replied, "Manjushri, these devas wish to hear dharma from you. Please speak of dharma here."

Manjushri said, "Deva, I will not teach dharma to those who wish to listen to me and retain what I say. Why? Because the wish to listen arises from fixation on the self and on beings."

By Manjushri's teaching the dharma of the utter purity of the three aspects in that way, ten thousand devas achieved patience with unborn dharmas.[56] Then the deva Stable Intellect said to Manjushri, "Let us go into the tathagata's presence."

Manjushri replied, "Do not engage in thought. I have brought the tathagata."

The deva asked, "Where is the tathagata?"

Manjushri replied, "He is in front of me."

Through this dialogue, Stable Intellect came to understand that the tathagata's body is coextensive with space. Manjushri thus taught him the profound way of viewing the tathagata. Then the youthful Manjushri emanated thirty-two thousand beautiful, symmetrical, four-sided mansions with four columns. In each was a precious throne covered by fabric coming from the wish-fulfilling tree of the devas. On each of the thrones was seated a bodhisattva whose body bore the thirty-two marks. Through the youthful Manjushri's blessing, all the bodhisattvas seated on lotuses throughout this realm of a billion worlds, and all of the bodhisattvas within the mansions he had emanated, gathered around the tathagata. They all circumambulated the bhagavat and his retinue of bhikshus three times, and then remained in the sky, where they were visible to the mandala of the buddha's retinue. The lotuses and mansions filled the sky surrounding that assembly in the four directions.

All the bodhisattvas seated on lotuses and all the bodhisattvas within the mansions then harmoniously exclaimed this:

"You venerated millions of buddhas,
As inconceivably many as the Ganges' sand grains.
You sought the conduct of supreme awakening.
You, the best of people, are beautiful.

"Adorned by the name Shakyamuni,

56. The three aspects are the three aspects of any action. In the case of giving, for example, they are the giver, the gift, and the recipient.

Your supreme body stands out among all those in
   the three worlds.
Guide, you teach beings that there are
No persons, lives, individuals, or dharmas.

"You lead beings by demonstrating generosity,
Morality, patience, diligence, and meditation.
Your knowledge of the three worlds is unlimited.
We bow to you whose wisdom is perfect.

"Lord of dharma, you are venerated by devas
   and humans.
Guide of the world, we bow to you.
Those devoted to emptiness
Will also become guides of worlds.

"All the tathagatas of the past and
All the guides now abiding in any direction
Have taught the dharma of the absence of characteristics.
Always contemplate this nature without characteristics.

"This is the nature of beings:
There is no birth, no death,
No coming, no going.
All dharmas are like space.

"Just as a magician's illusion
Appears without truly existing,
All dharmas are like illusions and dreams,
As the tathagata has taught.

"If one person gave generously to as many
Worlds as the Ganges' sand grains,
And another person was patient with the emptiness of
   composites,
That patience would be superior to that generosity."

In that way they extolled in melodious verse the nature of

dharmas, the clear light, profound emptiness, and encouraged its earnest contemplation. Twenty-two thousand beings in that assembly generated the intention to achieve unsurpassable awakening. Five hundred bhikshus freed their minds, without acceptance, from all defilements. Three hundred bhikshus, three thousand bhikshunis, seven thousand laymen, one thousand laywomen, and twenty-seven thousand devas achieved the immaculate eye of dharma. Three hundred bodhisattvas achieved patience with unborn dharmas. This realm of a billion worlds vibrated, shook, and rocked six times.

Then the elder Shariputra asked the bhagavat, "This place is filled with a great radiance. The earth just shook. By whose power have these dharmas occurred?"

The buddha replied, "Just now the youthful Manjushri and the deva Stable Intellect are preparing to demonstrate to the tathagata the dharma called Utter Destruction of All the Mandalas of Mara, so that they can accomplish the inconceivable buddhadharmas."

Shariputra said, "Bhagavat, the youthful Manjushri is not present within this assembly!"

The buddha replied, "Wait a while. The youthful Manjushri is about to overcome all the mandalas of Mara and appear, with great splendor, in the tathagata's presence."

As soon as the youthful Manjushri entered the samadhi called Utter Destruction of All the Mandalas of Mara, all the billions of abodes of Mara within this realm of a billion worlds became dark. All the Mara the Wrongdoers within them became old and infirm, so that they were forced to walk leaning on staffs. All the daughters of Mara became old and decrepit. All the palaces of Mara became dilapidated and were demolished, leaving only darkness in their place. Seeing all

this, all the Mara the Wrongdoers became terrified and desperate. Their body hairs stood up through their fear. The Maras thought, "What has done all this to our abodes? Shall this not bring about our deaths?"

Just as the Maras gave rise to those thoughts the youthful Manjushri emanated billions of devas, one of whom appeared before each of those Maras and said, "Friends, the irreversible bodhisattva, the youthful Manjushri, has caused this by entering the samadhi called Utter Destruction of All the Mandalas of Mara. You will not be harmed at all, so do not be afraid."

When the Maras heard those words, and especially when they heard the name of the youthful Manjushri, they became even more terrified. All the abodes of Mara began to shake even more violently. The Maras said to the emanated devas, "Friends, save us!"

The emanated devas said, "Friends, do not fear! Go into the presence of the bhagavat Shakyamuni. That tathagata, in his great compassion, bestows fearlessness on fearful beings." Then the devas vanished.

Then Mara the Wrongdoer, with a retinue of billions of other Mara the Wrongdoers, went in an instant into the presence of the tathagata Shakyamuni. All those Maras were aged and feeble. They leaned on staffs in their infirmity. With one voice, they said, "Bhagavat, we pray that you save us from this unpleasant appearance! Sugata, we pray that you protect us! Bhagavat, the names of billions of buddhas are unknown to us, but the name of the youthful Manjushri is not like that. Why? Because when we hear the youthful Manjushri's name, we become afraid, anxious, and terrified. We feel we are about to die. We feel we are about to cease to exist."

The bhagavat replied, "Wrongdoers, it is just so. It is just as you have said. Even billions of buddhas have not ripened or impartially benefited as many beings as the youthful Manjushri, nor will they do so. Therefore the name of the youthful Manjushri is uniquely renowned. For that reason, the proclamation of the names of one hundred billion buddhas would not cause you to suffer and be endangered as you are now."

The Mara the Wrongdoers then said to the bhagavat, "Bhagavat, this infirmity of our bodies has made us desperate and ashamed. We beg you to restore our former vigor and complexion."

The buddha replied, "Remain here until the youthful Manjushri's arrival. He will free you from your present ugliness."

Then the youthful Manjushri arose from that samadhi. He got up from his seat and walked into the bhagavat's presence. Manjushri was accompanied by many other bodhisattvas, and by millions of devas, nagas, yakshas, ghandharvas, asuras, garudas, nonhumans, and great serpents. They played millions of cymbals and cast rains of lotuses and utpala flowers. With this great retinue, and with great pageantry, Manjushri arrived there. He bowed his head to the buddha's feet, circumambulated him three times, and sat down together with his entourage.

The bhagavat asked the youthful Manjushri, "Manjushri, did you enter the samadhi called Utter Destruction of All the Mandalas of Mara?"

Manjushri replied, "Bhagavat, I did."

The buddha asked, "Manjushri, from what tathagata did you learn the accomplishment of that samadhi? How long has it been since you accomplished it?"

Manjushri replied, "Bhagavat, when I learned the accomplishment of that samadhi and subsequently accomplished it, the bhagavat had not yet generated bodhichitta."

The buddha asked, "Manjushri, what was the name of the tathagata from whom you learned the accomplishment of that samadhi?"

Manjushri replied, "Bhagavat, inconceivably many, unimaginably many, innumerably many kalpas ago I learned the accomplishment of that samadhi from a buddha, a tathagata, called Fragrance of Mandarava Flowers."

The buddha asked, "Manjushri, what is its accomplishment?"

Manjushri replied, "Bhagavat, bodhisattvas who possess twenty dharmas will achieve that samadhi. What are they? They are the utter annihilation of desire and a desirous mind, and the similar annihilation of anger, stupidity, pride, jealousy, dishonesty, rage, agitation, perception, views, conceptualization, taking, grasping, characteristics, becoming, permanence, termination, aggregates, elements, and the senses. Bodhisattvas who possess the utter annihilation of those twenty dharmas, and therefore utterly annihilate within themselves the three realms and the mind that conceives of the three realms, will achieve that samadhi."

Manjushri then also categorized the dharmas required for that samadhi into six groups of four. He continued, "Bhagavat, after the tathagata Fragrance of Mandarava Flowers, I further accomplished that samadhi in the presence of the tathagatas called Jewel, Precious, Lightning, and Light Greater Than the Sun and Moon."

When Manjushri taught this, ten thousand bodhisattvas achieved that samadhi. Then the bhagavat said to the elder Shariputra, "Shariputra, what do you think of this? Do not think that Manjushri has merely made ugly the Mara the

Wrongdoers of this realm of a billion worlds. Through the youthful Manjushri's blessing, all the Mara the Wrongdoers there are in as many buddha realms as the Ganges' sand grains have been transformed in this same way!"

Then the bhagavat said to the youthful Manjushri, "Manjushri, release them from this blessing of yours. Return these Mara the Wrongdoers to their former vigor."

As soon as Manjushri released them from his blessing, the wrongdoers were all returned to their former youthful vigor. Manjushri said to them and their retinues, "Wrongdoers, anyone who has eyes, the idea of eyes, attachment to eyes, fixation on the characteristics of eyes, concepts about eyes, and vanity about eyes, is subject to the obstacles of Mara. Similarly, anyone who is attached to ears and the rest, and forms and the rest, and accepts and rejects, is subject to the obstacles of Mara. Anyone without any fixation on eyes and the rest is impervious to the obstacles of Mara. They are unassailable by any strength, might, or power."

Because of the dharma Manjushri taught then, ten thousand maras generated the intention to achieve unsurpassable awakening and eighty thousand maras attained the immaculate eye of dharma. Then Mahakashyapa said to the bhagavat, "Bhagavat, the youthful Manjushri is here now. We would like to see those invisible bodhisattvas, as such holy beings are rarely seen."

The bhagavat said, "Manjushri, this gathering wants to see the bodhisattvas you have summoned from the ten directions. Please reveal them!"

The youthful Manjushri said to the bodhisattvas Dharma, Aryadharma, Dharmamati, Surya, Weapon Against Mara, Manjughosha, Pacification of Evil, Shantarakshita, Vijayarakshita, Dharmaraja, and the other bodhisattvas, "Children of

family, please display your bodies as they appear in your respective buddha realms!"

As soon as Manjushri said that, all those bodhisattvas arose from samadhi and revealed their bodies. The bodies of some of those bodhisattvas were the size of Mount Meru. Some were eighty thousand yojanas tall, some seventy thousand, and so on, down to ten thousand. Some were five thousand yojanas tall, some four thousand, and so on, down to a thousand. Some were five hundred yojanas tall, some four hundred, and so on, down to a hundred. Some were fifty yojanas tall, and some were one yojana tall. Some were three and a half cubits tall measured by the beings of this realm of Saha. All their bodies appeared. At that time there was not in all this world so much as the space needed to place the tip of a staff that was not filled by majestic and powerful bodhisattvas. The light of those bodhisattvas illuminated billions of buddha realms in the ten directions.

Then the youthful Manjushri arose from his seat, bowed to the bhagavat, and asked him amidst that vast assembly, "Bhagavat, to whom does the word *bodhisattva* refer?"

The buddha replied, "Manjushri, those who realize all dharmas are called "bodhisattvas." Bodhisattvas realize that the eyes, the ears, and so on, and forms and so on, are empty in nature. They do not, however, think, 'I have realized this!' They realize the emptiness beyond elaboration that is the nature of all dharmas."

Then Manjushri and the deva Stable Intellect engaged in a dialogue that included asking the bhagavat and several principal figures in that assembly questions. Although the asking of these questions was unnecessary for them, by asking them they revealed the profound meaning. Briefly put, Manjushri taught that since kleshas, the five desirable objects of the senses, and all dharmas of the three realms have never truly arisen, bodhisattvas, with profound and skillful wisdom, experience their equality. Because Manjushri taught the profound absence of origination in a way that was understood even by bodhisattvas who had just generated bodhichitta, thirty-two thousand bodhisattvas achieved patience with unborn dharmas. Five hundred bhikshus freed their minds, without acceptance, from all defilements. Six hundred million devas achieved the immaculate eye of dharma.

At that time Mahakashyapa said to the bhagavat, "The youthful Manjushri must have gone to some trouble in order to benefit so many beings by teaching dharma."

Manjushri said, "I have gone to no trouble. As all dharmas are uncreated, no being is bound. I therefore do not have to free any being. This is because there are no beings. It is beings who go to trouble, in order to find something that is not and never will be found by any buddha, shravaka, or pratyekabuddha. What childish, ordinary beings seek to find and even buddhas never find is a self — a being — as well as all dharmas such as forms. Beings do something that no buddha, shravaka, or pratyekabuddha ever does. Beings engage in permanence, termination, involvement, and vanity."

Manjushri then asked the bhagavat, "What is the achievement of patience with unborn dharmas?"

The buddha answered, "It is patience with the nonexistence of the achievement of anything." As a result of that and other things the buddha said then, sixty-two thousand beings generated the intention to achieve unsurpassable awakening and twelve thousand bodhisattvas achieved patience with unborn dharmas.

Then the deva Stable Intellect asked Manjushri, "How does one progress from level to level?"

Manjushri replied, "All dharmas are unchanging and illusory."

With that and other indirect words Manjushri answered Stable Intellect's question.

The bhagavat then said, "Excellent! Manjushri, excellent, excellent! If one teaches, one should teach like that."

Then the youthful Manjushri taught the deva Stable Intellect essencelessness, employing profound and indirect words. When Manjushri taught the profound fact that there are no such things as the factors of awakening or the three doors of liberation to be conceived of, meditated upon, or achieved, thousands of bhikshus within that assembly thought, "The bhagavat has taught that it is through the achievement of the thirty-seven factors of awakening and the three doors of liberation that we will achieve nirvana.[57] Manjushri is refuting that! How can he teach this? Is he not contradicting the doctrine?"

Manjushri, knowing their thoughts of doubt, said to Shariputra, "You have been proclaimed to be supreme among the intelligent. Venerable one, when someone becomes free from desire, are the four truths, the three doors of liberation, or the factors of awakening conceived of, meditated on, or achieved by them?" Shariputra replied, "Manjushri, they are not. This is because all dharmas are beyond acceptance, unborn, and empty. There is therefore nothing to be revealed."

Because of that dialogue, three thousand bhikshus freed their minds, without acceptance, from all defilements. Then the deva Stable Intellect and the youthful Manjushri discussed through question and answer the profound fact that, because all dharmas are unborn from the beginning, they do not exist. About five hundred bhikshus within that assembly misunderstood that dharma. Seeing it as contradictory, they repudiated it. They therefore fell into a great hell in those very bodies.

Shariputra said to Manjushri, "Those five hundred bhikshus

57. The thirty-seven factors of awakening are the practices cultivated during the various stages of the Buddhist path. They are the four mindfulnesses, the four relinquishments, the four bases of miracles, the five faculties, the five powers, the seven factors of awakening, and the noble eightfold path.

have fallen into hell because they misunderstood this dharma and repudiated it! Please do not teach matters of such profundity! Please think before you teach!"

Manjushri replied, "Venerable Shariputra, do not think in this way! There is no such thing as beings going to hell. Why? Because all dharmas are unborn. You said, 'Think before you teach.' If a son or daughter of family retaining the view of a self were to serve the tathagata and a sangha of as many bhikshus as the Ganges' sand grains with all necessities conducive to well-being for the length of their lives; and someone else were to hear profound dharma — hard to understand, contradictory to all worldly ideas — such as emptiness, repudiate it, and fall into a great hell, that second person would arise from that hell and achieve liberation long before the first person. This is because the first person would serve the tathagata while retaining the view of a self and without hearing this profound dharma."

When the youthful Manjushri said that, the bhagavat said to him, "Manjushri, excellent, excellent! As you have said, hearing dharma like this is like witnessing the appearance of a buddha. It is like becoming a stream-enterer, even an arhat! Why? Because there is no attainment or realization for someone who retains the view of a self and other concepts."

The bhagavat then said to Shariputra, "Shariputra, those bhikshus will arise from those hells very quickly. They will achieve parinirvana. However, the stupid who retain conceptual views and serve the tathagata while remaining in doubt will not. Furthermore, Shariputra, while those bhikshus will achieve parinirvana, this will not cause their extinction. This is because their achievement will be caused by their hearing dharma of such profundity."

Then the deva Stable Intellect asked Manjushri, "Are you chaste?"

Manjushri replied, "Deva, if I were to say that I was not chaste and did not practice chastity, it would imply that, like you, I wished to be."

The deva asked, "Manjushri, what do you mean?"

Manjushri replied, "Deva, behavior that is consciously adopted is conduct. Behavior that is not consciously adopted is not conduct. The concept of chastity is conduct. The absence of the concept of chastity is not conduct."

The deva asked, "Manjushri, are you really not chaste?"

Manjushri replied, "Deva, just so. I am really not chaste. This is because I am not pure and not active. I am therefore without pure conduct."

In that way, through question and answer Manjushri clearly taught the nonexistence of concepts by repeatedly demonstrating that every concept actually contradicts itself. He taught the profound meaning of the absence of origination using indirect language that merely appeared to contradict the doctrine. In that assembly were five bodhisattvas who practiced the four meditative stabilities and had achieved the five supercognitions. They had not yet achieved patience with unborn dharmas, and were engaged in entering and arising from various samadhis. While doing so they recollected that in the distant past they had killed their parents and killed arhats. Aware of the remaining karma from those deeds, and without patience for the profound, they were tormented by their knowledge. They maintained the idea of a self and were wholly conceptual. As they were unable to overcome their affliction, the bhagavat, in order to tame them, communicated mentally with the youthful Manjushri.

Manjushri arose from his seat, hung his shawl on his shoulder, and picked up a sword with his right hand. He sharpened it thoroughly and then ran, brandishing the sword, toward

the bhagavat. The bhagavat said to Manjushri, "Manjushri, I have already been killed! I have already been completely killed! Let me go! Why? Because, Manjushri, when someone decides to kill another person, the person they wish to kill has in fact already been killed long before the person who wants to kill them has even thought of doing so."

The five bhikshus thought, "All dharmas are like magical illusions. There is no self. There are no sentient beings. There are no parents, buddhas, dharma, or sangha. There are no actions of immediate consequence. Why? Because the youthful Manjushri — who is wise, clever, intelligent, praised by all buddhas, and patient with profundity; who has served many buddhas, is wise in his full discernment of all dharmas, teaches dharma properly, speaks perfectly, and has great respect for the tathagata — has taken up a sharp weapon and run toward the tathagata. The tathagata has said, 'Manjushri, I have already been killed! I have already been completely killed! Let me go!' If buddhas and so forth truly existed, it would be impossible for anyone who had ever engaged in an action of immediate consequence to ever escape from its consequences. Therefore none of those dharmas exist. They are hallucinations. They are like magical illusions. They are empty. There is no one to do anything. There is no one to whom anything could be done."

By understanding that, the five bodhisattvas achieved patience with unborn dharmas. In their great joy they ascended to a height of seven palm trees in the sky. They praised the bhagavat in verse, describing their recollection of past events and their profound realization. When this dharma was taught by means of Manjushri taking up a weapon, as many realms throughout the ten directions as the Ganges' sand grains shook six times.

Then all the bhagavat buddhas in all the buddha realms throughout the ten directions were asked by their respective

attendants, "By whose power has this great earth shaken so?"

Those buddhas replied, "This was caused by the youthful Manjushri in the realm of Saha who, in order to tame beings, took up the sharp sword of wisdom and ran toward the bhagavat Shakyamuni."

Then those buddhas taught dharma based on the sword of wisdom, causing innumerable beings to achieve the pure eye, liberated minds, patience, and an entry to awakening. At that time the bhagavat blessed the many beings in his retinue who, as beginners, had few roots of virtue and many thoughts so that they did not see the sword or hear the dharma taught about it.

Then the elder Shariputra said to Manjushri, "Manjushri, you have performed an action beyond tolerance in attempting to assassinate our teacher! What shall be its ripening for you?"

Manjushri replied, "Venerable Shariputra, just so! I do not know what the ripening of my intolerable action will be. However, the ripening for me will be the same as the ripening of actions for a person created by magical illusion. Why? Because just as a person created by magical illusion is without thoughts or concepts, all dharmas are without thoughts or concepts. I will ask you, venerable Shariputra, a question. Answer it according to your degree of patience. Venerable one, do weapons, karma, and karmic ripening truly exist?"

Shariputra answered, "They do not."

Manjushri said, "Venerable Shariputra, if weapons, karma, and karmic ripening do not exist, than how could karma ripen?"

Shariputra replied, "Manjushri, according to your thinking, karma does not ripen as anything whatsoever. Why? Because all dharmas are without karma and its ripening."

Then the bodhisattvas gathered from the worlds of the ten directions asked the bhagavat, "We pray that you kindly permit the youthful Manjushri to visit our buddha realms and teach dharma in them."

The youthful Manjushri said then to those bodhisattvas, "Children of family, look at your respective buddha realms!"

When they looked at their respective buddha realms throughout the ten directions, they heard the pleasant sound of Manjushri's voice in each of those realms. They saw that the youthful Manjushri was present before all of the buddhas in those realms. In every realm Manjushri was accompanied by the deva Stable Intellect, who was requesting and receiving this same dharma teaching. They also saw in each of their realms gatherings of bodhisattvas and devas equal to those in this world. They thought, "The youthful Manjushri has not left this buddha realm, and yet appears simultaneously in all realms! Amazing! Amazing!" They were astonished.

Then Manjushri said to those bodhisattvas, "Children of family, it is like this. For example, a well-trained illusionist can, without arising from his seat, cause various forms to appear. Similarly, a bodhisattva well-trained in prajnaparamita can emanate as many illusory dharmas as he wishes throughout all the buddha realms that there are. Why? Because he knows all dharmas to be like illusions."

Then the bhagavat said to the youthful Manjushri, "Manjushri, the hearing of this dharma is like the appearance of a buddha. Hearing this dharma is like attaining the result of a stream-enterer, of a returner, of a nonreturner, and of an arhat. Interest and belief in this dharma is like reaching the site of awakening."

Manjushri said, "Bhagavat, it is just so. Emptiness, no-characteristics, no-ambition, suchness, the dharmadhatu, the perfect

conclusion, equality, full liberation, and isolation are just like that."

Then the youthful Manjushri asked the bhagavat, "I pray that you bless any son or daughter of family who practices this dharma teaching in the future, during the final five hundred years, or even hears of it."

When Manjushri said that, all of the musical instruments of devas and humans throughout this realm of a billion worlds emitted their respective sounds. All the trees bloomed with flowers and grew. Many lotuses appeared in all the ponds. This realm of a billion worlds shook six times and was filled with a light so bright that the sun and moon disappeared. Millions of devas, delighted, appeared in the sky and cast down rains of flowers, powders, incense, and salves. The sound of cymbals and the songs of devas were heard. All those devas joined their palms and proclaimed in unison, "AH LA LA! The dharma taught by the youthful Manjushri! AH LA LA! Dharma! AH LA LA! Dharma! We have seen a second turning of the dharmachakra in this world! Any being who hears this dharma teaching and is interested in it possesses considerable roots of virtue. Anyone who hears this dharma and is not frightened by it has served previous victors well and is patient with profundity."

Then Manjushri said to the bhagavat, "Since all these wonders preceded this dharma teaching in order to bless it, it will be practiced in the future."

The buddha replied, "Manjushri, it is so. These wonders occurred in order to bless this dharma teaching."

Manjushri asked, "Bhagavat, so that this dharma teaching remains for a long time, I pray that the bhagavat will perform a blessing of the truth."

The bhagavat proclaimed, "Manjushri, by the truth, and the

true words, of the attainment of complete liberation in reliance upon the three gates of liberation, may this dharma teaching be practiced in the future, in the last five hundred years."

Manjushri granted his blessing by saying, "Bhagavat, by the truth, and the true words, of the nonexistence of the self, beings, samsara, and nirvana, may this teaching be practiced in the future, in the last five hundred years. By the truth, and the true words, of the nonexistence of desire and so forth; of the imputation of dharmas and terms by the tathagata; of this doctrine; of the engagement in and attainment of liberation by the buddhas of the three times; and of any teaching, listening, attainment, or conduct whatsoever, may this dharma teaching be practiced in Jambudvipa in the future, in the last five hundred years."

At that time this realm of a billion worlds shook six times. The bodhisattva Maitreya asked the bhagavat, "What caused that?"

The buddha replied, "Maitreya, it would not be good if beings interested only in lesser things misunderstood. Let it go."

Maitreya asked, "Bhagavat, for the sake of the benefit and happiness of many beings, and for the sake of the virtue of devas and humans, I pray that you tell us."

The bhagavat replied, "Maitreya, this dharma teaching has been taught in this very place by seven hundred and forty sextillion buddhas. It was received from each of them by the youthful Manjushri and the deva Stable Intellect."

Maitreya asked, "Bhagavat, how long has it been since the youthful Manjushri and the deva Stable Intellect first heard this dharma teaching?"

The bhagavat replied, "Maitreya, three novemdecillion kalpas ago, these sons of family heard this dharma teaching from the tathagata Utterly Manifestly Superior Flower Lion's Power. When he taught this dharma, as many beings as the Ganges' sand grains generated the intention to achieve unsurpassable, perfect awakening. Twice that number achieved patience with profundity. Twice that number achieved the immaculate eye of dharma."

From the *Sutra of Manjushri's Play*

Glorious Light of Finest Gold, the daughter of a prostitute, had a golden complexion. The clothing she wore and any place she went always appeared golden in color. The king, ministers, and merchants all found her pleasing and followed her around, gazing at her. Fear Remover, the son of a merchant, purchased her freedom. He placed her in a chariot and drove her along the road to a park. On the way they encountered the youthful Manjushri. In order to tame them he emanated from his body light so bright that it eclipsed that of the sun and moon. The light that emerged from his robes filled a yojana. He was adorned by a full set of jewelry. Finest Gold, observing that Manjushri's appearance was superior to her own, was attracted to him and thought, "I shall play with him."

Through Manjushri's power, King Vaishravana appeared in human form and said to the young woman, "He is not looking for passion. He is the youthful Manjushri, a bodhisattva. He fulfills beings' wishes and will give anything away to those who ask for it."[58]

58. Vaishravana is a deva associated with wealth and a dharma protector. He is one of the four great kings who rule the deva realm called Four Kings.

The young woman thought, "If I ask him for his clothing, he will give it to me." She then asked Manjushri for his clothing.

He replied, "If you enter the path to awakening, I will give you my clothing."

The young woman asked, "What is awakening?"

Manjushri taught her about essencelessness and equality, causing five hundred thousand celestial devas to generate the intention to achieve unsurpassable awakening. Two hundred people among the many men, women, boys, and girls who had accompanied Finest Gold also generated the intention to achieve unsurpassable awakening. Sixty devas and humans achieved the pure eye of dharma. The young woman Glorious Light of Finest Gold touched her five limbs to the ground. She undertook the bases of training and with the best of intentions generated the intention to achieve unsurpassable awakening. She promised to diligently engage in the means of taming beings through the knowledge that kleshas have no inherent existence. She questioned Manjushri about the nonexistence of kleshas for bodhisattvas. In response, Manjushri skillfully taught the profound dharma of emptiness.

At that time the bhagavat was walking on the grassy slopes of Vulture Peak Mountain, accompanied by Ananda. Speaking of Manjushri, the buddha exclaimed, "Excellent!"

The sound of his voice filled this realm of a billion worlds. The great earth shook six times. This alerted many devas, nagas, yakshas, and other beings, all of whom assembled before the bhagavat. They asked him, "The sound of the word *excellent* has filled this world. We have all heard it. Of whom were you speaking?"

The buddha replied, "Of Manjushri, who is teaching dharma to the young woman Finest Gold."

Those devas and all the others then assembled before Manjushri. King Ajatashatru and others gathered as well. They saw that the young woman Glorious Light of Finest Gold was undisturbed by desire and at peace. They saw that she was no longer engaged in passion with anyone.

Manjushri asked her, "Where have you put your kleshas?"

She replied, "As all kleshas abide in the dharmadhatu, they are never generated, stopped, or transformed. I have realized the nature of kleshas."

Manjushri then taught that the nature of kleshas is awakening. The young woman Glorious Light of Finest Gold explained that, through the wisdom resulting from her accumulation of roots of virtue, she viewed forms as like the reflection of the moon in water. Through their teaching of dharma, twelve thousand beings generated the intention to achieve unsurpassable awakening. Five hundred devas and humans achieved patience with unborn dharmas. Thirty-two thousand beings achieved the pure eye of dharma. That young woman, through her utter delight in listening to dharma, achieved concordant patience with all dharmas. She then asked Manjushri for the vows of renunciation.

Manjushri replied, "Sister, shaving your head is not the renunciation of a bodhisattva. Diligence in the eradication of the kleshas of all beings is the renunciation of a bodhisattva." In that way, he taught her that a bodhisattva's renunciation consists of benefiting others without attachment to one's own benefit.

Manjushri said to her, "Get back into your chariot and, out of kindness, ripen the merchant's son Fear Remover. That will be your renunciation and completion."

Manjushri had blessed those present who were temporarily unreceptive to that dharma teaching, such as the merchant's son Fear Remover, so that they did not hear any of it. Most of those present therefore thought, "How can the passionless and the passionate remain together?"

The young woman, aware of their thought, said, "Friends, a bodhisattva who is without desire, and yet lives among beings with desire, is without wrongdoing and will tame those

desirous beings. It is the same with anger and so forth." In that way, she taught how those with kleshas are tamed. She then bowed to Manjushri's feet, got back into her chariot, and went with Fear Remover to the park, where she played with him. While doing so, she lay down with her head resting on Fear Remover's lap. She then appeared to die, stiffen, and putrefy. She began to stink. Blood, pus, and the smell of putrefaction issued from her orifices. The merchant's son Fear Remover was terrified by this display of impurity. Manjushri appeared in a tree and reassured Fear Remover, encouraging him to flee into the buddha's presence. Knowing it was time for Fear Remover to be tamed, the tathagata emanated light rays that shone on him. Fear Remover cast aside the corpse and fled into the buddha's presence. He requested refuge. Through the victor's teaching of dharma, Fear Remover achieved concordant patience with all dharmas. Knowing that the merchant's son had been tamed, Glorious Light of Finest Gold, accompanied by about five hundred devis and the sound of cymbals and song, entered the bhagavat's presence.

The bhagavat said, "This Glorious Light of Finest Gold, the daughter of a prostitute, was established in the pursuit of awakening by Manjushri in the past. She has now achieved concordant patience. This Fear Remover, the son of a merchant, was established in the pursuit of awakening by me in the past. He also, having heard dharma, has achieved concordant patience. The young woman Finest Gold will, after nine million two hundred thousand kalpas, become the tathagata Precious Light in the world Precious Source during the kalpa Precious Source. The prosperity of that realm will be like that of the devas of Thirty-Three. However, all the jewels in Precious Source will be the jewels of bodhisattvas. The tathagata Precious Light will have an immeasurable life span. After that tathagata's buddhahood, Fear Remover will become the bodhisattva Light of Precious Qualities. He will hold the treasury of that tathagata's dharma and will receive from that

tathagata the prophecy: 'After my passing, you will achieve buddhahood!' That bodhisattva will then become the tathagata Precious Radiance."

When the buddha spoke this prophecy, this world shook six times and was filled with bright light. Thousands of beings generated the intention to achieve unsurpassable awakening. In that way, Manjushri demonstrated inconceivably skillful means of taming the passionate.

From the *Sutra of Manjushri's Magical Display*

While the bhagavat and his large retinue were staying at the Jetavana — the enclosure for the sangha built by Anathapindada — the deva Great Light asked Manjushri, "What are the actions of Mara for a bodhisattva?"

Manjushri replied, "Devas, as long as actions arise, they are the actions of Mara. As long as there are ambition, misapprehension, the apprehension of supremacy, desire, perception, vanity, and conceptualization, there will be the actions of Mara."

He taught that fixation on bodhichitta, generosity, and so on is also the action of Mara. He then taught the excellent, perfect dharma of combining means and wisdom. Eight thousand devas generated supreme bodhichitta. Five thousand bodhisattvas achieved patience with unborn dharmas. The bhagavat said to Manjushri, "Excellent!"

The deva Great Light asked, "Manjushri, are you pleased that the tathagata has declared your excellence?"

Manjushri replied, "It is like one magical illusion pronouncing the excellence of another magical illusion. I have no attachment to that which does not inherently exist."

In response to Manjushri's teaching of profound dharma, the

deva remarked, "Manjushri, it is amazing that Mara the Wrongdoer does not come to torment our eyes when you say such things."

Soon after those words were spoken, Mara the Wrongdoer appeared in the sky in the form of a great, roiling cloud that roared with thunder. Those gathered there moaned with terror and thought, "Who is this?"

The bhagavat asked Manjushri, "Manjushri, do you see this transformation of Mara the Wrongdoer?"

Manjushri replied, "Bhagavat, I see it! Sugata, I see it!"

Then Manjushri tightly bound Mara the Wrongdoer and cast him to the ground. Mara cried out, "I am tightly bound!"

Manjushri said, "Wrongdoer, there is a fetter even more constricting than this. You are always bound by it, and yet you do not know it. What is it? It is the proud thought of 'I'; it is error, craving, and views. This fetter always binds you, and yet you do not know it."

Mara cried, "Manjushri, let me go and I will return to my abode! I will no longer engage in the actions of Mara!"

Manjushri said, "Wrongdoer, if I need you to perform the deeds of a buddha, why would I let you go?"

Mara asked, "If I am engaged in obstructing the buddha-dharma, how could I perform the deeds of a buddha?"

Manjushri replied, "Wrongdoer, making Mara perform the deeds of a buddha is one of the magical displays of a bodhisattva's means and wisdom. When a buddha performs the deeds of a buddha, it is wondrous. When Mara performs the deeds of a buddha, it is utterly wondrous."

Then Manjushri blessed Mara so that he had the form of a

buddha, was seated on a lion throne, and had a buddha's confidence. Mara then said, "Venerable ones, ask me whatever you wish. I will delight you with prophecy!"

The elder Mahakashyapa asked Mara, "Wrongdoer, what fetters a bhikshu who practices yoga?"

Mara replied, "Noble Mahakashyapa, attachment to the tranquility experienced in meditation, the perception of nirvana as an essence, and the perception of samsara as something to be removed are the fetters of a practitioner of yoga. Why? Because one does not meditate on emptiness by discarding views. The nature of views is emptiness. One does not meditate on the absence of characteristics by discarding characteristics. The nature of characteristics is the absence of characteristics. One does not meditate upon the absence of aspiration by discarding aspirations. The nature of aspirations is the absence of aspiration. One does not meditate upon nirvana by discarding samsara. The nature of samsara is nirvana. Noble Mahakashyapa, nirvana is beyond all perception, vanity, and concepts of characteristics. It is not the exhaustion of origination and destruction. Nirvana is the nonexistence of inherent arising."

When this was taught, five hundred bhikshus freed their minds, without acceptance, from all defilements. The elder Subhuti asked those bhikshus, "Venerable ones, who tamed you?"

They replied, "No one, because there is no attainment and no manifest buddhahood."

Subhuti asked, "How then were you tamed?"

They replied, "Because of how things are, there is no guidance, nor is there the absence of guidance. We know how things are, that nothing is created or destroyed. We have been tamed by our knowledge of sameness."

When those bhikshus taught this, two hundred devas achieved the immaculate eye of dharma. Then Subhuti asked Mara, "When does a bhikshu abide in generosity?"

Mara replied, "Subhuti, when there is no accepting and no receiving, and yet there is a full engagement in faith and wonderment."

Shariputra asked Mara, "What is the samadhi without disturbance spoken of by the bhagavat?"

Mara replied, "It is the samadhi of utter exhaustion, in which there is nothing to be exhausted. It is the samadhi of no inherent origination, in which there is no origination of the unoriginated. It is the samadhi of nothing to be experienced, in which there is no experience. It is the wisdom that all dharmas are unified in their nature. Knowing this, all sensations cease. One enters and sees the equality of all dharmas, yet nothing whatsoever is seen. There is also nothing whatsoever that remains unseen. This is the samadhi without disturbance of which the bhagavat speaks."

Maudgalyayana asked, "When has a bhikshu achieved complete freedom of mind?"

Mara replied, "A bhikshu has achieved complete freedom of mind when he knows that all dharmas possess the characteristic of a fully liberated mind, yet does not fixate on this. Because the mind has been fully liberated from the beginning, he does not conceive of bondage or liberation. Because the mind is without form, beyond apprehension, and without location, he knows that all dharmas are without form, beyond apprehension, and without location. He knows the nature of all dharmas to be the dharmadhatu, the nature of the mind. He has achieved the power of independence from others through his knowledge of the dharmadhatu's nature. He possesses the miraculous abilities of the imagination, and complete freedom of mind."

Purna asked, "When does a bhikshu teach dharma with utter purity?"

Mara replied, "A bhikshu teaches dharma with utter purity when he knows all dharmas, yet is without fixation on the minds of self and other. He teaches that all dharmas are mere imputations. He knows that words, letters, speech, and language are like echoes. He sees the people listening to dharma as magical illusions. He sees his own body as the moon's reflection in water. He knows that all kleshas arise from thinking. He never teaches dharma for the purposes of the acquisition, retention, rejection, or removal of anything. He has mastered fourfold individual perfect awareness.[59] He teaches dharma without placing his hopes in any individual and without materialism. Because he knows that the nature of his mind is utterly pure, he also knows that the minds of all beings are of the same nature. He sees that they are without the skandhamara. He perceives the kleshamara as a fabrication. He knows that the mara of death is unborn and will never arise. He is free from the deception and vanity of the devaputramara. Such a bhikshu teaches dharma with utter purity."

Upali asked, "Wrongdoer, when is a bhikshu an upholder of the vinaya?"

Mara replied, "Noble Upali, when a bhikshu knows that all dharmas have been utterly subdued, and that no wrongdoing ever truly occurred; when he is therefore without any guilt about previous wrongdoing; when he knows adventitious kleshas to be without inherent existence like clouds or the moon's reflection in water; when he no longer tries to dispel kleshas or accomplish a state without kleshas; when he correctly understands improper mental engagement to be like darkness or a thief and yet without origin, location, or destination; when he has compassion for beings afflicted by

59. These are the perfect awareness or knowledge of individual dharmas, meanings, definitions, and explanations.

kleshas; and when he realizes that there is no self and there are no beings, he is a perfect upholder of the vinaya."

All those shravakas were delighted by the answers Mara gave to their questions. Then the deva Good Border said to Mara, "Manjushri has already described the actions of Mara for a bodhisattva. Please elaborate on this with confidence."

Mara replied, "When a practicioner of yoga desires liberation and venerates and serves those who are frightened of samsara, this is an action of Mara. To think about emptiness and abandon beings is an action of Mara. To think about the noncomposite and reject composite virtues is an action of Mara."

In that way, Mara went on to describe twenty actions of Mara. The bhagavat said to him, "Excellent! Anyone who hears of these actions of Mara and renounces them will achieve twenty dharmas, such as great love, that will ripen into awakening."

The deva Good Border said, "Mara the Wrongdoer, you acquired something worth acquiring when the bhagavat said 'Excellent' to you!"

Mara replied, "How could I have acquired something worth acquiring? Everything I have said is like the speech of a human possessed by a demon! I have taught through the blessing of Manjushri, and not through my own power."

The deva said, "Wrongdoer, you are teaching dharma with the form and confidence of a buddha and are seated on a lion throne. Does this not please you?"

Mara replied, "You see me as decorated; I know myself to be tightly bound."

The deva said, "Wrongdoer, apologize to the youthful Manjushri. He will release you."

Then through the power of Manjushri, Mara said, "It is unnecessary to apologize to mahabodhisattvas immersed in the mahayana. They are beyond disturbance and anger."

The deva asked, "What is the patience of bodhisattvas like?"

Mara replied by describing twelve qualities of patience, such as being unfabricated.

Then the deva asked, "Wrongdoer, would it please you if you were released?"

Mara replied, "I would be delighted, most delighted!"

The deva Good Border then said to Manjushri, "Let Mara the Wrongdoer go. He will return to his abode."

Manjushri asked Mara, "Wrongdoer, by whom are you bound? By what will you be freed?"

Mara replied, "Manjushri, I do not know by whom I am bound."

Manjushri said, "Wrongdoer, you are not bound, yet you perceive yourself to be bound. In the same way all childish, ordinary beings perceive the impermanent as permanent. In that same way they perceive a self, pleasure, beauty, and the five aggregates. Wrongdoer, if you were freed, from what would you be freed?"

Mara replied, "I would not be freed from anything."

Manjushri said, "Wrongdoer, in that same way, unless you recognize the idea of liberation to be inauthentic you will never be liberated from anything. Liberation is that recognition itself."

Then Manjushri withdrew his blessing. The wrongdoer was restored to his own appearance. Mahakashyapa said to

Mara, "It is excellent that you have performed the deeds of a buddha."

Mara replied, "It was not my doing, but Manjushri's."

Then the deva Good Border asked Manjushri, "Where does one seek the deeds of a buddha?"

Manjushri replied, "Deva, seek the deeds of buddhas among the kleshas of beings. If all beings were not afflicted by kleshas, the deeds of buddhas would not occur. Buddhas arise in order to bring the transcendence of birth, aging, sickness, and death. When the tathagata achieved awakening, nothing new began and nothing ended. This is because nothing ever arises or ceases. The appearance of buddhas is, in its nature, unoriginated. The greatest wish of bodhisattvas is to be free from the conceptualization of anything. The greatest benevolence is to be without attachment to anything, internal or external. The greatest generosity is to give up all kleshas without giving up beings."

Then Mara the Wrongdoer, miserable, unhappy, his face covered by tears, said, "Whoever practices this dharma teaching will be unassailable by maras. For those who uphold this dharma, all the actions of Mara will cease." Having said that, Mara disappeared.

In that way, Mara the Wrongdoer — hateful, jealous, and proud — was unable to obstruct the dharma and was even forced to perform a buddha's deeds by teaching the extremely profound mahayana. The skill and power of bodhisattvas is inconceivable!

From the *Mahayana Sutra of the Place of Manjushri*

Once the youthful Manjushri went for a stroll, going from house to house among the dwellings of five hundred bhikshus who lived as a community. Eventually he came to the dwelling

of Shariputra. Manjushri saw that Shariputra was alone and meditating. He spoke to Shariputra of meditation and explained the profound nature of all dharmas that is beyond conceptualization. Hearing him, five hundred bhikshus arose from their seats, declaring, "We shall never again look upon or listen to the youthful Manjushri! We shall abandon any place in which he is present! Why? Because Manjushri contradicts the dharma of our teacher by teaching that samsara, affliction; and nirvana, purity, are one." Disparaging Manjushri scornfully, they left.

Manjushri said, "What those five hundred bhikshus have said was well said. Why? Because the youthful Manjushri does not exist and cannot be perceived. It is therefore impossible to look upon or listen to me. If I do not exist, then my place does not exist either and cannot be specified."

Hearing what Manjushri said, the five hundred bhikshus returned and said, "Manjushri, we do not understand your teaching!"

Manjushri replied, "Bhikshus, excellent! Excellent! What you have said is appropriate for shravakas of our teacher! Bhikshus, there are no such things as wisdom or consciousness. The dharmadhatu is the only place, and it is inconceivable."

Through Manjushri's teaching, four hundred of those bhikshus liberated their minds, without acceptance, from all defilements. One hundred bhikshus became enraged and fell into the Great Wailing Hell while still alive.

Then Shariputra said to Manjushri, "Your teaching of dharma does not protect beings! Those hundred bhikshus are lost! You have brought about a disaster!"

The bhagavat said, "Shariputra, do not say such things! Those hundred bhikshus will only experience the Great Wailing Hell for a moment. They will then be born as devas

in Tushita. Had they not heard this dharma, they would have definitely gone to hell and remained there until their karma was exhausted. They would then have been born as human beings. Because they have heard this dharma, they will purify through a moment's experience the karma that would otherwise have caused them to experience a kalpa in hell. They will achieve arhathood among Maitreya's first disciples.

"To hear this dharma, even with doubt, is superior to the achievement of the absorptions of the form and formless realms and the cultivation of the four immeasurables. Without hearing dharma such as this, one will not be fully liberated from samsara."

Shariputra said to Manjushri, "It is wondrous that you have taught so thoroughly this dharma in order to ripen beings!"

Manjushri replied, "Suchness — the dharmadhatu, the nature of beings — is without fluctuation. It is neither affliction nor purification. It is inconceivable, nonabiding, and unceasing. It is awakening, liberation, and nirvana."

The bhagavat then taught, as had the youthful Manjushri, that all dharmas are mere imputations without true existence. A hundred thousand beings achieved the immaculate eye of dharma. Five hundred bhikshus freed their minds from all defilements. Eighty thousand devas of the form realm generated the intention to achieve unsurpassable awakening. They received prophecy of their achievement of perfect awakening.

In that way, Manjushri ripened, directly or indirectly, even the foolish who rejected profound dharma. The sutras repeatedly relate how the youthful Manjushri ripened innumerable beings through various means, such as asking the tathagata questions, conversing with other bodhisattvas, engaging in dialogue with shravakas, and teaching dharma to devas and humans.

From the *Root Tantra of Manjushri*

At one time the bhagavat abided with an assembly of bodhi-sattvas in the midst of the sky above the pure abodes. When he taught the youthful Manjushri's bodhisattva miracles and the basis of his mantra, light rays issued forth from between the tathagata's eyebrows. These light rays passed through as many worlds to the northeast as there are sand grains in a thousand Ganges Rivers. They reached the world called Endowed with Flowers. In that realm was the tathagata Lord King of All Flowers' Birth. Before him was the youthful Manjushri. The light rays alerted Manjushri, and he entered a samadhi that caused every part of every realm in the four directions to be filled with buddhas. The buddha of that realm and all the other buddhas said, "Child of the victors, excellent! Excellent! Shravakas, pratyekabuddhas, and bodhi-sattvas on the ten levels are incapable of such a samadhi as this!" Then the youthful Manjushri miraculously appeared before the bhagavat Shakyamuni, along with an immeasurable display of offerings. Manjushri prostrated to the buddha's feet, praised him, and then sat down.

The bhagavat said to Manjushri, "Please teach the functions of your mantra."

The youthful Manjushri entered a bodhisattva samadhi called Perfect Gathering of the Ornamental Array of the Radiant Light of the Blessing of All Buddhas. Immediately, radiant light filled as many realms as the Ganges' sand grains. They were filled from Akanishtha down to Avichi.[60] All the suffering of all the beings within those realms was pacified. All the shravakas, pratyekabuddhas, and bhagavat buddhas in those realms were alerted. Then the light was withdrawn into the top of Manjushri's head. The tathagatas of innumerable realms, accompanied by their retinues of bodhisattvas, shravakas, and pratyekabuddhas, gathered. All the deities of

60. Akanishtha, "nothing higher," is the highest of the seventeen "levels of the form realm. Avichi, "uninterrupted agony," is the lowest of the eight hot hells.

the tathagata, vajra, and padma families: innumerable tathagatas, bodhisattvas, ushnishas, queens of awareness, and
great kings of awareness, as well as innumerable pratyekabuddhas, shravakas, and ordinary beings were present in that
great gathering.[61] Amidst the display of miracles, Manjushri
taught the practice of his mantra and its boundless functions.

Then the bhagavat said:

"When the moon of Shakyamuni has set
And the mandala of the earth is empty,
This practice will remain in the world.
It will reveal the point of my teaching.

"Manjughosha is always good.
Amidst all elementals,
This youth will then display to the world
The deeds of a buddha.

"The power of this king of practices
Will, long from now, liberate
Those who wish for it and hear it even once.
They will always become accomplished.

"This youth pervades all substantial things.
He will benefit worlds that do not yet exist.
He appears for the benefit and the good of all beings.
He abides in pure places where liberation is known.

"Those who always delight in truth, kindness,
Patience, benevolence, love, and generosity
Will always attain siddhi.
There will be no siddhi for others.

"For those who always delight in and are bound
To this supreme mantra, the teachings, and the
    wheel's holder,

61. Ushnishas, "crown projections," and the other types of deities mentioned here are female and male deities of the kriyatantra, "action tantra." The buddha, vajra, and padma families are the families of wisdom deities taught in that tantra class.

62. *Supremely*
Gentle is another
name for Manjushri.

Supremely Gentle will subdue Mara and turn the
dharmachakra.[62]
They will be worthy of the wheel's holder.

"His speech is pleasing and good.
It is always beyond that of childish beings.
Pleasing and good, it soothes the ear.
One hears it with corresponding delight.

"He satisfies one's mind and bestows bliss.
All buddhas have proclaimed him Gentle.
But even the greatest tathagatas claim not to know
The limits of Manjushri's abilities.

"Their children on the ten levels
That transcend the world,
The greatest lords among mundane devas,
And good sages are all unable to know you.

"No being on the levels of form and formlessness;
No desirous deva, clever human, yogin, or siddha;
No great being of this world, and no ruler of humanity
Knows your greatness.

"There is no being anywhere
That fully knows your greatness.
Only buddhas really know
The one called Manju.

"The name Manjushri was given
To you by victors of the past.
This name, so given, is only learned
From the buddhas of the past, present, and future.

"Only those with a one-pointed, undistracted, pure mind
Can hear your name; and only amidst the gathering
    of a buddha.
Those who do will achieve auspicious peace

In this life and finally, supreme awakening.

"They will accomplish all mantras
And achieve the best of births.
They will always perfectly abide in supreme dharma.
They will transcend obstructions and attain siddhi.

"Your name causes all desired accomplishments
    of mantra.
It causes one to quickly reach the tree of awakening.
Then it causes the achievement of supreme awakening.
Then it causes one to remain for beings' benefit.

"With a buddha's awakening, one will turn the
    dharmachakra.
These are your qualities as stated by the great victors.
Manjushri, the recollection of your name
Is said by the victors to be of inconceivable value.

"All the great victors who have appeared in the past
Have continually taught the power of your name.
Pure youth, the meaning of your mantra
Could not be fully taught even in innumerable kalpas.

"Manjushri, the practice of your mantra
Is extensively taught by all buddhas.
This youth is ubiquitous!
Within my teachings, you are supreme.

"Beings who inhabit pure realms
Will all pass into peace,
But your mantra will never disappear.
Your mantra will never be lost."

The obscurity of this quotation requires explanation. *This
youth pervades all substantial things* states the future benefit
of beings that Manjushrighosha, who pervades all realms in
the form of a youth, will accomplish.

Those who always delight in truth, kindness describes the qualities of those who will accomplish Manjushri's mantra.

His speech is pleasing and good describes Manjushri's qualities. Because he expounds the treasury of dharma with a voice as pleasing as that of Brahma, he is known by the name Manju. Even great tathagatas pretend not to know the full extent of his qualities. The supramundane bodhisattvas on the ten levels; the supreme rulers among mundane devas; the devas, humans, and yogins of the three levels of existence; and all other beings, including shravakas and pratyekabuddhas, are all unable to fully know Manjushri's greatness. Only buddhas know it.

The name Manjushri was given states that the name Manjushri, bestowed by buddhas, is rarely heard other than in the gatherings of buddhas, and is only heard by beings with pure and undistracted minds. The benefits of hearing the name Manjushri, in brief, include auspiciousness in this life; the pacification of all sorts of adversity, including obscurations; and the ultimate achievement of unsurpassable awakening. The benefits are then stated more fully: Merely by hearing this name, all mantras will be accomplished. In all lives one will be free from bad births. One will acquire the best of births. One will always abide in the supreme dharma of perfect, virtuous qualities. Siddhi will be attained without any obstruction or impediment. All mantras one wishes to accomplish will be accomplished. One will become a vidyadhara.[63] Those are the temporary benefits. Ultimately, one will reach the tree of awakening. For beings' benefit, one will sit down there and immediately achieve unsurpassable awakening. One will then turn the dharmachakra that accords with a buddha's awakening. This is how great victors have described the qualities of Manjushri's name. This is then summarized in "Manjushri, the recollection of your name is said by the victors to be of inconceivable value."

63. A vidyadhara, a "holder of awareness," is a realized master of tantra.

All the great victors who have appeared in the past states that the buddhas of the past extensively explained Manjushri's power and qualities. As the significance and benefits of his mantra are unlimited, even a description of them that took innumerable kalpas to give would be incomplete. All buddhas of the three times teach his mantra. The youthful Manjushri possesses a wisdom body that is always free from aging and infirmity. With this body he enters the realms of all buddhas of the three times and illuminates them. Within the teachings of Shakyamuni, Manjushri appears as a supreme person, a bodhisattva, in order to benefit beings. Although innumerable noble beings who inhabit the pure abodes pass into nirvana, the expanse of peace, the mantra of Manjushri never disappears and is never lost throughout the three times.

The buddha continued:

"At the end of time
The accomplishment of mantra is certain.
I, the lord of sages, declare
The following about this youth:

"Manjughosha of great wisdom
Possesses a youthful form.
He roams all over this world,
Patiently caring for beings.

"In the future will be seen
Many siddhas of Manjushri.
When the constellations and stars are understood,
Those siddhas will appear. [64]

"The twenty-seven constellations
Will become famous in a moment.
At that end of time,
The twelve houses will appear.

64. This stanza and the following two are usually interpreted as predictions of the emergence of astrology through Manjushri's blessing.

"Based on the constellations,
The planets will be distinguished.
The distinctions among all of these
Will be made by Manjushri.

"The teachings of the protector,
Shakyamuni, will disappear.
At that terrifying, dangerous time
Manjushri will be accomplished.

"Therefore always, youthful Manjushri,
And especially then, it will be you
Who will subdue the lords of the earth
Who are engaged in wrongdoing.

"Your miracles are inconceivable.
The number of your disciples is inconceivable.
All elementals without exception
Will be tamed by you."

After the heroic buddha said that,
He said to the luminous Manjushri,
"Look at those present above the pure abodes!
They are perfect buddhas, the best of all with two feet."

Then the supreme speaker said to Manjushri,
"After many kalpas you will become a perfect buddha.
The number of your disciples will be unequalled,
Beyond imagining, greater than the number of
     human beings.

65. Manjudhvaja
means "gentle
victory banner."

"You will appear in the world
As the buddha called Manjudhvaja.[65]
At that time you will perform the deeds of a buddha.
You will liberate many beings and then pass into
     nirvana."

From the *Tantra of the Ferocious Heart-Spike*, a dharma of the
Early Translations of Secret Mantra

Manjushri is the greatest of noble bodhisattvas.
Marichi is the greatest goddess.
There is no siddhi other than from these two.
Without them, the vidyadharas' siddhi would disappear.

The three worlds emerge from my belly.
Whatever is peaceful
Is my peaceful body.
Whatever is wrathful   .
Is my wrathful body.

From the *Ornamental Tantra of the Vajra Nature*

He bestows the supreme wisdom of the buddhas.
Therefore the supreme wisdom of the buddhas
Is renowned as Manjughosha.

Merely by accomplishing him,
Your wisdom will become stainless.
You will proclaim all shastras
And abide in the presence of all great lords.

The mantrin will be the king of all.[66]
You will become like the king of all.
You will traverse all the stages of a vidyadhara
And all the stages of awakening.

You will gain all aspects of mastery, great bliss,
The supreme qualities of all dharmas,
Those of all vajra holders,
And even the perfection of all buddhas.

What need is there to speak of other siddhi?
Alchemy; rasayana;[67]

66. A mantrin is a practitioner of tantra.

67. Rasayana is the practice of deriving nourishment from minerals, water, air, or awareness alone. It and the other abilities mentioned in this stanza are examples of common siddhi, attainments other than awakening.

Stainless, supreme fleetness of foot;
Pills; invisibility — all will be bestowed.

This supreme Manjushri was born
From the supreme speech of dharma.
The melody, like Brahma's, of the buddhas
Is renowned as Manjughosha.

Merely by accomplishing him,
You will attain the greatest affluence —
The state of all buddhas.
What need is there to speak of other deities?

68. This is the mantra OM ARAPACHANA DHIH. In the *Trilokavijayatantra*, there is a brief description of the benefits of the Arapacha, the king of awareness mantras.[68] The many excellent qualities of the various manifestations and mantras of the peaceful and wrathful forms of Manjushri are repeatedly described in the old and new tantras.

In the *Shrikalachakratantra*, it is taught that one of the six lands of Jambudvipa is Shambhala, which is in the north. In that land of wondrous array, mahabodhisattvas on the ten levels appear continuously as kings. The first to do so was King Suchandra, an emanation of Vajrapani. The bhagavat, having arisen in the form of Shri Kalachakra, taught Suchandra the *Root Tantra* of twelve thousand stanzas. The eighth king to rule Shambhala — seven generations after Suchandra — was the Rigden Manjushrikirti, an emanation of Manjushri. At the beginning of his reign there were still in that land adherents of various forms of discipline, including brahmins following the Vedas. Manjushrikirti bestowed the empowerment of unsurpassable vajrayana on everyone in that land, causing everyone there to join the single family of the supreme vehicle. It was therefore during his reign that it became customary to refer to the king of Shambhala as the Rigden, "the one endowed with family." The Rigden

Manjushrikirti also condensed the *Root Tantra* into the
Condensed Tantra of five chapters.

From the great *Condensed Tantra*

In the glorious Shakya family there will appear seven
 illustrious rulers.
The eighth, Kirti, will be Shri Manjuvajra, who will
 be endowed with the vajra family of this supreme deity.
He will bestow the vajra empowerment, bringing
 everyone into the single family of Shakyamuni.
Shri Kirti with a spear will establish them in the perfect
 vehicle, terrifying the asuras. For the sake of beings'
 liberation, he will illuminate Kalachakra.

From the "Wisdom Chapter" of that tantra

The dharmaraja Manjushrikirti said to the brahmin
 Chariot of the Sun,
"Sun, the lords of the world are active in the three worlds.
 They show beings the path and rob them of hell's
 dangers. No other gods do this."

Chariot of the Sun praised him in response,
"You are old yet young. Among all the victors' children,
 you are first and are also the first buddha.
You unite with women and yet are chaste. In your
 supreme compassion, you are the world's friend
 and Yama's enemy.
Great vajra, you are tranquil yet rob us of death's
 dangers.
You are always a mara to Mara.
Kirti, you are free yet enter this existence in order
 to ripen beings."

The son of King Manjushrikirti was the Rigden Padma
Karpo, an emanation of Avalokita. Padma Karpo wrote

Stainless Light, the great commentary on the *Condensed Tantra*. The thirty-second ruler if numbered from Suchandra, and the twenty-fifth if numbered from the Rigden Manjushrikirti, will be the reappearance of King Manjushrikirti — Manjushri in person — in the form of the Rigden Rudrachakrin. He will conquer barbarians.

From the "Chapter on the World" in the *Condensed Tantra*

After thirty-two reigns will appear the asuras' enemy.
His life span will be a hundred years. He will
  hold a wheel.

And:

After twenty-five reigns have been counted,
The Rigden Rudra, bowed to even by the rulers of
  devas, will appear.
To the holy he will appear tranquil and will bring them
  bliss,
But he will be a destroyer of barbarians.
With the brilliance of the sun, he will ride a stone horse.
Holding a wheel and a spear, he will pierce all
  his enemies.

The Rigden Rudrachakrin will engage in fierce combat throughout southern Jambudvipa. He will have a vast army, and the armies of the twelve great devas will be his allies. After defeating all the barbarian forces, he will elucidate the buddha's teaching and especially the vajrayana. His two sons will be known as Brahma and Indra. Rudrachakrin will place Brahma on the throne of Shambhala and make Indra the king of the rest of Jambudvipa. By disseminating dharma, they will increase the life span and well-being of humans. The Rigden Rudrachakrin will retire to his palace in Shambhala and demonstrate the attainment of the siddhi of mahamudra. Along with his court and all connected to him, he will pass into a realm of bliss.

From the chapter quoted above

With his armies, assisted by fierce Vishnu, the Rigden will
defeat the barbarians at war.
Chakrin will then go to live in the divine citadel atop
Mount Kailash.
All people will then enjoy perfect dharma, pleasure, and
wealth.
Grain will grow in the wilderness. Trees will bow with
their fruit.
The barbarians and their allies will be eradicated.
After fifty years the Rigden will gain siddhi behind
The palace built by devas atop high Kailash.

As the extensive predictions in the *Kalachakratantra* indicate,
Manjushri's display of various forms that are individually
suitable for those to be tamed is worthy of admiration. He
does this in every realm throughout space. His emanations are
unlimited and appear like the moon's reflection in water.

From the *Tantra of Black Yamantaka*

At the time of the bhagavat Shakyamuni's manifest awakening, Mara appeared with a vast army in order to obstruct him.
The bhagavat entered the samadhi of Complete Victory over
Great Maras. From the bhagavat's vajra body, speech, and
mind appeared wrathful Yamantaka.[69] The bhagavat then
said to Vajrapani, "You too should adopt such a wrathful
form. Then conquer Mara and his forces. Bind them. Realize
their nature."

69. Yamantaka,
the "slayer of the
lord of death," is
the wrathful form
of Manjushri.

Vajrapani then received and held that tantra.

From the "Tale of the Deity" in the *Vajrabhairavatantra*

He crossed the southern sea
To Yama's city.

With his sixteen invincible feet
He crushed sixteen doorless iron castles.

With the single-pointed weapon of wisdom
He destroyed the great central castle.
Then victorious over great Mara,
He exclaimed, "Ha, ha, hi, hi!"

Dharmaraja and the others
Called out in subjugation,
"Great hero, where are you?
Hero, I will do what you want!
We correctly offer our life essences.
Hero, accept them!"

From the *Aryamanjushrivimalaguhyatantra,* a dharma of the
Early Translations

In the past, underneath the mandala of water and above the
mandala of wind, there were seventeen great, doorless, iron
castles. Yama, who moved about these castles with his mind,
was the embodiment of killing, mutilation, and fierce hatred.
His name was Dark Destroyer Nine Million Yojanas Tall. His
wife was called Kali Kalaratri. They ruled over all pretas and
brought fatality to all beings. Their food was fresh flesh and
blood. They held the three worlds in their bellies and lived in
the central castle. Their emanations included the four great
executioners, such as Dharmaraja, and the executioners' four
attendants, such as Yama Chasang. Their retinue included all
vicious devas, matrikas, rakshasas, and all the rest of the eight
classes.[70] Along with their emanations and retinue, Yama and
Kalaratri brought disaster to this world.

The bhagavat Arya Manjushri arose from the dharmadhatu and entered the samadhi called Annihilation of the
Vicious. He was immediately transformed into a ferocious
and powerful deity.

70. Matrikas are
ferocious female
beings. The eight
classes are: devas,
nagas, yakshas,
ghandharvas,
asuras, garudas,
nonhumans (beings
that can take
human form with-
out being human),
and great serpents.

His color changed from that of purest gold
To that of silver ore.
His scepter changed from a blue utpala
Into the black mace of Yama.
Manjushri the tranquil emanated
A form enraged at Yama.

He embraced fierce Vetali on his left and Ekajati on his right. The father and mothers, united in nonduality, were surrounded by four great Yamantakas with their consorts, the ten father and mother Yamantakas who guard the ten directions, the four goddesses of the gates, and the rest of their inconceivably vast retinue, all of whom blazed with wrath.

Manjushri then entered the samadhi called Enthralling the Three Realms. This entire world shook violently. He then crushed with his feet the city of the Lord of Death. He drew from Yama his life essence, which had the form of a scorpion with eight mouths. All the other Yamas then offered their life essences and promised to protect the buddha's teaching until the end of its final five hundred years.

From the "King of Examinations," the latter part of the
Elucidation of Yamantaka Tantra from the Early Translations

The wrathful one's name is Yamantaka.
He radiates weapons that blaze like fire.
Ferocious, he possesses fierce power.
Seeing him, all other wrathful ones
Drop their weapons.
All mundane devas bow to him.
They join their palms in fear
And praise him greatly.

According to the definitive meaning, Manjushri is the single wisdom body of all victors, the holy overlord of all families.

From the "Chapter of Earnest Praise" in the
Aryamanjushrinamasamgiti

The wisdom body of the bhagavats,
The great ushnisha, the lord of words,
The self-arisen wisdom body,
Manjushri, the wisdom being.

From the "Chapter on Mantra"

Buddha, wisdom body
Of all buddhas of the three times.

And:

Supreme, primordial holder of the trikaya;
Embodiment of the buddhas' five bodies;
Overlord and embodiment of the five wisdoms.

And:

Progenitor of all buddhas,
Supreme, holy son of buddhas.

And:

Supreme body, embodiment of all buddhas.

And:

Enactor of the three times' buddhas' activity,
Buddha without beginning or end,
Undifferentiated first buddha,
Single stainless eye of wisdom.

And:

Great king of all buddhas,
Holder of the body of all buddhas.

And:

Great mind of all buddhas,
Abiding in the mind of all buddhas,
Great body of all buddhas,
And the speech of all buddhas too.

And:

Holder of the treasury of omniscience.

And:

Emanator of the innumerable millions
Of nirmanakayas of all buddhas.

And:

Holder of the nature of all buddhas.

And:

That which is realized by all buddhas,
The unsurpassable awakening of buddhas.

And:

Great essence of all buddhas,
Holder of the diverse wheel of emanation.

And:

Holder of the continuity of buddhas' emanations
Who dispatches diverse emanations to the ten directions.

And:

The supreme, incomparable lord
Of all wisdom and all that is to be known.

And:

71. These are the
renunciations of
a shravaka,
a pratyekabuddha,
and a bodhisattva.

Glorious, pure, ultimate meaning
To which the three renunciations lead.[71]

And:

I prostrate to you, the awakening of buddhas.

From the "Explanation of the Malamantra"

It means, "I will hold onto utterly pure Manjushri, the wisdom body of all tathagatas."

From the *Supplemental Tantra* to the *Magical Net of Manjushri,* a dharma of the Early Translations

Manjushri is a glorious, perfect body.
He is uncommon, nondual, and pervasive.
In this father of all victors, the three times are equal
   and complete.
His consort is the dharmadhatu. He appears as
   the supreme bodhisattva.

And:

Rest naturally, without acceptance or rejection,
In all-achieving emptiness, spontaneous, touched by
   nothing.
That is the true Manjushri.
If you do not fixate on or think about the inconceivable,
Your qualities will be as perfect as Manjushri's.

And:

Manjushri is the perfect wisdom vajra.
This wheel of the magical net

Abides neither as samsara nor nirvana.
It is the vajra peak.
It cannot be thought of or accomplished,
But is wholly present if you rest in the expanse.

As these quotations indicate, the youthful Manjushri of the definitive meaning is the nondual, self-arisen wisdom body that equally personifies all knowledge and all objects of knowledge. He is the overlord of all families and all victors of the three times. Having learned his nature, give rise to unreserved faith in him.

THE FIRST CHAPTER: THE YOUTHFUL MANJUSHRI

AVALOKITA
THE NOBLE LORD OF COMPASSION

I PROSTRATE TO THE BODHISATTVA MAHASATTVA
AVALOKITESHVARA,[72] GREAT COMPASSION!
I VENERATE YOU! I TAKE REFUGE IN YOU!

The qualities of this supreme noble one are utterly
inconceivable.

From the *Box Sutra*

When Avalokiteshvara visited the burning iron buildings in
the Avichi Hell, that environment became cool and the buildings were transformed into pools covered by lotuses. Seeing
Avalokiteshvara's ability to liberate beings, even Yamaraja
praised him. Then Avalokiteshvara went to the preta realm.
He caused it too to become cool and all the beings there
to become loving. He stopped their suffering. From his twenty digits and the pores on his skin emerged great streams of
water. These relieved all the pretas and removed all their suffering. From these streams issued the sound of the words
of the *Box Sutra*, like a king among the three jewels. This
sound caused the pretas' view of the transitory composite to
be conquered by the vajra of wisdom.[73] They were reborn in
Sukhavati.

Every day, Avalokita fully ripens billions and billions of

beings. Even tathagatas do not possess such confidence. From Avalokita's eyes emerge the sun and moon. From his forehead emerges Maheshvara, from his shoulders Brahma, from his heart Mahabala, from his canine teeth Sarasvati, from his mouth the god of wind, from his feet the god of earth, and from his belly the god of water.[74] Wherever Avalokita goes there are a rain of flowers and other amazing wonders such as pools and trees in bloom. Avalokita displays whatever form will tame those to be tamed, including the forms of a tathagata, a shravaka, a pratyekabuddha, Brahma, Indra, a human being, and a nonhuman being. By displaying such variety he fully ripens beings. Even tathagatas do not do what Avalokita does.

74. Mahabala is a wrathful deity associated with protection. Sarasvati is a goddess associated with learning and music.

He appeared as an asura to the asuras living in the cave called Vajra Womb in this Jambudvipa. He taught them dharma, causing their rebirth in Sukhavati. Avalokita also went to a place where the ground was of gold and all the beings were upside down; a place where the ground was of silver and all the beings had four legs; and a place where isolated asuras dwelt. By teaching dharma, he irreversibly established all those beings on the path.

He then went into the darkness where yakshas and rakshasas live, and taught them dharma. Then he appeared in the pure abodes in the form of a brahmin. He tamed, by means of both dharma and material generosity, the impoverished deva Supreme Ear Ring. Then Avalokita went to the island of Singhala, where he established the rakshasis living there in dharma by appearing to them in a desirable form.

In the great city of Shravasti were thousands of insects living amidst excrement and urine. Avalokita appeared to them in the form of a bee and produced the sound of the words, "I prostrate to the buddha!" All those insects were reborn as bodhisattvas in Sukhavati with the collective name Fragrance of Incense. In the wilds of Magadha, where beings were preying on one another, Avalokita sent down a rain of food, caus-ing those beings to praise him in their delight.

Avalokita rests in many samadhis, such as those called Appearance and Light. In each of the pores of his skin are hundreds or thousands of samadhis. Even tathagatas do not possess the merit of Avalokita. What need is there to mention that other bodhisattvas do not possess it?

Once, the bodhisattva Samantabhadra entered the samadhi called Vajra Risen Above in the presence of the tathagata Dispeller of Mistrust. Avalokiteshvara entered the samadhi called Scattering. When Samantabhadra then entered the samadhi called Holy Moon Eye, Avalokiteshvara entered the samadhi called Holy Sun Eye, and so on. No matter how many samadhis Samantabhadra entered, Avalokiteshvara always surpassed him. Finally, Samantabhadra said to Avalo-kiteshvara, "Son of family, your confidence is wondrous!"

The tathagata Dispeller of Mistrust said then to Samantabhadra, "Son of family, you have seen very little of Avalokiteshvara's confidence! Even tathagatas do not possess the same confidence as Avalokiteshvara."

Once, the bhagavat Shakyamuni said to the bodhisattva Sarvanivaranavishkambhin, "I am unable to number the mer-its of Avalokiteshvara. If I speak a little of some of the pores on his skin, one of his pores is called Gold. Living in it are tril-lions of ghandharvas. They are not menaced by suffering or kleshas. They abide in dharma. Their wishes are fulfilled by wish-fulfilling jewels.

"Beyond that is the pore called Black. Within it live trillions of rishis. They all possess between one and six types of supercognition. Within that pore is a ground of silver adorned by seventy-seven golden mountains of which the peaks are silver and adorned by red lotuses. On each of those mountains live eighty thousand rishis. Within that pore are wish-fulfilling trees with red trunks and leaves of gold and silver. There are also pools and other wish-fulfilling trees adorned in various ways. These trees produce divine fabric, food, and fragrances at one's wish. In such ways, that pore possesses many qualities.

"One of his pores is called Precious Ear Ring. Within it live many beautiful ghandharva maidens. They are unafflicted by desire or other kleshas. Simply by recollecting Avalokita's name they receive all that they wish for. That pore is as imperceptible and untouchable as the reaches of space. The bodhisattva Samantabhadra once searched for that pore for twelve years without finding it. If he could not see it, what need is there to say that other bodhisattvas are unable to do so? If the natural body of Avalokita is unseen by the tathagata, what need is there to say that it is unseen by bodhisattvas such as Samantabhadra?

"In the pore of Avalokita's skin that is called Drops of Amrita live bodhisattva devas who abide between the first and tenth levels. That pore possesses an immeasurable array of such things as mountains, mansions, rivers, and wish-fulfilling trees.

"Similarly, in the pore called Vajra Gate live many nonhumans. In pores such as those called Sunlight and Ruling King are various immeasurable arrays. Those who hold Avalokita's name and the six syllables are born within these pores.[75] They will not thereafter return to samsara. Until they achieve nirvana, they will inhabit one of Avalokita's pores after another.

75. The six syllables:
OM MANI PADME HUM.

"From the big toe on Avalokiteshvara's right foot stream four great lakes of immeasurable depth. The waters within those lakes form waterfalls like the face of a mare. In such ways, through his inconceivable blessing, Avalokita fully ripens innumerable beings and establishes them on the path to awakening."

Once, the tathagata Crown said to the bodhisattva Jewel-in-Hand, "To offer robes, food, and other necessities to as many tathagatas as there are sand grains in the Ganges River for the duration of a kalpa of the devas would produce an amount of merit equal to that contained in the tip of one of the hairs on Avalokita's body. One could count the drops of rain that fall on all four continents during a period of twelve months, or the drops of water contained within the oceans' depths, or the number of hairs on the bodies of all the wild animals and predators that live in the four continents. One could not, however, measure Avalokiteshvara's merit.

"One could measure the merit of making, every day, as many golden images of tathagatas as there are smallest particles and filling them with relics. One could count the number of leaves in a forest of shrishapa trees. One could not, however, measure Avalokita's merit.

"One could weigh on a scale the king of mountains and all that surrounds it. One could not, however, weigh the merit of Avalokiteshvara.

"If all the men and women in Jambudvipa were turned into scribes, and innumerable supreme mountains were turned into birch-bark paper, and all the depths of the oceans were turned into ink, one could count the number of letters that would be written. One could not, however, measure the merit of Avalokiteshvara.

"For example, the aggregate of merit accumulated by offering all sorts of robes, food, bedding, and healing medicine to as many tathagatas as there are sand grains in twelve Ganges Rivers would equal the merit contained within the tip of one of the bodhisattva Avalokita's hairs.

"The merit of establishing all the men and women of the four continents in the awakening of a shravaka or pratyekabuddha

would equal the amount of merit contained within the tip of one of Avalokita's hairs. If all tathagatas like me were assembled in one place, we would be unable to measure the aggregate of Avalokita's merit. What need is there to say that I alone am unable to do so?"

The bhagavat Shakyamuni once said, "It is valuable for beings to hold the name of Avalokita. His great awareness mantra of six syllables was sought for sixteen kalpas by all tathagatas. Even the great mother of all tathagatas prostrates to this awareness mantra. Those who hold and recite it will acquire immeasurable merit. At the time of its recitation tathagatas and bodhisattvas equal in number to the smallest particles will gather. Millions of buddhas will enter each of the pores of the reciter of this mantra. They will bestow their approval, saying, 'Child of family, you have well acquired something worthy of acquisition. Even all the beings who live in your belly will become irreversible bodhisattvas.' The reciter will be guarded by devas, nagas, yakshas, and others. Anyone who keeps this mantra on their body will achieve a vajra body and a buddha's wisdom. They will acquire all complete qualities, including confidence, wisdom, love, and the paramitas. They will quickly achieve the unsurpassable awakening of buddhahood.

"Any being who touches or sees this mantra will become a bodhisattva who has reached the end of rebirth. This great awareness mantra pulls out the root of samsara. It guides one to liberation and omniscience. In search of this mantra, one should fill Jambudvipa with the seven jewels and offer it. If someone wishes to write this mantra down but lacks ink, it would be excellent for them to use their blood as ink, their skin as paper, and their bones as a pen. By reciting this mantra, one will attain a hundred and eight samadhis, such as the samadhi called Holding a Precious Jewel. By merely recollecting this mantra all one's wrongdoing will be purified. The merit of reciting this mantra even once is beyond comparison.

"One could count the number of smallest particles, or the number of sand grains in the oceans' depths. If there were a granary that was five hundred yojanas high and a hundred yojanas wide on every side, and it was filled with sesame seeds, and every hundred years a single seed was removed from it, one could count the number of years it would take to empty it. One could not, however, measure the aggregate of merit gained by reciting this awareness mantra.

"One could count all the ripened grain in Jambudvipa. One could count the drops of water that flow into the oceans every day and night from the eleven rivers, such as the Ganges, and their five hundred tributaries. One could count the hairs on the bodies of all the wild animals and predators in all the mountains and valleys in the world. There is a king among mountains called Mount Vajra Hook. It is ninety-nine thousand yojanas high. Its base extends into the ground to a depth of eighty-four thousand yojanas. Each of its faces is eighty thousand yojanas wide. If at the end of every kalpa one were to wipe that mountain once with the finest cotton cloth, one could estimate the length of time it would take to utterly erode this mountain in that way. One could not, however, measure the merit of a single recitation of the six syllables.

"One could count the number of drops of water in an ocean by removing it, drop by drop, with the tip of a hair. If it rained heavily and continuously, day and night, for a year or even thirteen months, one could still count the number of raindrops fallen in that period. One could not, however, measure the aggregate of merit accumulated by a single recitation of the six syllables. If all the men, women, boys, and girls in the four continents became bodhisattvas on the seventh level, the aggregate of all their merit would still be greatly exceeded by the aggregate of merit gained by a single recitation of the six syllables. Even if millions of tathagatas were to describe it for an entire deva kalpa, they could not enumerate the aggregate

of merit gained by a single recitation of the six-syllable awareness mantra. What need is there to say that I, a single tathagata abiding in this world, am unable to do so?

"Anyone who writes or causes to be written these six syllables
will have written or caused to be written the eighty-four thousand aggregates of dharma. OM MANI PADME HUM. If one made
every day as many golden images of tathagatas as there are
smallest particles and filled them with relics, the ripened result
of doing so would barely equal the ripened result of writing
a single one of the six syllables. They are inconceivable.
Someone who holds the six syllables, even if their moral discipline is impaired, will not be stained by kleshas. These six
syllables are indestructible vajra words. They are words of
unsurpassable wisdom. They are the essence of everything."

The tathagata Shakyamuni once said to the bodhisattva
Sarvanivaranavishkambhin, "Son of family, in the past, in
search of this awareness mantra of six syllables, I went to as
many worlds as there are smallest particles and served sextillions of buddhas. I did not, however, hear it from any of them.
I then entered the presence of the buddha Supreme Red One,
and wept in front of him. He said to me, 'Son of family, do
not cry! Go to the tathagata Supreme Lotus. He knows this
great awareness mantra. Go to him!'

"I went to the buddha Supreme Lotus and prostrated to him. I
joined my palms and said, 'Although I have gone to many
worlds in search of it, I have not received the great awareness
mantra of six syllables. The mere memory of its name purifies
all wrongdoing. It is rarely known even by bodhisattvas.
Please bestow it upon me.'

"In reply the tathagata Supreme Lotus greatly praised this
great awareness mantra. Then he said, 'Son of family, I too
went to sextillions of worlds in search of this mantra. Finally
I entered the presence of the tathagata Amitabha. I joined my

palms and wept through the power of my yearning for dharma. The tathagata Amitabha said to Avalokita, "Son of family, look! The tathagata Supreme Lotus has gone to sextillions of worlds in search of the great awareness mantra of six syllables! Son of family, please offer him these six syllables, the queen of awareness mantras! Even though he is a tathagata, he has gone everywhere in search of it!"'

"The buddha Supreme Lotus continued, 'The bodhisattva Avalokita then bestowed the six syllables, the king of awareness mantras, upon me along with the ritual of his mandala. The great earth and all its oceans shook. All obstructors and yakshas fled. I extended my arm, like an elephant extending its trunk, and offered Avalokita a garland of thousands of pearls. He accepted it and offered it to the buddha Amitabha. He too accepted it and then returned it to me. After receiving this awareness mantra of six syllables, I returned to my own world, Lotus.'"

The tathagata Shakyamuni concluded, "Son of family, I heard this awareness mantra in that way from the tathagata Supreme Lotus."

In reply, Sarvanivaranavishkambhin said, "Bhagavat, where must I go to receive the awareness mantra of six syllables?"

The buddha answered, "Son of family, in the great town of Shravasti there are dharma teachers who hold the awareness mantra of six syllables. Dharma teachers who hold the awareness mantra of six syllables are rare. Such dharma teachers should be viewed as equal to the tathagata. They should be viewed as the ground and aggregate of beings' merit. They should be viewed as perfect speech, as heaps of jewels, as all-bestowing wish-fulfilling gems, as treasuries of dharma, and as liberators of beings.

"Son of family, even if such dharma teachers have impaired morality and ungoverned conduct, even if they have spouses

and are surrounded by their children, even if their saffron robes are filled with excrement and urine, do not give rise to doubt when you see their behavior. If you do so, you will fall from the bodhisattva levels into an inferior birth."

The bodhisattva Sarvanivaranavishkambhin, bearing various offerings and accompanied by a retinue of thousands, went to the town of Shravasti. He bowed his head to the feet of the dharma teachers there. He saw that their morality was impaired, that their conduct was imperfect, and that their behavior was ungoverned. Nevertheless, he venerated them with parasols, ornaments, and balms. He joined his palms and extensively praised them, saying, "E MA HO! You cause us to taste the treasure of dharma! You are like immeasurable oceans, treasuries of amrita!"

One of the dharma teachers replied, "Son of family, do not give rise to doubt! My friend, kleshas are engagement in desire, in the characteristics of samsara, and in the wheel of beings. Anyone who knows the awareness mantra of six syllables will be unstained by desire, anger, and stupidity, like the stainless gold of the Jambu River."

Sarvanivaranavishkambhin took hold of his feet and begged, "Be eyes for us, the blind! Show us, the lost, our way! I thirst for dharma! Quench my thirst with the taste of dharma!"

When, in that way, Sarvanivaranavishkambhin requested the awareness mantra of six syllables, the dharma teacher replied, "The six syllables, the queen of awareness mantras, are rare words, vajra words, indestructible words, words of unsurpassable wisdom, words of inexhaustible wisdom, unsurpassable words."

Along with those praises, the dharma teacher said, "If one recites the six syllables even a little, one will attain the peace and liberation that is the meaning of the twelve branches of the mahayana teachings. Just as rice is the fruitful essence of the soil in which it grows, all other yoga is like chaff when compared to this queen of awareness mantras, which is like the fruitful essence. Son of family, bodhisattvas gather great accumulations for the sake of the six paramitas. A single recitation of this mantra will make the six paramitas totally complete. It is rare for beings to even hold the name of this awareness mantra. By holding its name even once, one will present all types of offerings, such as robes, to all tathagatas."

Then Sarvanivaranavishkambhin supplicated that dharma teacher for the awareness mantra of six syllables. The dharma teacher sat there, considering the request. While he was doing so, the sound of the words, "Bestow the great awareness mantra of six syllables!" came from the sky. Both Sarvanivaranavishkambhin and the dharma teacher wondered where the sound had come from. Then the sound of the words, "This bodhisattva has undergone many austerities! Give him the awareness mantra of six syllables!" came from the sky. The dharma teacher looked at the sky and saw the body of Avalokiteshvara. Knowing then that he should do so, the dharma teacher bestowed upon Sarvanivaranavishkambhin the awareness mantra of six syllables. As he did so, the earth shook six times. Sarvanivaranavishkambhin attained many samadhis, such as the samadhi called Inexhaustible Dharmata.

Then Sarvanivaranavishkambhin prepared to offer his teacher the four continents filled with jewels out of gratitude for the dharma he had received. The dharma teacher said, "If such an offering would be insufficient for even one of the six syllables, how could it be sufficient for all six? Son of family, I will accept nothing from you. You have become a bodhisattva. You were tamed by me."

Then Sarvanivaranavishkambhin offered the dharma teacher a garland of thousands of pearls. The dharma teacher said, "In my stead, offer these to the tathagata Shakyamuni."

Sarvanivaranavishkambhin then prostrated to that dharma teacher's feet and left. Having received what he had wanted to receive, with his wishes fulfilled, Sarvanivaranavishkambhin went to the Jetavana and entered the presence of the bhagavat Shakyamuni. He bowed to him and told him that he had well received what he had sought.

On another occasion, the bhagavat Shakyamuni said, "In the past, when I was a bodhisattva, I went on an ocean voyage in a company of five hundred merchants. An ill wind cast us on the shore of an island of rakshasis. Five hundred rakshasis, having transformed themselves into youthful maidens, led the merchants off one by one to their respective homes, deceiving them with their affectionate words and demeanor. While the senior rakshasi was attempting to seduce me, she fell asleep. Dozing, she began to laugh. I asked her why she was laughing. She said, 'We are the rakshasis of the island of Singhala. We will kill all of you! If you don't believe me, walk to the crossroads to your right and look!'

"I did what she had told me to and saw, in a city of iron, the merchants whom the rakshasis had already captured. The merchants were crying, 'They are going to eat a hundred of us every day!'

"When I heard that, I asked the rakshasi who was revealing all this to me if there were anything I could do about it. She said, 'There is a king among horses called Balaha. He helps the weak and desperate. He is to be found at the shore, on a beach called All Medicines Concealed, which has golden sand. He runs back and forth along the shore, shaking his mane and exclaiming, "Who will cross the ocean?" If you answer him, "I will cross it," he will bring you to freedom.'

"When I had heard all this, I secretly repeated it to the merchants. We decided to leave three days from then. We also promised one another that we would not look back at the island of Singhala.

"When we went to the shore we saw the king among horses. When he shook his mane, the entire island of Singhala became subdued. He asked us three times, 'Who will cross the ocean?'

"The merchants replied, 'We will cross it.'

"The king among horses then cautioned us, saying, 'None of you may look back at the island of Singhala!'

"Then I and the five hundred merchants climbed onto Balaha's back. The rakshasis pursued us, wailing piteously. The five hundred merchants turned to look back and fell into the water, where they were recaptured by the rakshasis, who eventually ate them. I alone reached Jambudvipa. When we reached its shores, Balaha, the king among horses, circumambulated me three times, bowed to me, and left. I eventually reached my home, where I was happily reunited with my parents.

"In that way, when I was a leader of merchants, I was saved from suffering and death by Avalokiteshvara, who took the form of the horse Balaha. Avalokiteshvara is a protector of the defenseless, a refuge for those without refuge, a giver of succor to the fearful, a torch for those captured by darkness, a parasol for those burnt by the sun, medicine for the sick, a parent to those who suffer, and a revealer of nirvana for the lost. All who recollect Avalokiteshvara's name will be happy. They will be freed from the sufferings of aging, sickness, and death. They will reach the end of samsara. Born in Sukhavati, they will hear dharma from Amitabha and will continuously remain there."

From the *Compassionate White Lotus Sutra*

As many kalpas ago as there are sand grains in the Ganges River, there occurred in this buddha realm a great kalpa known as Holding. At that time, the tathagata Ratnagarbha appeared in the world. There lived in his realm a chakravartin called Nemi, who had a thousand sons. He and his sons

extensively served and venerated that tathagata and his retinue. At that time our teacher was that king's chaplain, a brahmin called Ocean Dust, who was also the father of the tathagata Ratnagarbha. Ocean Dust turned the minds of the king, the thousand princes, and many other beings away from inferior motivations. He caused them to generate the intention to attain unsurpassable awakening.

The king's eldest son was called Eyes Never Shut. He once said to the tathagata Ratnagarbha, "Bhagavat, I have looked upon all the beings in the lower and higher states. For their sake, I have donned the armor of dedicating all roots of virtue to unsurpassable awakening. When I engage in the conduct of a bodhisattva, if any being who is afflicted by suffering, or afraid of danger, or wrapped in the darkness of spiritual famine, or weak and defenseless recollects me and calls my name, if I do not hear them with the divine ear, see them with the divine eye, and free them from suffering, may I not achieve the buddhahood of unsurpassable awakening. Through this special aspiration of mine, may my hopes be fulfilled as I engage, for a long time, in the conduct of a bodhisattva in order to help beings. When King Nemi attains buddhahood in Sukhavati as the tathagata Amitayus, may I continue to engage in the conduct of a bodhisattva until he passes into nirvana. After that, may I attain buddhahood."

In response to his aspiration, the tathagata Ratnagarbha said, "Son of family, you have generated a mind of compassion in order to free all beings from suffering and kleshas. You will therefore be known as Avalokiteshvara. Even while you are a bodhisattva, you will perform the deeds of a buddha. As many innumerable kalpas as the sand grains of two Ganges Rivers after the buddha Amitabha's nirvana, at dawn on the day following the night in which the holy dharma disappears, you will attain the buddhahood of unsurpassable awakening on a vajra seat before a beautiful tree of awaken-

ing. You will become the tathagata Glorious Massive King of Supreme Light-Rays. Your life span will be ninety-six sextillion kalpas."

From the *Sutra on the Noble Samadhi Like a Magical Illusion*

Once, light rays emitted by the tathagata Shakyamuni summoned the mahabodhisattvas Avalokita and Great Power from the realm of Sukhavati. They emanated eighty-four million miraculous mansions, each of them ornamented by the most splendid and diverse array, and arrived in a company of bodhisattvas equal in number to the mansions. They all bowed to the buddha's feet and praised him in verse.

Then the tathagata said to the bodhisattva Glorious Lotus Essence, "Son of family, these two holy beings have throughout innumerable kalpas cultivated all roots of virtue. They have achieved the samadhi that is like a magical illusion and display various miracles. Look at what is appearing in the east!"

Glorious Lotus Essence looked and saw in the east as many buddha realms as the Ganges River's sand grains. In each of them was a buddha, and in the presence of each of those buddhas were the bodhisattvas Avalokita and Great Power, inquiring as to the health of that buddha. Glorious Lotus Essence saw an equal number of realms and so on in each of the ten directions. Amazed, he asked the buddha, "In which tathagata's presence did these two holy beings first generate bodhichitta? How long ago did they do so?"

The buddha replied, "Innumerable, far more than innumerable kalpas ago, a number of kalpas ago that is inconceivably greater than the number of smallest particles in a thousand worlds, there was a world called Innumerable Jewels Always Joyous. In that realm appeared the tathagata Golden Light King of Lion's Play. The qualities of his buddha realm were

beyond measure. To give you an analogy, if a hair were split into one hundred parts, and the features of the present realm of Sukhavati were like a drop of water picked up by the tip of one of those parts, the features of the buddha realm Innumerable Jewels Always Joyous would be like all the water that would remain in a great ocean. Praise of that realm's qualities could not be completed in as many kalpas as the Ganges River's sand grains!

"In that realm lived a ruler of a thousand of its worlds, the dharmaraja Glorious Majesty, who had one hundred million sons. All of them entered the path to unsurpassable awakening. They all simultaneously served and venerated the buddha Golden Light King of Lion's Play for eighty-four trillion years. They held the dharma called Immeasurable Seal.

"Once, that king was meditating in a park. To the right and left of him were resplendently colorful lotuses of snakeheart sandalwood. From the lotuses two boys appeared miraculously. Their names were Ratnachitta and Paramaratna. Seeing them, the king questioned them. Based on their answers, he accomplished the five supercognitions. Then the king, accompanied by the two boys, went into the presence of the bhagavat Golden Light King of Lion's Play and bowed to him. When the two boys asked in verse how they might best venerate that victor, he replied, 'The holiest offering is the generation of bodhichitta.'

"The two boys then vowed to benefit beings for as many kalpas as had occurred throughout the beginningless past, to never again give rise to kleshas or unvirtuous states of mind, and to create pure realms like that of the buddha Golden Light King of Lion's Play. When they described their vows, signs such as the vibration of the earth occurred.

"The king Glorious Majesty is now the tathagata Amitabha.

The boy Paramaratna is now Avalokita. Ratnachitta is now Great Power. It was then that they first generated bodhichitta. It is possible to count the sand grains in the Ganges River, but it is not possible to count the number of buddhas these two holy beings have served and venerated since their first generation of bodhichitta in front of the tathagata Golden Light King of Lion's Play. These two beings have donned the inconceivable armor of commitment. Their qualities are innumerable and impossible to measure.

"The bodhisattva Avalokita will attain buddhahood as the tathagata Glorious Massive King of Supreme Light-Rays in the realm of Sukhavati, which will then be renamed Gathering of All Jewels. The features of that realm could not be fully known even if a tathagata were to explain them for as many kalpas as the Ganges River's sand grains. The features of the realm of Golden Light King of Lion's Play would not withstand comparison to even a hundredth or a thousandth of the features of Gathering of All Jewels.

"The bodhisattva Great Power will attain buddhahood after the nirvana of Glorious Massive King of Supreme Light-Rays and after the disappearance of that buddha's dharma. Great Power will become the tathagata King of Vast Qualities Like Piled Jewels. His realm and retinue of bodhisattvas will be like those of Glorious Massive King of Supreme Light-Rays. Anyone who hears the names of these two buddhas will never turn back from the pursuit of unsurpassable awakening. Anyone who hears the name of the past buddha Golden Light King of Lion's Play or the names of these two future buddhas will not be reborn in a state of inferiority. They will reach the end of samsara within forty million kalpas. They will never turn back from the pursuit of unsurpassable awakening. They will always see buddhas, hear dharma, and serve the sangha. In every life they will renounce the world, recollect previous lives, have boundless confidence, and achieve retention."

From the *Saddharma Pundarikasutra*

The bodhisattva Inexhaustible Intellect once asked the bhaga-vat, "Why is Avalokiteshvara called Avalokiteshvara?"

The buddha replied, "No matter what sufferings any of the sextillions of beings that there are experience; whether they fall into a great fire; or are drowning in a river; or are traveling on the ocean in search of jewels; or are cast on an island of rakshasis by an ill wind; or about to be killed by execution-ers; or are thrown off the peak of a mountain; or are bound by iron fetters; or are menaced by poison, spells, revenants, or spirits; or endangered by ferocious predators, lightning, strong hail, or vicious carnivores — whatever their danger or suffering — if they hear Avalokiteshvara's name they will be quickly freed from danger and misery. Even if these billion worlds were filled with yakshas and rakshasis, they would be unable to even look with hatred upon anyone who holds Avalokita's name. If a great vajra mountain were thrown down upon one's head in order to kill one, and one recollect-ed Avalokiteshvara, not so much as one of one's pores would be harmed. Even if these billion worlds were filled with one's enemies, all of them holding weapons, if one heard the name of Avalokita one would be freed from danger.

"Anyone who is afflicted by desire, anger, or stupidity will be freed from those kleshas if they hold Avalokita's name. When someone is desperate — unleisured, at war, or about to die — this embodiment of great love and compassion will be their holy protector and defender. If someone wishes for sons or daughters and holds Avalokita's name, beautiful sons and daughters will be born to them and will generate roots of virtue.

"The merit accumulated by prostrating to and holding the names of as many buddhas as the sand grains in sixty-two Ganges Rivers, and by offering that many living buddhas robes, alms, and so forth is equal to — neither greater than nor superior to — the merit of a single prostration to Avalokiteshvara and of holding his name. The merit of prostrating to Avalokita and holding his name cannot be easily exhausted in even a quintillion kalpas. Such merit is immeasurable.

"Avalokita appears in whatever form will tame particular beings, as anything from a buddha down to an ordinary being. In these forms he teaches dharma. Because he bestows fearlessness upon all beings, he is known by all in this realm of Saha as Giver of Fearlessness."

Then the buddha praised Avalokita extensively in verse.

From the *Avatamsakasutra*

Once, Sudhana the merchant's son went to Mount Potala. He bowed to Avalokiteshvara and asked him about the conduct of a bodhisattva. Avalokita extended his right hand, which had the color of gold from the Jambu River and emanated immeasurable webs of multicolored light, and placed it on Sudhana's head, saying, "Son of family, the gate to my bodhisattva training is great compassion. I never move from the presence of the tathagatas, but I am always responsive to the needs of all beings. I ripen beings and bring them to accomplishment through attraction, various forms and colors, the radiation of light, melody, my behavior, the teaching of dharma, and various miracles that correspond to beings' wishes.

"I have accomplished the aspiration to remove the various dangers that menace beings — precipices, confusion, bondage, the endangerment of life, lack of resources, poverty, being unknown, social anxiety, death, inferior rebirth, losing their way in darkness, unfit company, separation from what is pleasing, encountering what is displeasing, physical and mental illness, and the danger of samsara — all the suffering and misery of all beings. I have accomplished the aspiration to

bring all beings to the utter transcendence of all agitation and the aspiration to establish them in utter stability. I have blessed my recollection by the world in order to pacify the fears of all beings. I have caused my name to become known in the world so that beings may be freed from danger. I have blessed as many forms of myself as there are forms of beings, so that beings will think of me when necessary. With this body I cause beings to generate the irreversible intention to attain unsurpassable, perfect awakening so that they achieve all the buddhadharmas."

The wise Avalokiteshvara also said these words:

"I, the buddhas' son, am the single gate to liberation.
I am the essence of wisdom, the compassion of all victors.
I have arisen in order to protect and liberate all beings.
I am the ubiquitous personification of love.

"I protect all beings from suffering.
If those who are tightly bound,
Given to their enemies, tortured, and imprisoned
Hear my name, they will be freed from captivity.

"If those who, having offended monarchs,
Are sentenced to death recollect my name,
The arrows shot at them will not pierce their bodies.
Sharp weapons will fail to penetrate.

"Those who argue in the courts of rulers
Will defeat their adversaries and gain fame.
Fame, friendship, family, and wealth will increase.
Those who recollect my name will be invincible.

"Whoever recollects my name, even if they enter
Dangerous forests filled with robbers and enemies,
Will defeat all lions, bears, leopards, other predators,
Wild oxen, snakes, and enemies. They will be fearless.

"If someone who recollects my name is cast by enemies
  Onto the slopes of a great mountain
  Or onto blazing coals,
  The fire will become a pool filled with lotuses.

"If someone who recollects my name for even a moment
    is cast into the sea,
  They will not drown in its water or be burnt by fire.
  Nothing pointless will happen to them.
  They will accomplish their aims.

"Those bound in fetters of wood or iron,
  Those who are reviled or deceived,
  And those who are cursed and shunned
  Will find freedom if they merely recollect my name.

"If those who are menaced by their relatives,
  And those who are continually insulted through anger
  Hear my name and recollect it, they will be praised.
  All who see them will immediately give rise to love.

"If the enemies of someone who recollects my name
  Attack them with revenants, spells, and curses,
  Those enemies will always be overcome.
  No poison will affect the recollector.

"For someone who recollects my name,
  Nagas, rakshasas, garudas, pisachis, kumbhandhas,
  Spirits, ferociously malevolent beings,
  Stealers of vitality, and nightmares will all be pacified.[76]

"If someone recollects my name for a moment,
  They will never be in conflict with their parents,
    relatives, or friends.
  They will never encounter those who hate them.
  Their wealth will never be exhausted. They will
    never be poor.

76. Pisachis and kumbhandhas are aggressive non-human beings.

"Someone who recollects my name
Will not go to the Avichi Hell after this life,
Nor to an animal birth, that of a preta, or any
    unleisured state.
They will be reborn as pure gods or humans.

"Someone who recollects my name
Will not become blind, deaf, lame, or impaired.
They will be well-spoken and attractive.
For millions of kalpas they will possess full senses.

"Someone who recollects my name will be born
    after this life
In one of the worlds in the ten directions that
    has a buddha.
They will meet that buddha and hear his dharma.
My taming of beings in these and other ways
Cannot be measured or exhausted."

From *Utter Conquest of These Billion Worlds*

If someone who is about to be harmed
By armed killers ready to strike
Recollects Avalokiteshvara,
The weapons of the attackers will crumble.

If the attackers hold onto their weapons,
Their hands will break and fall to the ground.
The recollector's body will remain totally unharmed
Unless his past actions are at fault.

From the *Summary of the Benefits of the Dharani of Great Compassion*[77]

77. "Great Compassion" refers to Avalokita.

"Anyone who has heard this dharani will not be harmed
Even if they pass through mountains and wilderness

And encounter tigers, wolves, ferocious predators,
Lizards, snakes, ghosts, or rakshasas.

"If anyone who has heard this dharani crosses
Rivers and oceans, and encounters vicious nagas,
Fierce crocodiles, yakshas, rakshasas, fish, or turtles,
These predators will flee.

"If someone at war is surrounded by their enemies,
Or is about to have their wealth stolen by vicious bandits,
And they one-pointedly recite the dharani of
     Great Compassion,
Their attackers will become benevolent and leave.

"If someone is sentenced by a monarch,
Fettered and imprisoned,
And they one-pointedly recite the dharani of
     Great Compassion,
The monarch will become benevolent and release them.

"If someone enters the home of a sorcerer
And is about to be murdered by poison,
If they one-pointedly recite the dharani of
     Great Compassion,
The poison will become delicious food and drink.

"If a mother giving birth to her child
Is obstructed by maras and suffers unbearably,
If she one-pointedly recites the dharani of
     Great Compassion,
The spirits will flee and the birth will be easy.

"If someone is struck by the breath of fierce nagas
And comes close to death through a sickness of heat,
If they one-pointedly recite the dharani of
     Great Compassion,
The contagion will be removed and their life will be long.

"If someone is harmed by nagas and develops swellings
Or unbearable ulcers exuding pus and blood,
If they one-pointedly recite the dharani of
     Great Compassion
And rub the swellings three times with saliva, their
     suffering will be pacified.

"If a troubled being engages in wrongdoing
And is attacked by curses, spells, or enemies,
If they one-pointedly recite the dharani of
     Great Compassion,
The curses and spirits will return to their sender.

"In the dregs of time, when wrongdoing flourishes
And holy dharma is being destroyed,
The fires of desire will spread. In their delusion,
Husbands and wives will think with desire
Of other partners throughout day and night.
If someone recites the dharani of Great Compassion,
The fire of their desire will be pacified.
Their delusion will be removed.

"If I were to fully explain the power of my dharani,
I could speak for a kalpa without reaching an end."

Although Avalokiteshvara is specifically describing the benefits of the dharani of his thousand-armed, thousand-eyed
form here, these benefits should also be understood to be
those of calling his name in general.

From the *Lotus Net Avalokita Root Tantra*

Once, Avalokita spoke of his past bodhisattva training and
of his awareness mantra. In response Manjushri, Samantabhadra, Sarvanivaranavishkhambin, and other male and
female bodhisattvas praised him. The Avalokitas of innumerable buddha realms in the ten directions — each of whom

has a different form and name — then assembled in this realm accompanied by their retinues. When the Avalokitas taught their respective great awareness mantras, all the buddhas of the ten directions placed their hands on the Avalokitas' heads and said, "Excellent!" The wrathful kings danced and removed obstacles. The lokapalas and their retinues promised to guard those teachings.

From the *Detailed Ritual of the Thousand-Armed Thousand-Eyed Avalokita*

The miraculous power of the mahabodhisattva Avalokiteshvara is inconceivable. Innumerable kalpas ago, he achieved the awakening of manifest, perfect buddhahood, and was known as the buddha bhagavat Radiant Dharma. Through his great compassion and aspirations he now appears as a bodhisattva in order to help beings and bring them happiness. Therefore you devas and humans, always venerate him! Recite his name! You will accumulate roots of virtue, purify much wrongdoing, and be born after your death in Sukhavati.

From the concise *Prajnaparamita Mahayanasutra*

The bhagavat once said to Avalokita, "You will become the tathagata arhat samyaksambuddha Glorious Massive King of Supreme Light-Rays. Whoever hears your name, retains it, reads it, teaches it widely to others, or writes it down and venerates it will in the future become a tathagata."

From the *Sutra of the Noble King of the Qualities of All Dharmas*

Vajrapani once asked the buddha, "Bhagavat, why is Avalokiteshvara called Avalokiteshvara?"

The buddha replied, "He is called Avalokiteshvara because he

looks upon, understands, satisfies, protects, and grants assurance to all worlds; because his mind is compassionate, joyous, loving, and affectionate; and because he fulfills all wishes."

Vajrapani then said, "Bhagavat, all the wishes of anyone who thinks of even the name of Avalokiteshvara will be fulfilled."

From the *Sutra on the Hundred and Eight Names of Avalokita*

If you want to always be happy,
Always praise the lotus-born Avalokita,
The lord of all beings.

THE SECOND CHAPTER: THE NOBLE LORD OF
COMPASSION

GLORIOUS VAJRAPANI

I prostrate to the bodhisattva mahasattva Vajrapani![78] I venerate you! I take refuge in you!

78. Vajrapani means "vajra in hand" or "vajra holder."

Vajrapani, the Lord of Secrets, holds the treasury of all the secrets of the body, speech, and mind of the tathagata. He is therefore the very personification of the inconceivable.

From the *Ratnakutasutra's* "Chapter on the Inconceivable Secret"

Once, Vajrapani remained to the bhagavat's right, holding a vajra. The bodhisattva Shantimati said to Vajrapani, "Lord of Secrets, you are a close attendant of the tathagata. Please confidently expound the secret qualities of the tathagata that are beyond the reach of shravakas, pratyekabuddhas, and, it need not be said, ordinary beings."

As the tathagata Shakyamuni then also requested Vajrapani to speak, the Lord of Secrets said, "As long as the bhagavat remained a bodhisattva whose awakening had been predicted by Dipankara, I remained his attendant.[79] During that period I saw his secret body, speech, and mind of a bodhisattva." Vajrapani then partially described them. By doing so he benefited innumerable beings.

79. Dipankara was a buddha in the distant past.

While Vajrapani was speaking, some of the bodhisattvas present in that assembly wondered, "Through what roots of virtue has the Lord of Secrets achieved this confidence? How many buddhas has he served? Through what aspirations has he become what he is?"

In response to their thoughts, the bhagavat said, "Inconceivably innumerable kalpas ago, there was a kalpa called Beautiful Appearance. During it, in the world called Fully Ornamented, appeared the tathagata called King of Boundless Qualities and Diverse Jewels. His life span was thirty-six million years. During his time people did not suffer untimely death. His realm was extremely affluent and pleasant. The beings there had few kleshas and were all capable of understanding his profound teachings.

"Within that realm was a wealthy, spacious, and pleasant world of four continents called Beautiful Appearance. On that world was its capital city, which was called Utter Purity. This city was both large and affluent. In it resided the chakravartin Regional Guardian, who ruled that world of four continents. He had achieved irreversibility on the path to unsurpassable awakening. He had seven hundred thousand queens, all of whom were like jewels among women, and a thousand sons, all of whom were both heroic and extremely handsome. All the queens and princes were immersed in the pursuit of unsurpassable awakening.

"Once, the bhagavat King of Boundless Qualities and Diverse Jewels, together with his sangha of bhikshus, visited the royal palace in the city of Utter Purity. The king Regional Guardian served them with all types of fine things for a period of one million years. The king also attentively listened to that buddha's dharma and accomplished the five types of supercognition.

"After this period the young princes, in order to assist their father in his further presentation of offerings, built a vast mansion made of snakeheart sandalwood. The mansion was ten yojanas wide on every side and was beautifully decorated. The sandalwood of which the mansion was made was so precious that all of Jambudvipa would not pay for half a measure of it.

"After it had been built, the king Regional Guardian, the princes, the queens, and all their court, servants, and friends moved into the mansion. They filled it with diverse offerings and caused it to rise into the sky and travel to where the buddha King of Boundless Qualities and Diverse Jewels was. The mansion then settled onto the ground. The king and his retinue then bowed to that tathagata and listened to his dharma. Utterly delighted by that tathagata's dharma, the king offered his entire kingdom to that buddha.

"On a full-moon day, while he was staying there, the king Regional Guardian was enjoying himself in a park, listening to music. Two of his noble queens, named Respected and Incomparable, had just bathed and were seated on lion thrones and fine lotuses. Suddenly, two handsome young princes appeared miraculously, seated with crossed legs in the two queens' laps. At that moment, the devas proclaimed from the sky, 'This is Dharmachitta! This is Dharmamati!' These therefore became the princes' names.

"Immediately after their appearance, and without uncrossing their legs, the two princes recited dharmic verse, descended from their mothers' laps, bowed to their father, and asked to be brought into the presence of the tathagata King of Boundless Qualities and Diverse Jewels. The king, queens, and princes therefore entered that tathagata's presence. By listening to his dharma they benefited many beings.

"The king Regional Guardian then went into solitude in one of his mansions. While there, he thought, 'All my princes have

entered the path to unsurpassable awakening. I shall determine which of them will attain buddhahood first.' He wrote down the princes' names and placed them in a vase made of the seven jewels. He venerated the vase for seven days and then, in the presence of the queens and princes, had a member of his court draw the names from the vase.

"The first name to appear was that of the prince Pure Intelligence. As that name was drawn, the great earth shook, and cymbals gave forth sound without being played. Pure Intellect became the tathagata Samsara Destroyer, the first buddha of the present kalpa.

"The next four names drawn were those of the princes Vijaya, Tranquil Powers, All-Accomplishing, and Belt. They have become, respectively, Golden Sage; Kashyapa; me, your teacher, Shakyamuni; and the future buddha Maitreya.

"All the rest of the thousand names were drawn then. The sixth to appear was Supreme Intelligence and the second to last was Ornamental Crown. Supreme Intelligence will become the sixth buddha of this kalpa, Lion; and Ornamental Crown will become the nine hundred and ninety-ninth, the tathagata Boundless Famous Qualities.

"The youngest of the thousand princes was called Boundless Intelligence. His name was also the last to be drawn. When his name was announced, his brothers said, 'By the time you attain buddhahood, we will have already ripened all beings! What will remain for you to do?'

"The youngest prince, Boundless Intelligence, replied, 'Buddhadharma is like the sky. Beings are inexhaustible. I therefore make the aspiration that my life span and activity as a buddha may equal all of yours' combined!'

"As soon as he said that, the sound of the devas proclaiming, 'Excellent!' came from the sky.

"Boundless Intelligence will become the last of the thousand buddhas, the tathagata Enthusiasm. His life span, deeds, and sangha will equal those of all the preceding tathagatas of this kalpa combined.

"Then the thousand princes asked the princes Dharmachitta and Dharmamati, 'Sons of family, what aspirations shall you two make?'

"Dharmachitta, the son of Respected, replied, 'Friends, I will assist all of you by becoming Vajrapani. It is my aspiration to hear, be devoted to, and realize all the outer and inner buddhadharmas and to hold all the secret teachings of all tathagatas.'

"Dharmamati, the son of Incomparable, said, 'It is my aspiration to request each of you, upon your buddhahood, to turn the dharmachakra.'

"The king Regional Guardian became the buddha Dipankara. The thousand sons became the thousand buddhas. Dharmachitta became Vajrapani, the Lord of Secrets. Dharmamati became Brahma."

Shariputra then asked the bhagavat, "Bhagavat, does the Lord of Secrets accompany all the bodhisattvas of this fortunate kalpa from the ten directions who presently abide in pure conduct as they approach buddhahood?"

The buddha replied, "Shariputra, this is inconceivable. Let it go. The deeds of bodhisattvas would confuse the whole world and its devas. Nevertheless, those with faith who have been caught by spiritual friends will not be frightened by this. Shariputra, do you see the Lord of Secrets, Vajrapani, who always accompanies me?"

Shariputra answered, "Through the buddha's power I see him now. I never saw him before."

The buddha said, "In the same manner Vajrapani appears behind all the bodhisattvas of this fortunate kalpa. Do you see Vajrapani behind Maitreya?"

Shariputra answered, "I see him now. I never saw him before."

The buddha said, "Although you never saw him, Vajrapani is always present behind Maitreya. Bodhisattvas and lokapalas see him, always present and holding a vajra. Although the bodhisattvas of this fortunate kalpa emit sextillions of emanations, Vajrapani appears behind each of them. He also appears behind every emanation of every tathagata. All of this is through the Lord of Secrets' blessing. Vajrapani even displays his form behind each being in these billion worlds, but they are unable to perceive the full blessing of his dharma and wisdom."

Then the bhagavat said to the bodhisattva Shantimati, "Shantimati, while holding a vajra Vajrapani will serve all the buddhas of this fortunate kalpa and hold their holy dharma. He will disseminate the secret dharmas of tathagatas and ripen innumerable beings. Finally, when the holy dharma of the tathagata Enthusiasm disappears, Vajrapani will be born in Abhirati, the realm of the tathagata Akshobhya. Vajrapani will receive from that tathagata the teaching of the hundred mudras and accomplish it. After that, Vajrapani will serve innumerable tathagatas and guard their dharma. He will ripen innumerable beings and bring them to perfect awakening. After as many kalpas as the Ganges River's sand grains, Vajrapani will achieve manifest, perfect buddhahood. During the kalpa called Fully Purified, in the world called Utterly Pure, he will become the tathagata arhat samyaksambuddha Overwhelming Vajra.

"In his realm there will be no lower states or unleisured beings. His realm will be completely pure and adorned with affluence.

The enjoyments of his realm will be like those of devas in Tushita. There will be no untimely death in his realm. All the beings born there will be devoted to the vast mahayana. Even the names of the shravakayana and pratyekabuddhayana will be unknown there. Overwhelming Vajra will teach only the dharma of bodhisattvas. All the devas and humans in his realm will be adorned by twenty-eight marks.

"The life span of that tathagata will be eight intermediate kalpas. Whenever he teaches dharma, his body will emit light that will summon his retinue. He will then rise to a height of a hundred thousand palm trees in the sky, seated with crossed legs. His body will fill an entire four-continent world. When he teaches, all those in the worlds surrounding him in the ten directions will be able to hear his voice. No being anywhere in his realm will contravene or reject his dharma teaching. All the beings there will possess acute faculties. That tathagata will be the dharmaraja of his realm; there will be no other ruler there. The beings there will be without fixation on a self.

"When that tathagata wishes to accept alms, the deva or human from whom he wishes to receive them will appear in front of him, bearing a begging bowl. Those donors will immediately possess and offer whatever they wish to present as alms. Whenever that tathagata rests in perfect absorption, all the bodhisattvas in his retinue will also abide in samadhi. His realm will possess innumerable other qualities as well."

After the buddha bestowed that prediction, Vajrapani cast his vajra into the sky, causing this world to shake, flowers to descend like rain, and cymbals to issue their sounds.

The Lord of Secrets then invited the bhagavat and his retinue to his palace, Changlochen, for seven days. Then Vajrapani entered the samadhi called King of Great Arrays and emanated within his realm all the features of the eastern buddha realm called Boundless Array of Precious Qualities. He then

summoned the four kings with their retinues and all the devas from the realms starting with that of Brahma and all the way up to Akanishtha.

They all gathered to listen to dharma. Vajrapani then spoke words of secret mantra, benefiting innumerable beings.

The bhagavat then returned to Vulture Peak Mountain. In response to a question asked by King Ajatashatru, the buddha said, "Great king, one could count all the worlds in the ten directions, as numerous as the Ganges River's sand grains. One could not, however, count the number of buddhas that Vajrapani, the Lord of Secrets, has venerated and served. He has engaged in pure conduct in the presence of them all.

"Innumerable kalpas ago there was a tathagata called Conduct of Complete Peace. He taught only the doctrine for bodhisattvas, saying such things as, 'Bodhisattvas must diligently give away even their bodies and lives!'

"Vajrapani was one of the bodhisattvas in his retinue, and was called Heroic Strength. Contemplating what that tathagata had said, Heroic Strength did not see any virtue in nirvana; he saw that remaining in samsara was of greater benefit. He therefore undertook to remain in samsara and began to engage in innumerable bodhisattva deeds. The tathagata Conduct of Complete Peace pronounced the excellence of this and taught dharma about the utter purity of conduct.

"Just as all forms are within space, all dharmas are part of a bodhisattva's conduct. Knowing this, Heroic Strength donned the armor of stable commitment and thereafter served many buddhas."

King Ajatashatru then wondered, "Is the vajra that Vajrapani always holds in his right hand heavy or light?"

The Lord of Secrets knew Ajatashatru's thought and said to

him, "This vajra is both heavy and light. In order to subdue the proud and vain, it is heavy. For the honest and free of pride it is light." Vajrapani then blessed the earth in that place so that it was vajralike and placed his vajra on the ground. This caused the great earth to shake six times.

The Lord of Secrets then said to Ajatashatru, "Lift this vajra off the ground."

Although Ajatashatru was strong enough to pick up an elephant with one hand, he was unable to move that vajra the distance of a hair's tip, even though he exerted all his strength. Amazed, Ajatashatru urged Indra to lift the vajra. Indra was also unable to move it. Astonished, Indra said to the buddha, "I can carry the chariot of Takzangri, the ruler of the asuras, for a distance of seven hundred yojanas without difficulty. Why can I not move this vajra?"

The buddha replied, "This vajra is so heavy that it is beyond analogy. If Vajrapani were to throw this vajra at a mountain made of vajra, that mountain would explode like a handful of chaff."

Indra then urged Maudgalyayana to lift the vajra. When Maudgalyayana took hold of the vajra, the great earth shook six times. Water shot into the sky. All the oceans became turbulent. However, Maudgalyayana was unable to move the vajra. Amazed, he said to the bhagavat, "With my miraculous abilities I could hold all the water of a great ocean in the palm of my hand. I could flip this realm of a billion worlds with one finger as easily as someone flipping a coin. I could stop the sun and moon. I could pick up Mount Meru with one hand and cast it all the way to the world of Brahma. I have tamed the naga kings Nanda and Upananda. I have been to the world of Light Rays. I could go to as many realms as there are particles in Mount Meru. I am unable, however, to move this little vajra. Have my miraculous abilities become impaired?"

The buddha replied, "Your miraculous abilities are unimpaired. Nevertheless, no shravaka or pratyekabuddha, let alone any other being, can disturb the blessing of a bodhisattva. You could move all the supreme mountains in as many buddha realms as the Ganges River's sand grains, but you cannot remove this vajra from this place."

Maudgalyayana said, "The great strength of the Lord of Secrets, who holds this vajra, must be wondrous! Did Vajrapani inherit his strength from his parents, or is it miraculous?"

The buddha replied, "Maudgalyayana, no matter how much strength one might inherit from one's parents, it barely justifies the use of the term *strength*. If I revealed all the miraculous strength of bodhisattvas, this world with its devas would go mad!"

The bhagavat then said to Vajrapani, "Pick up that vajra."

The Lord of Secrets shook the world and then picked up the vajra with his left hand. He threw it into the sky above. It circled him seven times and came to rest in his right hand. Everyone in that assembly was amazed. They praised Vajrapani, made aspirations to achieve his strength, and asked about the causes of attaining such strength.

From the *Trilokavijayamaharaja*

Once the bhagavat stayed on the peak of Mount Meru, in a mansion made of vajras and precious jewels. He was accompanied by a large retinue of bodhisattvas, devas, nagas, yakshas, and others.

The mahabodhisattva Vajrapani descended from the midst of the sky, prostrated to the bhagavat's feet, circumambulated three times, and said, "Bhagavat, I wish to cause Mahadeva and other unruly beings to hold samaya. I pray that the bhagavat speak to me about this."

Hearing this, the tathagata, the dharmaraja, said, "Yaksha, you are extremely wrathful, brave, and fierce. In order that you thereby benefit beings, please speak the words of such a mantra." ·

Vajrapani said, "In that case, bhagavat, I will subdue the unruly. Why? Because by overpowering those immersed in the pleasure of desire, I will establish them in unsurpassable pleasure. By killing the unruly, I will purify them and establish them in peace."

The bhagavat said to Vajrapani, "Excellent! Excellent! Excellent! For the benefit and happiness of the world, speak your essence mantra."

Then Vajrapani addressed those devas and humans with faith in the buddha's teaching, saying, "Friends! Take refuge in the buddha! Obey my commands!"

Then Vajrapani prostrated to the bhagavat's feet and recited the essence mantra of Trilokavijaya. Just by his doing so, the three worlds vibrated, trembled, and shook terribly. All beings, including the devas, trembled with terror and gathered around the bhagavat. All the land and mountains in this world of four continents became filled with beings.

The bhagavat Vajrapani gazed upon this whole assembly and said, "Friends, vow to take refuge in the buddha, dharma, and sangha! Obey my commands!"

All the beings in that vast assembly were terrified by the mighty Vajrapani. Trembling, they took refuge in the bhagavat, the tathagata. Then powerful devas including Mahadeva and Brahma said to the buddha, the bhagavat,

"Bhagavat, who is this awesome and miraculous being that has reformed us?"

The bhagavat replied in verse:

"For all beings' benefit
He has been blessed by all buddhas.
He is Samantabhadra, the lord of all.
All buddhas are born from him.

"Vajrapani, the great yaksha,
Has the power to reform the unruly.
Anyone who says Vajrapani's name
Will achieve buddhahood."

Then Vajrapani said, "Devas! Take refuge in the buddha! Obey my commands! This entirely blazing vajra will burn you all up!"

Then Mahadeva and the other devas said, "You are a yaksha; we are devas. We are unable to obey the commands of a yaksha."

Hearing this, Vajrapani became enraged and said to the bhagavat, "Bhagavat, you have empowered and appointed me to subdue the unruly. If the bhagavat commands, I will subdue this Mahadeva."

Then the bhagavat said to Mahadeva, "Great being, promise, or he will kill you!"

Then Mahadeva and all the devas that rule the three worlds said, "Bhagavat, we will not obey the commands of this unruly yaksha!"

Mahadeva then bowed to the bhagavat's feet and said to Vajrapani, "Yaksha, I am the creator, great ruler, and destroyer of everything! I am Brahma, the lord of all beings! I am Vishnu! I am Maheshvara!"

The mahabodhisattva Vajrapani then became enraged and said, "You are a rotten-bodied eater of human flesh. You are vicious and violent! How could a rotten-bodied carnivore be Brahma, Vishnu, and Maheshvara? *Brahma* means 'unchanging.' *Vishnu* means 'liberation.' *Maheshvara* means 'lord of the desire realm, the ruler of all beings.' It is I who am these things; I am therefore able to subdue you!"

When Vajrapani said this, the deva Maheshvara became enraged. He bowed to the bhagavat's feet and then, assuming a terrifying form, laughed ferociously. Blazing with terrifying rage, Maheshvara filled these billion worlds with his various forms, all of them of peerless intensity. They all produced and brandished invincible weapons such as vajras, tridents, wheels, axes, and maces. They appeared along with masses of matrikas and elementals. These various emanated forms of Maheshvara — maras and obstructors — were unbearably ferocious. They formed a vast, malevolent assembly and began to wage war and advance through these billion worlds. They caused this world of four continents to become as dark as night. They then lit huge fires that filled the world with their light.

Then the bhagavat Mahavajrapani slightly bared his fangs. His brow gathered in a frown. His left eye gaped wide. With a wrathful vajra gaze, he pronounced HUM, the profound essence mantra of Shritrilokavijaya. The sound of that HUM filled this entire world, causing it to shake and vibrate.

The deva Maheshvara and the other devas then said to the bhagavat, "Please protect us! Sugata, please protect us!" They took refuge in him.

Just by pronouncing the essence mantra of Trilokavijaya, the bhagavat Vajrapani caused Mahadeva and all the other rulers of devas to appear before him with their heads pointing to the earth and their feet to the sky. He placed them in a great mandala on the peak of Mount Meru. Vajrapani overthrew them and trampled them under his left foot.

The bhagavat then said to Vajrapani, "Excellent! It is excellent that you have tamed these beings in such a way! Therefore tame them and free them."

Through Vajrapani's blessing, the devas he had overthrown regained consciousness. He mastered them, placed them in samaya, and empowered them with vajra names. Maheshvara received the name Supreme Vajravidyamantra, Vishnu the name Vajra Illusion, Brahma the name Vajra Silence, Kumara the name Vajra Bell, and Indra the name Vajra Weapon. Vajrapani empowered with vajra names all the rulers of the devas that live in the sky, on the earth, or below the earth and placed them all in the mandala.

In other tantras there are many similar stories of Vajrapani wrathfully subduing those so hard to tame, the rulers of the three worlds.[80]

80. The three worlds are the subterranean world, the terrestrial world, and the celestial world.

From the *Vajrapani Empowerment Tantra*

The bodhisattva mahasattva Samantabhadra made the aspiration to emulate, throughout this world called Flower Ground Essence Ornament, the past conduct of the bhagavat Vairochana. Samantabhadra then set about taming the yakshas. He went to the abode of the great yaksha chieftains — Changlochen, which is in this Jambudvipa within the Saha world. Illuminated by the tathagata's light rays, Samantabhadra's eyes and face expanded. After stating his intention, he abided in contemplation of the inconceivable nature of the tathagata.

The tathagata indicated in verse that the bodhisattva Samantabhadra was about to appear. The bodhisattva Samantabhadra gathered the yakshas together. In order that

they accompany him in entering the tathagata's presence, Samantabhadra entered the samadhi called Diverse Ornamentation, which brings a display that is in accordance with the causes of bodhisattvas' conduct.

As soon as Samantabhadra entered that samadhi, a mansion appeared. It was adorned with all the ornaments of Vairochana and was the size of a billion-world system. It was decorated by oceans of inconceivable features such as sextillions of jeweled columns. Samantabhadra, surrounded by a great gathering of yakshas, picked the mansion up with his two hands and rose into the sky. He traveled to the dense forest of various sal-tree victory banners where the bhagavat Shakyamuni was abiding at the time.

The mansion appeared in the sky at a height of six million eight hundred thousand yojanas. It blazed like a huge fire, and was as bright and lustrous as a thousand suns. Its light filled all directions. The bodhisattvas gathered around the buddha Shakyamuni asked him, "What is that?"

The buddha replied, "The bodhisattva Samantabhadra is coming here. What you see is in accordance with his past deeds. This intense brilliance is the display of his dharma qualities, which could not be fully understood even if one devoted a hundred kalpas to attempting to do so. Ask the bodhisattva Samantabhadra about the aspect of dharma called the Complete Purity That is the Gate to the Mahayana."

The bodhisattva Samantabhadra remained in the sky at a height of seven palm trees. Rains of divine flowers, incense, and other fine things fell from the sky into that forest. Samantabhadra offered the mansion to the bhagavat and praised him. Then from the mansion and from large and small cymbals issued the sound of verses on how to begin the

conduct of the mahayana. At the same moment, the mahabodhisattva Samantabhadra requested that the bhagavat explain the entry to and practice of the mahayana.

The bhagavat entered the samadhi called Source of Great Vajras. At that moment, all the tathagatas in all the worlds in all directions uttered, with one great vajra voice, the essence mantra of Vajrasattva that radiates great, blazing vajra light. They all went to the dense forest of various sal-tree victory banners where the bhagavat Shakyamuni was, sat down with crossed legs on seats of great vajras and lotuses, and greeted the tathagata Shakyamuni. Then all those tathagatas and the bhagavat Shakyamuni uttered the mantra that blesses the vajra mandala and entered into the samadhi called Display of Buddhas' Blessings.

All the others in that vast gathering thought, "This is amazing!" With subdued hearts, they remained still, gazing at the youthful Manjushri. Manjushri, knowing that the whole gathering had become one-pointed in amazement, prayed in verse to the bhagavat Shakyamuni and all the other buddhas, requesting that they bestow the empowerment of the children of the sugatas. Those tathagatas blessed that forest so that it became a vajra mandala with a courtyard, decorations, and seats. From the tathagatas' ushnishas emerged light rays called Unstoppable Power that illuminated the entire mandala assembly and then dissolved into the top of the mahabodhisattva Samantabhadra's head. Utterly delighted, Samantabhadra uttered the mantra called Unstoppable Power. All those tathagatas united their samadhis, retention, power, limbs of awakening, paths, noble truths, emptinesses, unique qualities of buddhahood, generosity performed within great emptiness, discipline, restraint, peace, and all six paramitas. Through their blessing, all these virtues took the form of a vajra, which they placed in Samantabhadra's hand.

Immediately, all the tathagatas, bodhisattvas, shravakas,

pratyekabuddhas, devas, nagas, yakshas, humans, and other beings in all the buddha realms and worlds in the ten directions proclaimed with one voice, "Oh! This bodhisattva mahasattva is Vajrapani! He shall be called Vajrapani!"

Then those tathagatas blessed this samaya and uttered the essence mantra called Secret Vajra. Throughout all realms the sound of the words "Lord of Secrets" resounded. Through the power of that essence mantra and through the blessing of all tathagatas, the minds and perfect wisdom of all tathagatas manifestly entered the bodhisattva Vajrapani.

Then those tathagatas uttered the essence mantra called Vast Vajra, which guards the teachings and protects beings. At that very moment, in all worlds and all the mandalas of all buddhas, Vajrapani displayed his crowned form both in front of and behind each and every tathagata, bodhisattva, shravaka, pratyekabuddha, all who had just generated bodhichitta, all beginners, and all beings, no matter whether they were awake or asleep, teaching dharma, achieving buddhahood, benefiting beings, or emitting emanations.

Then those tathagatas uttered the essence mantra that binds an area with vajras. All unruly beings were bound by vajra bonds. When the tathagatas then uttered the Vajrakila essence mantra, there was heard the roaring sound of the words, "Oh! The mahabodhisattva Vajrapani is the vajra reliance!"

Then those tathagatas uttered the subterranean vajra-essence mantra. Throughout all worlds and in all the spaces beneath the earth's surface there was heard the roaring sound of the words, "Vajrapani is the subterranean vajra!"

When the tathagatas uttered the essence mantra that cuts through all beings who hold awareness-mantras, throughout all worlds and in all the places of awareness mantra holders there was heard the roaring sound of the words, "Vajrapani is

the vajra that cuts through all beings who hold awareness mantras!"

Then the tathagatas uttered the vajra essence mantra that eradicates yakshas and others. Throughout all worlds and all the respective abodes of those beings there was heard the roaring sound of the names Vajra of Yakshas, Vajra of Nagas, Vajra of Ghandharvas, Vajra of Garudas, Vajra of Semihumans, Vajra of Great Serpents, Vajra of Rakshasas, Vajra of Dakinis, Vajra of Bhutas, Vajra of Pisachas, Vajra of Pisachis, Vajra of Rakshasis, and Overpowering Vajra.

When the tathagatas then uttered the terrifying essence mantra that overcomes contamination, throughout all worlds there was heard the roaring sound of the name Vajra Who Ends All Ruination.

Then the tathagatas uttered the essence mantra of Vajra of Unstoppable Force. Throughout all realms there was heard the roaring sound of the words, "The mahabodhisattva Vajrapani is the mahavajrachakravartin!" Those tathagatas then uttered the mahachakravartin essence mantra. They then gave Vajrapani all the great vajra essence mantras they had uttered. A great web of light rays illuminated that grove and its surroundings. Blessed by the tathagatas, Vajrapani became of the dharmadhatu nature within the mandala of the dharmadhatu. He disappeared.

The bhagavat Shakyamuni said then to Vajrapani, "Son of family, all tathagatas have empowered you as a chakravartin within the great vajra mandala by placing this vajra in your hand. They have given you this vajra, made from billions of their samadhis. They have blessed you. You are now a mahavajrachakravartin. They have taught you all the vajra essence mantras. All tathagatas have entrusted you with the care and protection of all their teachings. Your past aspirations are fulfilled. Son of family, display your miraculous abilities. Reveal the great mandala of vajra empowerment."

Vajrapani answered the bhagavat, "I will do what the lord of dharma has commanded. Bhagavat, my receiving these supremely wondrous things and this holy, victorious dharma is due to the bhagavat's kindness."

Vajrapani then entered the samadhi called Essence of Loud Piled Great Vajras. The world vibrated and shook. It was filled with a great light that ended all darkness and the sufferings of lower states. Kings among wrathful deities emerged from all of Vajrapani's pores, shouting HUM loudly. Holding vajras and frowning, they were heard all over the world. They placed all unruly elementals under samaya and caused all those elementals to reveal their essence mantras. The world was filled with the roaring sound of the words, "Oh! This mahabodhisattva is fierce Vajrapani!"

Then Vajrapani entered many samadhis, such as the samadhi called Vajra Fire. The world vibrated, shook, and caught fire. From Vajrapani's eyes emerged Vajra Terrifying Gaze. From Vajrapani's pores and all his limbs emerged vajra wrathful deities. From his ushnisha emerged Trilokavijaya, whose body was the size of ten billion-world systems and blazed with fire like that at a kalpa's end. From Vajrapani's forehead emerged the wrathful Chandrabindu, who had thousands of arms. Vajrapani also displayed the forms of Vajra Mace, Great Power, Trampling Vajra, Vajra Chain, Vajra Peak, and Vajra Fists. Each of them was accompanied by ten thousand female messengers. Vajrapani also revealed their essence mantras.

From Vajrapani's two hands emerged the youth Good Hands. From Vajrapani's mouth emerged the youth Vajrasena. They and all the other emanated youthful sons of Vajrapani were wrathful and held vajras in their hands. They diligently benefited beings and attained manifest buddhahood in various worlds. They were born with bodies endowed with strength

and other qualities. They fulfilled the wishes of all beings. In that way Vajrapani emanated many sons dear to his heart and taught their mantras.

Then Vajrapani entered the samadhi called Burning All Who Threaten Beings' Lives. When he uttered that samadhi's essence mantra, all the mountains and oceans caught fire and dried up. Seeing this, everyone present in that gathering — other than those abiding on the ten bodhisattva levels — fell face downward onto the vajra mandala. From Vajrapani's heart emerged a king among wrathful deities called Great Terrifying Tongues of Flame. He laughed long and loudly with a sound like the neigh of a horse, collecting the hearts of everyone in that gathering. Their hearts became like space and were placed in the mandala of Vajrapani's heart.

Vajrapani, abiding in the mandala of great compassion, remained in a state equal to that of all tathagatas. All tathagatas praised him by saying, "Excellent!"

Then the youthful Manjushri, knowing that everyone in that gathering had fallen onto the vajra mandala, gave rise to great compassion. He gazed into the distance with his two eyes and said to Vajrapani, "Son of family, give those gathered here a chance to enter samaya. They will gain the hope of survival through this teaching. In their faith, they will offer their respective secret essence mantras."

Vajrapani replied in verse. Then while uttering the dharani of Supreme Vajra Power, he handed his vajra to Manjushri. Manjushri then said to that gathering, "Children of family, recollect this queen of awareness-mantras, the Invincible Vajra's Stupefying Fire! Through it you will reap benefit and happiness! Because of it you will survive!"

Vajrapani then uttered that great awareness mantra. Through Manjushri's blessing, everyone in that gathering arose and

gave rise to delight and supreme faith. All the haughty, powerful, and mighty beings of the three worlds — Brahma, Rudra, Vishnu, Indra, the four great kings, the devas, nagas, yakshas, ghandharvas, and others — offered Vajrapani their re-spective essence mantras together with the rituals for their accomplishment. Vajrapani decreed their vajra samaya.

Then the youthful Manjushri entered the samadhi called Emanation of Light Rays of Great Vajra Wisdom. With his hand he received from Vajrapani his vajra. Manjushri then created a stainless utpala, arisen from his wisdom, and placed the vajra on it. Immediately, all the buddha mandalas in all worlds buzzed with the sound of the words, "Oh! The youthful Manjushri is the Vajra of Holy Giving!" These words were spread from one being to another in every realm.

All the buddhas abiding in all the worlds in the ten directions, while remaining in their respective realms, extended their right hands and stroked Manjushri's head. All those buddhas said, "Excellent!" Urged by them, Manjushri revealed the stages of accomplishing siddhi through the various essence mantras.

Manjushri also said then, "Shantimati, the essence mantras of all tathagatas possess endless hardness and power. Shantimati, this Vajrapani is called Vajra Arisen from the Terrifying Fire of All Tathagatas. He tames the untamed. He fulfills the aspirations of all tathagatas and all bodhisattvas. He has made aspirations to always perfectly guard the teachings. He properly fulfills the wishes of all beings. In all the endless oceans of worlds, he enters the gate of the proclamation of the aspirations of all tathagatas. He runs before all tathagatas."

Then all the tathagatas in all the innumerable realms in the ten directions extended their right hands and placed them on Vajrapani's head. They urged him to explain the secret mantras and mandalas, which he did. When Vajrapani taught

Manjushri the dharani of the empowerment of great wisdom, the youthful Manjushri realized the great wisdom vajra arisen from ninety-nine million wisdoms. Offering clouds appeared in the mandalas of all tathagatas. All tathagatas bestowed the empowerment of great wisdom upon Manjushri. This realm of a billion worlds buzzed with the sound of the words, "Manjushri has been empowered!"

Through that empowerment, Manjushri saw the forms of as many tathagatas as the number of finest particles in ten buddha realms, all of them seated within great utpalas. At that moment, through the power of his realization of the dharmakaya, the forms of tathagatas appeared within, and emerged from, all of Manjushri's pores, crown, jewelry, limbs, and digits. If someone who had achieved all the mental powers of the ten bodhisattva levels could not count the number of tathagatas present within even one of Manjushri's pores, what need is there to say that shravakas, pratyekabuddhas, and worldly beings could not do so?

Then the youthful Manjushri gazed with unblinking eyes upon the bodhisattva Vajrapani, and praised him in verse.

From the *Great Tantra of Supreme Awareness*

The tathagata Shakyamuni said, "Anyone who mentally prostrates to Vajrapani, the supreme king of awareness, generates more merit than someone who prostrates to as many tathagatas as the sand grains in nine million two hundred thousand Ganges Rivers."

The bodhisattva Stainless Realization asked the bhagavat, "Bhagavat, how long ago was Vajrapani appointed great king of awareness and great lord among awareness-mantra holders? In what samadhis does he abide? Who were his spiritual friends in the past? Where does he remain?"

The buddha replied, "As many kalpas ago as the number of sand grains in nineteen Ganges Rivers, there arose the great kalpa called Hard to Tame. During that kalpa there appeared the tathagata called Light Rays of the Great Wisdom Beacon. During his time our world, Saha, had become a world called Vajras. The tathagata Light Rays of the Great Wisdom Beacon once taught the secret dharma called Perfect Illumination Dispelling All Darkness to sixty sextillion bodhisattvas. Vajra holders gathered from innumerable worlds to hear this. At that time, in order to encourage the presentation of as many samadhis and dharanis as there are particles in innumerable worlds, the tathagata smiled. Present at that assembly was a great vajra holder, the best among great vajra holders, the king and ruler of endless worlds. When the tathagata smiled, that great vajra holder arose from his seat. He bowed to the tathagata's feet and then stood up once more.

"The great vajra holder, with a great gesture, took a vajra from a world countless worlds beneath ours. Brandishing it, he overpowered tens of boundless oceans of worlds in each of the ten directions. Like a majestic king summoning an ocean of subjects, while brandishing the vajra with great pride he gazed with eyes blazing like the fire at time's end. Taking the vajra with a grand gesture from beneath the blazing mandala of destructive light-rays, he placed that vajra before the tathagata's feet. He bowed to the tathagata's two feet and asked him, 'Why did you smile at this assembly? Light rays of various colors, unlike any seen before now, emerged from your mouth and from between your brows. I ask you this at this assembly's urging. I pray that, bhagavat, you kindly explain.'

"From the glorious knot that marked the tathagata's body emerged light rays the color of the sky or of precious beryl. These great light rays, like tongues of flame, brightly illuminated all the worlds in the ten directions surrounding that mandala. With his left hand, the tathagata picked up the vajra

from that mandala, which was radiant with stainless light rays. As he did so, from the vajra appeared the Lord of Secrets, Vajrapani, the King of Awareness. From the hooklike mark on the tathagata's hand emerged Hook. From the fish-shaped mark emerged Vajra Desire. From the mark of auspiciousness emerged Chain. From the very beautiful, blazing svastika that marked the tathagata emerged Mekhala. From his water vase emerged Yellow. From his parasol emerged Fierce Victory Banner. Finally, from the vajra there emerged Delight. These seven great messenger-queens appeared.

"In front of them appeared the uncontrollable wrathful one Great Power and the wrathful one Kilikili, who is like a jewel that blazes with the fire at time's end. These two wrathful ones emerged from the tathagata's vajra fists. From his blazing and beautiful shoulders emerged Vajra Sky-Iron. There thus appeared ten messengers along with their retinues. There also appeared, in a similar manner, two hundred and forty others.

"After Vajrapani had appeared along with his attendants, his messengers, and their retinues, blessed by the tathagata Light Rays of the Great Wisdom Beacon, he supplicated that tathagata in that mandala of great samaya. That tathagata entered the samadhi called Stainless. He then first explained the ten secrets of the tathagatas' bodies, speech, and minds. He then explained innumerable billions of billions of secrets. He taught that king of sutras in that mandala, that assembly of those with samaya, so that those hard to tame could be tamed and in order to reveal the wisdom of omniscience.

"Since that time, Vajrapani has conquered maras for, and guarded the teachings of, ninety-nine million buddhas, starting with the tathagata Light Rays of the Great Wisdom Beacon. Ninety-six kalpas after the time of the tathagata Light Rays of the Great Wisdom Beacon, in this world of Saha, there appeared a perfect buddha called Sees the Point. While that buddha was teaching, there appeared a mara called Says

Nothing Whatsoever. Vajrapani defeated him. Since then, Vajrapani has defeated maras for ninety-one million and eighty buddhas. He has guarded all their teachings.

"More than ninety-six kalpas after the time of the buddha Sees the Point, there appeared a buddha called Play of Golden Light. Starting from that buddha's time, Vajrapani continued to defeat maras and guard the teachings for sixty-eight million kalpas. For a thousand kalpas after that, Vajrapani held the secrets of all those tathagatas and guarded their teachings. Since then he has tamed the untamed for, and held the secrets of, the tathagatas Ushnisha, All-Seeing, All-Protecting, Golden Sage, Dispels Faithlessness, Akshobhya, and Kashyapa. Vajrapani has done this during my teaching as well. He will continue to serve all the buddhas of this fortunate kalpa in this realm of Saha. Finally, having served the teachings in this way, Vajrapani will achieve manifest, perfect buddhahood. He will become the buddha called Goes Through Vajra Power."

Vajrapani then said to the buddha, "Bhagavat, I have seen no one in the world remain in a state of hatred after hearing my name; no deva, no brahma, no mara, no renunciate, no brahmin, and no one else."

The bhagavat said, "Friends, anyone who mentally prostrates to the bodhisattva mahasattva Vajrapani will have bowed to nine thousand tathagatas."

Vajrapani said, "With my powerful vajra I will cleave the head of any spirit that does not flee after hearing my name!"

The bhagavat said to the fierce Vajrapani, "Anyone who hears your name and mantras will purify the wrongdoing of immediate consequence; will see you, Vajrapani; and will scatter all obstructors, misleaders, and especially the eighty-four sextillion misleaders, to the ten directions. Anyone who hears your name will become chaste if they are unchaste; will become

capable if they are incapable; will become austere if they lack austerity; will gain the fruit of renunciation even if they lack renunciation; will be guarded by all buddhas and bodhisattvas; and will achieve the siddhis of action.

"You have the ears of an elephant. You have fine ornamentation. You overcome everything. You are the source of precious qualities. You are a mass of truth. You are adorned by a pleasing form. You possess blazing tongues of flame. You are beautiful. Any wise person who hears your name will not be born in hell for seven sextillion kalpas. When they die, all buddhas and bodhisattvas will appear before them and teach them dharma. Such wise persons will be reborn among the devas in Tushita and will live among the bodhisattvas there."

Vajrapani said, "If anyone reads and praises my name, I, Vajrapani, and all deities will be pleased and bestow siddhi. Obstacles will not arise. Bad dreams will not occur."

He then described many other benefits as well.

From the *Dharani of the Mansion on the Peak of Great Vajra Mount Meru*

The bhagavat once abided in a mansion on the peak of Vajra Mount Meru together with a retinue of many mahabodhisattvas, mahashravakas, devas, humans, and others. From between the buddha's brows emerged a great radiance of light that illuminated as many realms as the Ganges River's sand grains. The brilliance of this light disturbed all the abodes of Mara. Mara therefore gathered a great and terrifying army that filled eighty-four thousand yojanas and attacked the bhagavat. All Mara's weapons became rains of flowers, and all the sound made by his army became the sound of buddhas. Mara the Wrongdoer was bound with five lassos and cast on the ground in the mansion's courtyard.

With a loving mind, the bhagavat said to Vajrapani:

"Vajrapani, Lord of Secrets, raise this wrongdoer up from the courtyard and place him on a seat! Display the inconceivable blessing of the miraculous samadhi of the Great Gate of Vajra Liberation, for it conquers the mandalas of Mara and causes Mara and all vicious beings to take refuge in the three jewels."

Vajrapani joined his palms in salutation of the bhagavat and praised him properly in verse. He then sat down on the center of a precious lotus and entered that samadhi. This world shook violently six times. From all of Vajrapani's limbs and extremities emerged blazing vajra fire. Becoming one vast tongue of flame, its vajra radiance illuminated innumerable worlds in the ten directions, all the bhagavat buddhas abiding in them, and their retinues. When those buddhas told the bodhisattvas in their retinues the reason for the light, all those bodhisattvas gathered here as a vast assembly. The innumerable buddhas of the realms in the ten directions extended their golden right hands, adorned by auspicious marks, and stroked Vajrapani's head. They all simultaneously said, with a roaring sound that filled all worlds, "Son of family, it is excellent that you have entered this samadhi in order to eradicate Mara the Wrongdoer and all the vicious who hate the tathagatas' teachings, in order to encourage beginner bodhisattvas, and in order to benefit all beings!"

Then the bhagavat said to Vajrapani, "Release Mara the Wrongdoer from his bonds and let him take refuge in the three jewels. Cause all without faith in the teachings to gain it."

Vajrapani, obedient to the bhagavat's command, entered the samadhi of the Great Gate of Vajra Liberation, which conquers all the mandalas of Mara. As soon as he did so, this world shook six times. Vajrapani's body blazed unbearably brightly with tongues of flame. Clouds of various invincible wrathful ones emerged from all the joints of his enraged body. His furious emanations burned and crushed all misleaders. Suffering unbearably, Mara the Wrongdoer and all

obstructors and misleaders wanted to shake like trees in the wind. They wanted to weep, but were unable to move and remained as still as paintings.

Then from Vajrapani's two feet emerged two terrifying wrathful ones. They circumambulated the tathagata hundreds of thousands of times and then said to Vajrapani, "Please give us our orders."

The Lord of Secrets, however, remained silent. From his forehead emerged a terrifying wrathful one with an invincible form. The radiant vajra blaze of that emanation's limbs filled these billion worlds, eclipsing the splendor of all others. Even the light of the sun, moon, stars, and jewels was darkened. All light other than that of tathagatas and bodhisattvas on the ten levels became darkness.

That emanation circumambulated the tathagata countless times and then said to Vajrapani, "Son of family, please give me my orders."

Vajrapani said to those wrathful ones, "Make Mara the Wrongdoer and all obstructors without faith in the teachings take refuge in the three jewels and abide in samaya!"

Those wrathful ones then simultaneously uttered the basis of secret mantra with voices like a lion's roar that filled the world. This world shook six times. In all directions great meteors fell like war clubs. The sky sounded as though it were shattering. The earth broke apart. From the fissures that appeared in the ground fountains of water shot upward like those that appear at the time of a world's destruction. The earth became covered by water. Great subterranean beings such as nagas, devas, and asuras emerged on the surface. The bodies of all elementals, obstructors, and misleaders burned until they became single tongues of flame, as did all the abodes of Mara. The mansions of the devas became dark. Seeing that the heads of all maras would be crushed by the vajras held by the great vajra wrathful ones, Mara the Wrongdoer became desperate in his misery. Crying in terror, he prostrated to the tathagata Shakyamuni and the Lord of Secrets. Mara exclaimed with sincerity, "Protect me! I take refuge in the three jewels until I reach the heart of awakening! I generate bodhichitta for the benefit of all beings!"

Everyone in that gathering was amazed. They praised and cast flowers upon the buddha and the Lord of Secrets. Mara the Wrongdoer was also delighted, and created through his powers a finely decorated mansion of jewels. He offered it to his spiritual friend, the Lord of Secrets, in veneration and praised him accurately in verse. At the Lord of Secret's command, the wrathful ones he had emanated placed all unruly devas, nagas, yakshas, and others within samaya. Then Vajrapani arose from that samadhi. Shariputra asked him the samadhi's name. In reply, Vajrapani said, "This samadhi cannot be realized through names, letters, or language."

He then taught dharma about the profound meaning of suchness, which is without characteristics such as name, form, or designated samadhis. The tathagata Shakyamuni and all the tathagatas in all the worlds of the ten directions placed their right hands on Vajrapani's head and praised him by saying, "Excellent!"

Through this dharma, more devas than the number of finest sand grains in innumerable Ganges Rivers achieved the immaculate and stainless eye of dharma. A great many bhikshus, bhikshunis, devas, and other ordinary beings achieved patience with unborn dharmas. A much greater number of beings generated the irreversible intention to attain supreme awakening. This world and countless, inexpressibly many other buddha realms shook six times. Through the power of the devas and bodhisattvas, diverse offering clouds as vast as oceans filled the sky and were presented to Vajrapani. Brahma, Indra, Vishnu, and all the other beings in the world prostrated to the bhagavat and accepted samaya.

From the *King of Tantras, the Glorious Drop of Wisdom*

Vajrapani is the great protector.
He is the lord of all vajra holders.
He is the cause of the birth and destruction
Of innumerable worlds.

He is without any birth.
He is the self-arisen, supreme lord.
The vajra in his hand
Is the unborn twelve wisdoms.

From its five upper prongs
Come the five tathagatas.
From its five lower prongs
Come the five elements.

From its center come the six types of beings.
In order to protect all views,
Vajrapani exhibits various forms.
For some he appears as a vajra holder.

81. A heruka is a type of wrathful deity.

For some he has the form of a buddha.
For some he has the form of a heruka.[81]
For some he has the form of a tathagata.
For some he has the form of a bodhisattva.

82. Lotus Joy is the name of the person being addressed in this quotation.

For some he has the form of a shravaka.
For some he teaches, Lotus Joy.[82]
For some he appears to study.
For some he composes tantras and shastras.

For some he upholds them.
What need is there to say more?
It is the victorious Vajrapani who teaches this.

THE THIRD CHAPTER: GLORIOUS VAJRAPANI

MAITREYA
THE REGENT AJITA

I prostrate to the protector Maitreya,[83] the bodhisattva mahasattva! I venerate you! I take refuge in you!

From the *Mahayana Sutra of Arya Maitreya's Entrance*

The buddha said, "The bodhisattva mahasattva Maitreya has for a long time behaved with chastity and served the victors. He has generated roots of virtue and has achieved patience with the profound. I, your teacher Shakyamuni, generated bodhichitta eighty-four thousand kalpas after Maitreya's entrance into the perfect path.

"Innumerably many, inconceivably many kalpas ago a buddha called Good Golden Light appeared. He radiated a golden light of benevolence that illuminated the world in which he lived. At that time Maitreya was a chakravartin king called Golden who ruled a world of four continents. He supported, served, and venerated in all ways the buddha Good Golden Light and his great sangha of bodhisattvas for eighty-four million years. He was assisted in this service by Brahma, Indra, and the four great kings. King Golden's palace had a courtyard that was eighty yojanas wide. He filled it with innumerable inconceivably precious and fine offerings and

presented them continuously to that buddha and his sangha.

"At the end of that period of patronage, King Golden thought, 'Shall I dedicate my roots of virtue to the achievement of the state of Indra, or that of Brahma, or that of a chakravartin?'

"The buddha Good Golden Light knew of the king's thought. He emanated a tathagata like himself into the sky before them. The emanated tathagata said to King Golden:

"'The states of Brahma and so forth are impermanent
    and unstable.
Do not desire such an inferior state.
Generate the intention to achieve supreme awakening.
It has immeasurable qualities and is of benefit to
    all beings.'

"King Golden therefore generated the intention to achieve unsurpassable awakening. When he told the buddha Good Golden Light that he had done so, he said to him, 'I pray that you teach me a path through which the amrita of supreme awakening can be gained easily by means of an easy vehicle, without any suffering such as that of giving away my head and limbs repeatedly over a period of many kalpas.'

"That buddha therefore taught the king how to achieve buddhahood by means of an easy vehicle and without austerities such as giving away one's body. This requires the accumulation of the immeasurable merit of bodhichitta, and the cultivation of such circumspection that one never abandons one's training, one's vows, or love.

"The king renounced the world and lived purely for ten thousand years. He accomplished supercognition and perfected learning. He also accomplished the samadhi of love. Through his roots of virtue and good intentions he was continuously reborn as a chakravartin. He served twenty thousand buddhas and renounced the world in front of each of them.

"After that, but still innumerable kalpas ago, during the teaching of the tathagata called Precious Parasol, the bodhisattva Maitreya became the bhikshu Stable Intellect. Once, while he was begging in a village, he thought, 'I shall not eat until I have placed one hundred beings in the five bases of training!'[84]

"Sometimes he was able to place one hundred beings in the bases of training in a single day, but sometimes it took him two or as many as seven days to do so. Nevertheless, he kept his vow. Even if it meant that he did not eat for seven days, he was never discouraged, because of his compassion for beings. He therefore sometimes ate only every eight days. He lived in that way for eighty-four thousand years. Without discouragement, he went from village to village and town to town, placing beings in the five bases of training. At the end of that number of years, he had placed thirty-six sextillion men, women, and children in the five bases of training. He then thought, 'I have placed these beings in the five bases of training. I shall now place them in unsurpassable, perfect awakening!'

"For the next forty-two thousand years, he went from place to place, praising the three jewels and the mahayana. Thirty million of those beings were established in perfect awakening. The rest of them generated the intention of the shravakayana or pratyekabuddhayana. Stable Intellect then thought, 'I have interested them in the three vehicles. In order that they abide in circumspection, I will now teach them samadhi.'

"For the next twenty-one thousand years, he instructed those thirty-six sextillion beings in the cultivation of samadhi. They all accomplished the samadhi of love. When the bhikshu Stable Intellect went into the villages, he did so while abiding in the samadhi of love. Whenever he placed his foot on the threshold of a dwelling, all those within came to abide in love. All of them were established in the samadhi of love. When the devas above the earth saw the miraculous power of

84. These are the vows not to kill, steal, fornicate, lie, or drink liquor.

that bhikshu's samadhi of love, they exclaimed, 'A LA LA! This bodhisattva mahasattva will be known as Maitreya! Whenever he enters a village, all the beings there enter the samadhi of love!'

"Those words were repeated by one deva to another, starting with the devas that inhabit the sky of this world and culminating with those that inhabit the pure abodes. The giving of the name Maitreya to this bodhisattva was joyously confirmed by the tathagata Precious Parasol. He predicted, 'This bhikshu Stable Intellect will be renowned as the bodhisattva mahasattva Maitreya in every life. When he achieves awakening, this will remain his name; he will be the tathagata Maitreya. His buddha realm will be called Precious Array. It will possess a sangha of innumerable shravakas. Its beings will possess all types of happiness.'

"If those who merely hear the name of the bodhisattva mahasattva Maitreya have gained something supreme, what could be said about those who have the pleasure of actually seeing him with the fleshly eye?"

From the *Sutra on the Birth of the Bodhisattva Maitreya in the Tushita Heaven*

The omniscient tathagata said, "I predict the perfect awakening of the mahabodhisattva Maitreya, who is present in this assembly. Twelve years from now, he will pass away and be reborn in the heaven of Tushita. The devas of Tushita will venerate him as a bodhisattva in his last life. Offering him their crowns and jewelry, they will make aspirations. Through the power of those devas' merit, a palace with especially fine and beautiful features will appear. The merit of Tushita is unique. Even if a tathagata were to describe it for a kalpa, the description would not be complete. Those who seek birth in that abode of devas in order to attend Maitreya, who receive the full five-branched eight vows, and energetically practice the ten virtues for the sake of consummate joy and happiness, possess what is called "perfect view."[85] Other views are called "incorrect views."

"Tushita is a place of consummate joy and happiness. The great being Maitreya will, twelve years from now, on the fifteenth day of the middle month of spring, be born in Tushita in the town of Ranikapali, in the home of a great brahmin named Babali. Immediately upon birth, Maitreya will sit up with crossed legs and rest in samadhi. His body will be golden in color, and will remain unmoving. In Tushita, in a fine mansion made of the seven jewels, Maitreya will be miraculously born with a body like the gold of the Jambu River, sitting with crossed legs on a lotus atop a lion throne. His body will be sixteen yojanas in height and adorned with the marks and signs. From his jeweled crown innumerable tathagatas, along with their retinues of bodhisattvas, will be emanated. They will demonstrate eighteen types of miracles to the bodhisattvas of other realms. From Maitreya's brow rays of white light will emerge. From those light rays will appear numerous devas, blazing with light, adorned with marks and signs, their bodies as colorful as hundreds of jewels. Those devas will teach, throughout day and night, the dharmachakra of irreversibility. Finally, they will explain the predictions in the sutras of Maitreya's birth in Jambudvipa.

"After I, the bhagavat Shakyamuni, have passed into nirvana, all those of the four retinues who abide in vows, venerate stupas, recite sutras, create images of the tathagatas, and recite Maitreya's name will after their deaths be miraculously born in Tushita.[86] They will see Maitreya's face, hear his dharma, and will eventually receive prophecy from the buddhas of this fortunate kalpa.

"Anyone who, hearing the name of the bodhisattva mahasattva Maitreya, prostrates to him with joy and respect will not fall into realms of darkness after their death. They will not

85. The five-branched eight vows are those taken, for example, during Nyungnay practice. The eight vows fulfill five functions, hence their name.

86. The four retinues are male and female monastics and male and female householders.

be born in a borderland, or a place of wrong views, or a place where all forms of wrongdoing are done. In all their births they will be born in places endowed with upright views, places where the sangha is abundant, places where the three jewels are not denigrated.

"If those who have broken their vows and engaged in wrongdoing call this bodhisattva by name, prostrate to him, and confess with a one-pointed mind, all their wrongdoing will be quickly purified. Anyone who creates an image of Maitreya, venerates it with offerings, and recites his name will be welcomed at death by rays of white light emanated from Maitreya's brow. They will be received by devas casting rains of mandarava flowers. In an instant, they will be born in the deva abode of Tushita. They will see Maitreya's face, hear his dharma, and find the path to unsurpassable awakening. In the future, they will see as many buddhas as the Ganges River's sand grains.

"Any being in the future who takes refuge in Maitreya will find the unsurpassable path, the dharmachakra of irreversibility. When Maitreya achieves buddhahood, they will see that tathagata's light rays and receive his prophecy of their future buddhahood.

"After my nirvana, any member of the four retinues who wishes to be born in Tushita; or any deva, naga, or yaksha who seeks birth there; or any other being who wishes to be born there should do the following:

87. This means the vow to become a buddha, the bodhisattva vow.

"Keeping Tushita in mind, receive the vow of a tathagata.[87] Then for between one and seven days engage your mind and behavior in the ten virtues. Dedicate the merit of doing so with the aspiration to be born in Tushita in Maitreya's presence. Those who do this will see the devas and lotuses of Tushita.

"Anyone who recites Maitreya's name for even an instant will be freed from 12,000 kalpas of birth and death and will purify the wrongdoing of that many kalpas. Anyone who, hearing Maitreya's name, joins their palms in faith will be freed from fifty kalpas of birth and death. Anyone who respectfully prostrates to Maitreya will be freed from one billion kalpas of birth and death and purify the wrongdoing of that many kalpas. They will be unattached to the deva abodes. In the future they will receive, in front of the naga tree of awakening, the vow of unsurpassable bodhichitta."

From the *Sutra on the Heroic Samadhi*

The buddha once said, "Maitreya, demonstrate the heroic samadhi to the bodhisattva Jinamati."

The bodhisattva Jinamati and the rest of that assembly saw that Maitreya appeared in every Jambudvipa in this realm of a billion worlds. In some of them he abided in the deva worlds, in some in the worlds of humans. In some he remained a householder. In some he had renounced the world. In some, like Ananda, he served tathagatas. In some he had great wisdom like Shariputra. In some he had great miraculous abilities like Maudgalyayana. Like the supreme shravakas in our world, he appeared in various forms and was perceived as such by the worlds in which he displayed them. He begged for alms in the towns, taught dharma, and rested in perfect absorption. Seeing this, Jinamati and the others were amazed.

From the chapter of the *Ratnakutasutra* called the "Great Lion's Roar of Maitreya"

The bhagavat once asked the elder Mahakashyapa, "Are you willing to uphold the holy dharma in the future, during the final five hundred years?"

Mahakashyapa replied, "I would be willing to bear on my shoulders or even my head all the villages, towns, mountains, rocks, oceans, and forests in the four continents of this world for a kalpa or even longer than a kalpa. I cannot, however, listen with enthusiasm to the prospect of dwelling among such unholy beings. I could also willingly sustain myself for a kalpa or even longer than a kalpa with a single date, or a single sesame seed, or a single grain of rice. I could willingly live for a million years in a billionfold realm that was on fire with a great blaze like that at a kalpa's end. I cannot, however, listen with enthusiasm to the prospect of dwelling among the unholy beings of the future and their wrong views. I could endure being hated, scorned, vilified, and beaten by all beings, but I do not wish to listen to foolish people, thieves of dharma who adopt the pretence of dharma. As my conduct and wisdom are weak, I am incapable of bearing such a burden. Bodhisattvas, however, are capable of bearing such a burden.

"Bhagavat, if, for example, someone's treasure were entrusted to an old, weakened, sick man without sons, daughters, or other assistants, that treasure would be lost. Similarly, if the treasure of holy dharma is entrusted to shravakas, who possess weak wisdom and conduct and are without companions, it will not abide for long.

"If someone entrusted his treasure to a person without illness, a person who would live for hundreds of thousands of years and had both a retinue of youths and abundant ability, and the treasure's owner then went to another country, their treasure would be returned to them upon their return. Similarly, if the treasure of dharma is entrusted to bodhisattvas, it will not be lost for billions of kalpas. It will bring benefit to many beings. The lineage of the three jewels will be unbroken. It would therefore be appropriate for you to speak of this to the bodhisattva Maitreya."

The bhagavat responded to Mahakashyapa's words by saying, "Excellent!" The buddha then placed his golden right hand, the result of the virtue of innumerable kalpas, on Maitreya's head and said, "Maitreya, in the future, during the final five hundred years, when holy dharma is disappearing, enthusiastically guard, uphold, and sustain holy dharma. Ensure that the lineage of the three jewels is unbroken."

As the buddha placed his hand on Maitreya's head, this world shook three times and was filled with bright light. The devas of all realms up to Akanishtha joined their palms and said, "Maitreya, be enthusiastic for the benefit of many beings!"

Maitreya then arose from his seat. He bowed to the bhagavat and said, "Bhagavat, for the sake of even one being I would be willing to remain in samsara until its end. What need is there for me to say that I am willing to do so in order to uphold holy dharma? I will guard and spread this unsurpassable awakening that the tathagata accomplished over innumerable kalpas!"

Maitreya said this while placing his right knee on the ground. As he did so, this realm of a billion worlds shook six times. Maitreya then said, "Bhagavat, I do not compete with anyone. I am without pride. Why? Because this upholding of holy dharma is the responsibility of holy beings. It is a burden that bodhisattvas must bear, because shravakas and pratyekabuddhas are unable to bear it."

The bhagavat said to Maitreya, "Excellent! Excellent! Just as you have proclaimed in my presence this lion's roar in order to uphold holy dharma, other bodhisattvas will proclaim this lion's roar and take up the dharma in the presence of as many buddhas in the ten directions as there are sand grains in the Ganges River!"

Maitreya asked, "Bhagavat, please explain the faults of unholy beings — fools who declare themselves to be bodhisattvas and bhikshus for the sake of gain — so that others will be protected from those faults and feel awe, thinking, 'The tathagata knows!'"

The buddha replied, "In the future final five hundred years there will be many wrongdoers who will call themselves bodhisattvas. They will seek gain and honor by means of deception and evildoing. They will call themselves bodhisattvas yet behave like dogs. Like dogs, they will take possession of others' homes. They will be angry at others, and will quarrel, fight, incite disputation, and speak harshly and unpleasantly. In their words they will praise buddhas, bodhisattvas, the paramitas, and the means of attracting beings to dharma. By doing so, they will gain food and clothing. Yet they will not practice these things themselves. They will go to the homes of householders, not in order to increase householders' faith, but for the sake of gain. They will dislike others' gain, and will rejoice in others' poverty. They will be the opposite of bodhisattvas, who compassionately accomplish others' happiness. These self-proclaimed bodhisattvas will not cultivate morality or wisdom with body or mind. They will therefore enter peoples' homes with the aim of acquisition, not for the purpose of dharma, and will converse about worldly matters. Because their three gates are ungoverned, they will commit downfalls. They will think that by merely confessing these they will be purified. They will therefore not vow to abstain from downfalls thereafter. They will be very mistaken in choosing to emphasize material gain over dharma.

"There will also appear in the future many undisciplined bhikshus who will think to support themselves by painting images of the tathagata. They will discard the activities of renunciates — meditation and recitation; and take up the activities of householders — painting images and making offerings. They will hope to support themselves in such ways.

"A son or daughter of family who sponsors the creation of excellent images of the tathagata — each the size of Mount Meru — out of the seven jewels, and causes them to be kept thoroughly clean, and fills with such images as many buddha realms as there are sand grains in the Ganges River, filling those realms as densely as a thicket of sugarcane or a thicket of reeds or a rice paddy or a field of sesame, will accumulate far less merit than a bodhisattva who recognizes the emptiness of the tathagata's body and thinks of it with patience for the profound for even the duration of a finger snap. Someone who cultivates the aggregate of morality and memorizes even one four-line stanza, understanding its meaning, and teaches it to even one being, will accumulate even more merit than that.

"If one person filled with jewels
   As many worlds as the Ganges' sand grains,
   And enthusiastically offered them to the victors,
   And another person gave a single stanza of dharma
   To a single being, that vast offering of jewels
   Would not equal even a part of that compassionate
   Gift of a single stanza of dharma.
   How could it compare to the gift of two, three, or more?

"Maitreya, in the palm of the tathagata's right hand is a ray of light called Ornament of All Merit as Concordant Cause. If the tathagata wished, that ray of light could fill all these billion worlds, creating all the things that give beings pleasure. I could in that way give beings everything they want — food, clothing, and wealth. However, that would not free beings from the crocodile's mouth of suffering in the ocean of beginningless and endless samsara. I have therefore cast aside the creation of mundane pleasures. In order to create supramundane happiness, I correctly teach precious dharma. Hearing it, beings will be freed from suffering forever.

"Maitreya, for that reason you should follow my example. Don't be concerned with material things; be concerned with dharma. Maitreya, in this way bodhisattvas think, 'I will free myself so that I can then free others, liberate them, grant them assurance, and bring them to nirvana.'

"Other than bodhisattvas, no one in the world, including the devas, has ever undertaken this responsibility, this burden: the welfare of all beings. For example, if someone were to bear these billion worlds — with all their mountains, oceans, and forests — on their head or shoulders for a hundred thousand kalpas without resting, that would be a heavy burden. That person would have to be extremely strong and brave. Someone, however, who takes up the burden of bringing all beings to the happiness of nirvana bears a much greater burden, and must be even stronger and braver.

"Someone who could in the time of a finger snap accomplish all the actions of all the beings in a billion worlds would have to be very powerful. Someone, however, who says, 'I will free all beings from samsara's suffering!' and sets about doing it is even more powerful.

"For example, imagine that there is a householder with one beloved son. His king says to him, 'Householder, go to a certain city one hundred thousand yojanas from here and return to me within seven days. If you do so, I will return to you your son, wife, retinue, and wealth. I will also give you half my kingdom. If, however, you do not reach that city and return here within seven days, I will give you nothing. I will also execute your son, wife, and retinue.'

"That householder would travel as quickly as possible, using all his strength. Until his return, he would ignore all distractions, hunger, fatigue, and sorrow. Even such great diligence, however, would not equal a hundredth or thousandth part of the great diligence of a bodhisattva. Why? Because bodhisattvas turn all beings back from the momentum in which they are immersed and bring them to the unmoving expanse of nirvana.

"For example, imagine a man strong enough to reverse the flow of all the water that flows into the four seas and cause it all to flow into Lake Manasarovar. That would be both difficult and amazing. However, a bodhisattva's great compassionate bodhichitta and resolve are far more difficult and amazing than that.

"It is even more difficult and amazing to realize the truth of the three jewels and the ripening of karma.

"It is even more difficult and amazing than that to dispel the three poisons in the mind.

"It is even more difficult and amazing than that to give up friends, family, and luxury and walk seven steps away from one's home for the sake of full renunciation.

"It is even more difficult and amazing than that to don saffron robes and achieve full renunciation of home life through faith in the vinaya that was well taught.

"It is even more difficult and amazing than that to practice the instructions and bases of training.

"It is even more difficult and amazing than that to walk seven paces toward solitude out of a dislike of distraction and a liking for solitude.

"It is even more difficult and amazing than that to contemplate that all dharmas are empty. It is even more difficult and amazing than that to realize the three gates of liberation and achieve the results of a stream-enterer, once-returner, nonreturner, or arhat.

"Why? Because faith in the noble dharma, the vinaya; achieving the state of a bhikshu; and achieving the fruitions are all

extremely difficult. Therefore having achieved full renunciation, don't abandon the actions of a bodhisattva and return
to the actions of the childish. Engage in the twenty actions of
a bodhisattva — such as eradicating greed — and avoid, like
poison, transgressing the training. Keep the four vows: ab-
stention from ingratitude, deception, lies, and transgressions.
Those four things are impediments to the achievement of
omniscience. Abandon acquisitiveness, negative influences,
and distracting environments. Especially, remain at least a
hundred yojanas away from any place where there is fighting
caused by hatred. Never give rise to hatred. It is far worse to
give rise to anger and hatred toward another bodhisattva even
once than to abuse, beat, and attack with weapons all the
beings in a billion worlds. A bodhisattva who does so will be
damaged and impaired. For example, iron can only be cut by
iron and not by other materials such as earth. In the same
way, a bodhisattva's roots of virtue will be destroyed by hat-
ing another bodhisattva. Nothing else can destroy them.
Therefore treat one another with courtesy and respect. Regard
even a bodhisattva who has just generated bodhichitta as the
teacher."

The mahabodhisattva Maitreya said, "Bhagavat, I treat all
beings with courtesy and respect. What need is there to speak
of bodhisattvas? Why? Because I don't like malevolence; I
have very strong patience. I am not deceptive; I have great
benevolence. I am not attached to a home; I am free from
ownership and possession. I don't seek material wealth; I seek
dharma. I am not interested in food and clothing; I am in
search of my inheritance. I have no jealousy or greed; I delight
in the prosperity of others and am extremely generous. I don't
seek the title of 'renunciate'; I am cultivating the qualities of a
renunciate. I don't seek talk; I make practice my essence. I am
not especially attached to honor and gain; I seek few actions
and the qualities of buddhas.

"I don't enter towns in a state of acquisitiveness; I enter them with my mind focused on omniscience. I am not deceptive in order to gain dharma robes and alms; I have the undeceptive contentment of the four aryas. I don't emulate the behavior of the childish; I emulate the behavior of buddhas. I don't think about what others do or don't do; I diligently subdue and pacify myself. I don't speak of others' downfalls; I control my speech. I don't delay the training; I cultivate the pratimoksha.[88] I don't seek the praise of myself by the buddha, dharma, or sangha; I joyously praise, contemplate, and rely upon the three jewels. I don't weep in the sight of others in order to impress them; I weep through the power of dharma. I am unpolluted by the distraction of various activities. I am diligent in seeking dharma. I dislike mundane activities; I like the search for supramundane dharma.

88. The pratimoksha, "individual liberation," is the moral discipline taught in the vinaya.

"I don't accumulate and store provisions; I behave without hypocrisy. I don't remain in one home or place; I wander like a wild animal. I am not diligent in the search for alms; I am diligent in the search for the buddhas' qualities. I don't sleep in a stupor of unconsciousness; I diligently abstain from sleep during the beginning and end of the night. I don't engage in distracting activities; I delight in solitude. I am not content with a few qualities; I am relentless in my search for all qualities. I don't behave like a dog; I roar like a lion. I don't make friends easily, but I am an extremely stable friend. I am never ungrateful; I am very grateful and appreciative. I don't offer my friendship in repayment of generosity; I offer my friendship out of benevolence. I don't fake benevolence; I strengthen it. I am uninterested in lowly things; I am interested in the vast and perfect accomplishment of the buddhakaya. I am not disrespectful to the tathagata and the training; I respect them.

"I am not two-tongued, thinking one thing and saying another; I do what I say. I am not a hypocritical bodhisattva; I am perfectly benevolent and diligent in being subdued and tranquil. I am not proud; like the child of outcasts, I have conquered pride. I don't consume alms through desire; with pure morality, I regard them as a burden in that they are offered through faith. I don't allow my mind to wander, sleeping in the afternoon in an unconscious stupor; I diligently apply myself to the accomplishment of all buddhadharmas. I don't hold the view of a personal self; I remain in emptiness. I don't conceptualize or speak through bewilderment; I remain in the absence of attributes.

"I am without pretense in my physical behavior; my actions of body, speech, and mind are pure. I don't teach dharma with a mind focused on acquisition; I teach dharma with a mind free from materialism. I don't befriend others through materialism; I befriend them through the giving of dharma. I don't torment myself or others; I practice in order to heal myself and others. I am not hypocritical in my reliance upon solitude, alms, and cast-off clothing; I perfectly cultivate the twelve qualities of training.[89] In doing so, I don't seek honor, gain, or praise."

89. The twelve qualities of training are twelve austerities, such as wearing cast-off clothing and living at the foot of a tree, which were permitted by the buddha.

The bhagavat said to the mahabodhisattva Maitreya, "Excellent! Excellent! Your lion's roar of diligence in seeking the qualities of buddhas shows that you have attended the victors of the past, have generated roots of virtue, and are independent in dharma and qualities! Excellent! Excellent!"

This lion's roar of the great regent was proclaimed by him out of compassion for beings in the final five hundred years. As it is important for beginner bodhisattvas in times of decadence who have fully renounced and teach dharma to consider it, I have quoted it in full.

When Maitreya taught his lion's roar, five hundred bhikshus present in that gathering arose from their seats and walked away. The elder Mahakashyapa called to them, "You have left your seats because you have heard talk of few possessions. Where are you going?"

They replied, "The bodhisattva Maitreya's talk of few possessions is hard to implement. We think that we lack the ability to live with so few possessions, and so we are returning to our homes. Why? Because we think that the donations of the faithful are dangerous to touch and hard to purify."

The youthful Manjushri then said to those bhikshus, "Excellent, sons of family, excellent! Someone who dislikes using the donations of the faithful should avoid and regret their use. To abandon full renunciation a hundred times a day is less serious than the use of the donations of the faithful by someone with impure morality."

The youthful Manjushri then asked the bhagavat, "Bhagavat, under what conditions do you permit the use of the donations of the faithful?"

The buddha replied, "Manjushri, I have given my permission for those with awareness and liberation to use the donations of the faithful."

Manjushri then said to those five hundred bhikshus, "Venerable ones, apply yourselves! Exert yourselves! Try! The appearance of a buddha is rare, so don't turn back from full renunciation."

They asked, "Manjushri, to what are we to apply ourselves?"

Manjushri replied, "Bhikshus, to what are you to apply yourselves? At what are you to work? What are you to try to do? Apply yourselves to nothing whatsoever! Exert yourselves in nothing whatsoever! Apply yourselves to making no distinctions, to starting nothing, stopping nothing, attaining nothing, abandoning nothing, decreasing nothing, and increasing nothing. Bhikshus, through such training you will realize nothing whatsoever. Realizing nothing whatsoever is going nowhere and coming from nowhere. Someone who is beyond

going and coming is fit to be called a bhikshu. He depends on nothing, yet is not independent."

Through Manjushri's teaching, those five hundred bhikshus, without acceptance, freed their minds from defilement.

From the "Prophecy Requested by Maitreya," a chapter of the *Ratnakutasutra*

The bodhisattva mahasattva Maitreya once asked the bhagavat about bodhisattva training. Delighted by the bhagavat's response, Maitreya praised him with appropriate verse. Ananda then praised the bodhisattva Maitreya's confidence and dharma teaching. The bhagavat said, "It is so! The bodhisattva Maitreya's perfect confidence and his dharma teaching with precise language are amazing! He has just praised me with appropriate verse. In the past, novemdecillion kalpas ago, when the tathagata Supercognition Display of Light appeared in the world, the bodhisattva Maitreya was the brahmin boy Goodness. Seeing that tathagata, he was inspired and thought, 'In the future, may I have a form like his! If this is going to happen, may this tathagata touch me now with his feet!'

"That tathagata knew the brahmin boy's thought. He walked over to him and touched him with his feet. Immediately, Goodness achieved patience with unborn dharmas. That tathagata looked around him and said to his bhikshus, 'Don't touch this boy with your feet. Why? Because he has achieved patience with unborn dharmas!'

"At that time the brahmin boy Goodness also accomplished miraculous powers and supercognitions. He praised that tathagata with appropriate verse. Since that day, the miraculous powers and supercognitions of that brahmin boy Goodness, now Maitreya, have remained undiminished."

Ananda asked, "Bhagavat, if the mahabodhisattva Maitreya achieved patience with unborn dharmas so long ago, why has he not achieved unsurpassable awakening?"

The buddha replied, "Ananda, there are two types of bodhisattvas. What are they? They are those who remain among and care for beings, and those who create and remain in pure realms. The mahabodhisattva Maitreya, when engaged in bodhisattva training, created and remained in pure realms. Ananda, I remained among and cared for beings, although I also created and remained in pure realms. Ananda, I know with supercognition that I first generated unsurpassable, perfect bodhichitta forty-two kalpas after Maitreya's entry into perfection. I should therefore have achieved buddhahood ninety-four kalpas after this fortunate kalpa. However, through great diligence I achieved buddhahood quickly. I repeatedly gave away the ten things hardest to give: all my possessions, my wealth, my throne, my children, my spouse, my head, my eyes, my blood, my bones, and my limbs. I also practiced the rest of the ten paramitas, such as morality and patience. In that way I achieved unsurpassable awakening quickly.

"Once in the past I became the prince called Giver of All Wealth. During that life I gave a sick person all the blood in my body, which cured the sickness. In such ways, although you could measure all the water in the four oceans, you could not measure the amount of flesh and blood I have given away for the sake of awakening.

"When I became the prince called Youthful Flower, I had my body pulverized and my marrow removed so that it could be used as an ointment on the body of a seriously ill person, whose illness was cured by this. In such ways, the amount of marrow I have donated for the sake of awakening is immeasurable, greater than all the water in the four oceans.

"When I became the king called Moonlight I gave my eyes to a sightless person. In such ways, I have donated innumerable eyes, greater in number than the particles that make up Mount Meru.

"When the bodhisattva Maitreya first began bodhisattva training, he wished to accomplish the unsurpassable, perfect awakening of buddhahood through an easy vehicle easily practiced on an easy path."

Ananda asked, "Bhagavat, what are the skillful means through which the bodhisattva Maitreya is easily accomplishing unsurpassable awakening?"

The buddha replied, "When Maitreya engaged in bodhisattva training, three times every day and night he devotedly brought all buddhas to mind and made aspirations. At the time of the bodhisattva Maitreya's engagement in bodhisattva training, beings had little of the three poisons and engaged in the ten virtuous actions. It was his aspiration to achieve buddhahood at such a time. Therefore through his aspirations, the mahabodhisattva Maitreya will achieve the unsurpassable, perfect awakening of manifest buddhahood at a time when beings have little of the three poisons and are engaged in the ten virtuous actions.

"Ananda, when I engaged in bodhisattva training I cultivated the aspiration, 'Why can't I achieve the unsurpassable awakening of buddhahood in a world of fivefold decadence among people whose three poisons are coarse and strong; who are attached to the unvirtuous; who are overwhelmed by passion; who are held in the embrace of inauthentic dharma; who conspire against their parents, siblings, and spouses; who hate their own preceptors, their own disciples, bodhisattvas, themselves, and others; who are stained, wild, and unwise?' During such awful times I aroused great compassion. With great compassion I taught dharma to the residents of villages, towns,

cities, and palaces. They denigrated me, reviled me, and spoke to me harshly and coarsely.

"Ananda, they accused me of teaching nihilism. They accused me of teaching eternalism. They said I just wanted to accumulate disciples. They called me greedy. When I stayed in their homes they threw dirt on me, fed me poisoned food, and tried to burn me alive. Even after my buddhahood they accused me of being as lustful as the courtesan Radiant Beauty!

"Ananda, I aroused great compassion, and with great compassion taught dharma to such beings."

Ananda said, "Bhagavat, by teaching dharma to such beings the tathagata took up the great burden of taming the untamed. You have done something difficult!"

The buddha replied, "It is so. I have done such difficult things because of great compassion."

From the *Avatamsakasutra*

The boy Source of Glory and the girl Shrimati said to Sudhana the merchant's son, "Son of family, at the seashore of this southern region is a grove of fruit trees called Mahadhvaja. Within it is a great mansion called Essence of the Ornaments of Vairochana. It was created by the ripening of bodhisattvas' roots of virtue. In it resides the bodhisattva Maitreya, in order to care for human beings and ripen bodhisattvas. Go to him and ask him about all the conduct of a bodhisattva. Why? Because Maitreya practices all bodhisattva training. He knows the minds and thoughts of all beings and is therefore able to act appropriately. He ripens all beings and helps them perfect the paramitas. He has achieved all the bodhisattva levels and all qualities. That spiritual friend will increase your roots of virtue, bodhichitta, bodhisattva faculties, and all qualities. He will teach you the conduct of Samantabhadra.

"Don't be complacent with your conduct, aspirations, and qualities. The deeds of bodhisattvas must become as perfectly innumerable as the realms of beings. Therefore you must never tire of the search for spiritual friends. All bodhisattva training depends on spiritual friends, comes from them, and is generated by them."

In that way they extolled the many qualities of spiritual friends and taught Sudhana at length how to rely upon spiritual friends, saying, "Therefore in order to meet spiritual friends, maintain ceaseless fervor that is never discouraged by any burden."

The bodhisattva Sudhana came to embody the utmost devotion to spiritual friends. He achieved immeasurable wisdom and searched with the eye of wisdom for the great mansion Essence of the Ornaments of Vairochana. Having found it, he threw his body to the ground at its door in prostration. Through the power of his benevolence and aspirations, he blessed himself so that he simultaneously appeared before all tathagatas, bodhisattvas, spiritual friends, stupas, gatherings of arhats, gurus, and his parents. In this way he filled the dharmadhatu, prostrating and bowing to them all unceasingly until the end of time. Sudhana, immersed in equality and other aspects of a bodhisattva's profound state, said:

"You've achieved great compassion and are utterly pure.
  Maitreya, splendid spiritual friend diligent in helping
    the world,
  Foremost empowered son of the victor,
  You contemplate and are attaining buddhahood.

"You've achieved the great wisdom and deeds
  Of renowned children of the victors.
  They move unimpededly throughout the dharmadhatu.
  Unsurpassed, you are just like them!"

Reciting that and other spontaneous verses, Sudhana was delighted at the prospect of seeing Maitreya. The bodhisattva Maitreya, however, was not within that mansion. He was returning from another place, where he had received the offerings of thousands of beings, including Indra, Brahma, the protectors of the world, and other rulers of devas, nagas, and yakshas. Maitreya was walking back to the mansion, surrounded by thousands of brahmins. Seeing him, Sudhana was overjoyed and threw himself upon the ground as he watched the bodhisattva's approach.

The bodhisattva Maitreya looked at Sudhana and then pointed to him with his right hand, saying to his companions:

"Look at this person with pure intentions,
  Sudhana, a child of the wealthy.
  Seeking the holy bodhisattva training,
  He has come to me, the wise."

Maitreya praised Sudhana with that and other verses. Then Sudhana seated himself before Maitreya and said, "Noble one, in order to achieve unsurpassable awakening, what bodhisattva training must I practice? In order to ask this, I approach you, Arya Maitreya, a bodhisattva who has passed through all the training and is in your last life preceding unsurpassable awakening. You are a flawless bodhisattva who has perfected all qualities such as the paramitas, patience, the bodhisattva levels, the doors to liberation, samadhi, retention, confidence, and supercognition. You hold the secret treasury of all buddhadharmas. You are the physician who heals the sickness of the kleshas of all beings. You are the best of beings, the ruler of all rulers of the world, the foremost among all bodhisattvas, the leader of all shravakas and pratyekabuddhas, and the ferryman who rows us all across the ocean of samsara. You appear in the mandalas of all buddhas and in all the realms of beings. You are unstained

by anything mundane. You are beyond all attacks by maras. You have reached all the qualities of buddhahood. You have achieved all the unobscured qualities of bodhisattvas. You rule the great kingdom of dharma and have received the empowerment of omniscient wisdom. As you have mastered omniscient wisdom, I ask you, noble one, to please tell me how to practice the bodhisattva training in order to achieve all buddhadharmas, fulfill the wishes of all beings, and ensure the continuity of the lineage of the three jewels."

The bodhisattva Maitreya looked at the mandala of his retinue, again pointed to Sudhana the merchant's son, and said, "This merchant's son Sudhana is irreversibly benevolent and diligent in his cultivation of the bodhisattva training. He is indefatigable in his search for and veneration of spiritual friends. He was sent by the youthful Manjushri to the town called Source of Glory. Starting there, he wandered all over the south and consulted a thousand virtuous friends. Finally, he has come to me. All this time, he has remained undiscouraged and benevolent. He has come here with firm commitment to the mahayana in order to save all beings."

Maitreya praised Sudhana extensively and then said to him, "Son of family, bodhichitta is like the seed of all buddhadharmas." Beginning with that, Maitreya extolled the qualities of bodhichitta using many analogies. He then said, "Son of family, since you ask how bodhisattvas should train, please enter this mansion called Essence of the Ornaments of Vairochana, and look about you. You will understand!"

Maitreya then snapped his fingers at the door of the mansion. The door opened, and Sudhana went inside. From the inside, Sudhana saw that the mansion was as vast as space and beautifully decorated, with innumerable features and ornaments. Within it were thousands of other mansions, each of them equal in size and features to the first. None of these mansions obscured or obstructed any of the others. They all appeared

identically like reflected images of one another. Seeing this tremendous display, Sudhana was even more delighted than before and prostrated. Through Maitreya's blessing, Sudhana experienced himself simultaneously entering each of the mansions and saw all of the many unimaginable miracles that were taking place within them.

In some of the mansions Sudhana saw the family of Maitreya's first birth as a bodhisattva, learned his name, about his family, how he created roots of virtue, and from which tathagata he received the generation of bodhichitta. Sudhana saw all of this and understood it. While seeing all this, Sudhana seemed to be actually present at all these events, and remained in the presence of that tathagata for the duration of that buddha's life and throughout the entire lives of all the beings involved.

In some mansions Sudhana witnessed Maitreya's first achievement of the samadhi of love and his acquisition of the name Maitreya. In some mansions Sudhana saw Maitreya's practice of the training, in some his perfection of the paramitas, in some his practice of patience, in some his achievement of the levels, in some his creation of buddha realms, in some his upholding of the buddhas' teachings, in some his achievement of patience with unborn dharmas, and in some his receipt of the prophecy of full awakening. In some of the mansions Sudhana saw Maitreya become a chakravartin who places beings on the path of the ten virtues. In some he saw Maitreya become a world ruler, and in some he saw him become Indra; Sudhana witnessed many different births in which Maitreya had helped beings.

In some of the mansions Sudhana saw Maitreya pacifying suffering in bad migrations. He saw him teach dharma in higher realms, such as those of devas. He saw him present various dharma gates to bodhisattvas of all levels, from beginners up to those on the tenth bhumi. Sudhana witnessed Maitreya's

immeasurable deeds, including discussing dharma, mastering crafts, chanting, writing holy dharma, and resting in innumerable samadhis. In some of the mansions Sudhana saw Maitreya simultaneously take the form of many bodhi sattvas. From every pore in the skin of every one of them emerged clouds of devas, yakshas, chakravartins, tathagatas, and countless different gates to dharma. In some mansions Sudhana saw many different tathagatas with their respective realms and mandalas.

Of all the mansions contained within the outer mansion, there was one that was larger than the rest. Within that mansion appeared all the worlds of this billionfold realm. Sudhana saw their billion sets of four continents and their billion Tushitas. In each of their billion Jambudvipas he saw a bodhisattva Maitreya take birth, achieve buddhahood, turn the dharmachakra, ripen beings tormented by their different sufferings, bless his teachings in various ways so that they remain, and finally pass into the deva abodes. In each of those billion worlds, Sudhana the merchant's son saw himself accompanying Maitreya in all his deeds and venerating him. Sudhana saw all of this and understood it all with perfect recollection.

From the strings and webs of larger and smaller bells that adorned all those mansions, and from all the musical instruments and singing heard within them issued an inconceivable variety of dharma, like thunder issuing from clouds of dharma. Hearing all of it, Sudhana heard the sound of teaching on bodhichitta in some mansions, the sound of teaching on how to practice the paramitas in some, and many different sounds of dharma in others. He heard all the sounds of various bodhisattvas first generating bodhichitta, of them attaining buddhahood, and of all their deeds throughout the duration of their teachings. Because of all this Sudhana achieved many qualities, such as retention and confidence.

All the other ornaments decorating the mansions produced

their own displays. In all the mirrors in the mansions Sudhana saw the images of various worlds — pure and impure — arising, remaining, and being destroyed. They showed all the beings inhabiting those worlds and all the deeds of bodhisattvas there. The strings of pearls emitted sprinkles of water with the eight attributes, deliciously fragrant with the scent of incense. The strings of vaidurya blazed like garlands of lamps. From the parasols came jewels, rich fabrics, and hanging nets of jewels. The pools were adorned by jeweled flowers of many colors and sizes. Reflected in the pools Sudhana saw devas, shravakas, pratyekabuddhas, various other beings bowing, and tathagatas seated with crossed legs.

All the vast ground within and between the mansions was made of vaidurya divided into squares. In each square Sudhana saw a different image displayed. He saw realms, tathagatas, bodhisattvas, and jeweled trees from which emerged the upper bodies of beings holding many different offerings. Within the semicircular openings in the mansions Sudhana saw countless suns, moons, stars, and planets in every direction. On all the walls of each of the mansions he saw displayed all the deeds of bodhisattvas.

In some of the squares that made up the ground Sudhana saw Maitreya giving away his head. In others he saw him give away his eyes, his body, his limbs, his children, spouse, land, and throne. Sudhana saw Maitreya free beings from prison. He saw him rescue beings as a ship and as a steed. He saw Maitreya's countless emanations as buddhas and beings, and his many different deeds in order to tame beings.

Sudhana saw every feature of those mansions and every image displayed within them — all those mentioned and countless others — with perfect recollection and the pure eyes of a bodhisattva's wisdom and blessing. The wisdom that arose upon seeing this tremendous display like a magical illusion, upon experiencing both the blessing of bodhisattvas and the

variety of the three realms, caused all other perceptions to cease for Sudhana. Sudhana saw all these wondrous deeds of bodhisattvas like someone dreaming of various places and things. A dreamer is unaware of the passing of time and even that they are dreaming. They nevertheless remember their dreams once they awake.

When someone is very ill, they may hallucinate that they pass from this life and experience their next life. If this is caused by wrongdoing, they will seem to burn in hell. Their suffering and its apparent duration will equal that of those actually born there. If their hallucination of a subsequent life is caused by virtuous actions, they will experience the pleasures of devas in the deva abodes for what will appear to be the same length of time as a deva's life span. In neither case, however, has the person actually died and been reborn. What is seen through a bodhisattva's blessing is like that. It is also like the hallucinations of someone possessed by a demon. The possessed person sees all sorts of things and can even answer any questions they are asked about the future.

The appearances perceived through a bodhisattva's blessing can seem to last for a long time. For example, someone who enters a naga's palace may experience remaining there for any amount of time from one day up to a hundred years. Once they have returned to the human realm, however, they will discover that they were absent for only a brief amount of time.

Just as all the appearances of these billion worlds are simultaneously and distinctly present as images in the palace of Mahabrahma called Best Decor of All, all of the mansions Sudhana saw and all their features were distinct. A bhikshu immersed in the experience of exhausting the elements or of pervasiveness will see and experience the inconceivable appearances of his meditation, no matter where he is or

whether he is seated or standing, for as long as the immersion continues. Sudhana saw all the various appearances of the individual mansions in a similar way.

The decorations and fabrics of a ghandharva city appear from space and do not obstruct one another or anything else. A yaksha's palace can arise within a human dwelling, or can contain one. In spite of their occupying the same space, they do not obstruct one another. Whichever of the two dwellings — human or yaksha — appears will depend upon the karma of the perceiver. All the billion worlds of a realm can appear as reflected images in a single ocean. An illusionist can display all sorts of things by using spells and devices.

Like these appearances, what was seen by Sudhana the merchant's son through the bodhisattva Maitreya's blessing — through the power and blessing of a bodhisattva immersed in the inconceivable wisdom of magical illusion — was the manifestation of magical illusion. It all arose through the power of the wisdom that knows all dharmas to be illusory. These appearances caused by that wisdom were seen by Sudhana as vast and vivid. He saw them, experienced them, examined them, and understood their attributes.

Then the bodhisattva Maitreya entered the main mansion and ended the display of blessing. He said to Sudhana, "Son of family, this is the dharmata of dharmas. All dharmas exist merely as appearances. The blessing of a bodhisattva's wisdom is nonexistent in its nature, like a magical illusion." Snapping his fingers, he woke Sudhana from his samadhi and asked him, "Did you see these bodhisattva miracles?"

Sudhana replied, "Noble spiritual friend, through your blessing I saw them! What is this miracle's name?"

Maitreya answered, "It is called Essence Ornament of

Undiminished Recollection, Awareness Penetrating All Concepts of the Three Times. Bodhisattvas in their final life before buddhahood have innumerable miraculous powers such as this."

Sudhana asked, "Noble one, where did all those decorations go?"

Maitreya replied, "They returned to their origin, through bodhisattva blessing. They neither come nor go. Nor do they remain anywhere. Nevertheless, they appear like magical illusions through the power of a bodhisattva's wisdom."

Sudhana then asked, "Noble one, how far have you traveled to get here?"

Maitreya replied, "Bodhisattvas travel without coming or going anywhere. It is like an optical illusion or a reflection. Son of family, in the land of my birth, called Garland of Strength, is a town called Homes, where there lives a merchant called Earth Guardian. Having led him to the buddhadharma, I taught dharma to the people of that land. I encouraged my parents, my relatives, and brahmins and householders in the mahayana. Then I came here."

Sudhana asked, "Noble one, what is the birthplace of bodhisattvas?"

Maitreya replied, "As one is born into the family of bodhisattvas through bodhichitta, bodhichitta is the birthplace of bodhisattvas. As one is born into the family of spiritual friends through benevolence, benevolence is the birthplace of bodhisattvas." In that way, Maitreya spoke of ten birthplaces of bodhisattvas. Then he continued, "Skillful means is the father of bodhisattvas. Prajnaparamita is their mother." He explained that by entering the flawless family of bodhisattvas, one passes far beyond the level of the childish and,

experiencing things as magical illusions, has control over such things as birth.

Then he said, "Son of family, in that way my emanations fill the dharmadhatu. They appear in every place where beings are born, with bodies identical to those beings in shape and color. My emanations are of varying types, names, behaviors, and births. I have been born in this Jambudvipa in order to ripen beings previously connected to me who have abandoned bodhichitta; in order to tame those born in the brahmin caste, including my parents and relatives, in the town called Homes in the southern area called Garland of Strength; and in order to free those with caste pride from that pride and bring them into the family of the tathagata. I tame beings in this southern region by these means while living in this mansion. After my death I will demonstrate birth in Tushita in order to tame those born there as devas, in order to be in the company of bodhisattvas in their final life, and in order to open the lotuses of the tathagata Shakyamuni's disciples. When my intentions have all been achieved, and at the proper time, I will attain omniscience. After my awakening, son of family, both you and the youthful Manjushri will see me again."

From the *Maitreyasutra*

After the nirvana of the tathagata Shakyamuni, his teaching will remain for five thousand years, divided into periods of fruition, practice, tradition, and vestiges. After those periods, and after his teachings have disappeared, there will be a period called Time of Relics, during which the only remnant of the buddha's teachings will be the veneration of his remains. After that period has ended, human behavior will degenerate. Wrongdoing will increase. Human life span will decrease until it is ten years. At that time there will occur epochs of famine, sickness, and war. Most people will die during these. The few remaining will become so desperate that their minds will turn

90. Uttarakuru is
the northern conti-
nent. The implica-
tion of the text is
that the life span
there exceeds eighty
thousand years.

to virtue. This will cause human life span to gradually increase. People will become happier and happier until they will be like the inhabitants of Uttarakuru.[90] Human life span will then gradually decrease again until it is eighty thousand years. At that time Maitreya will appear.

The mahabodhisattva Maitreya perfected the paramita of generosity and the thirty paramitas for sixteen periods of novemdecillion kalpas and more than one hundred thousand additional kalpas. In his last life, having been born as Liberates All, he completed the practice of the paramitas by performing the great generosity of giving away his body. Upon the destruction of that body, he was reborn in Tushita. At the end of his present life in Tushita, he will be born in Jambudvipa in the royal palace called Spire to his father — the brahmin Brahmabhadra, the chaplain of the chakravartin called Conch — and his mother, Purity.

When he enters his mother's womb, ten thousand realms of worlds will vibrate. After ten months Maitreya will be born in the Deer Park at Varanasi. Through his merit, four mansions composed of the seven jewels will appear on the ground. Maitreya will inhabit these for one thousand years, enjoying the pleasures of the devas in the company of the devi Moonface and many other women, all of them as lovely as devis. On the day after one thousand years have passed, Maitreya will see a renunciate. He will come to dislike the mansions and will give rise to renunciation. When he does so, devas from ten thousand billionfold realms will gather around his mansions bearing divine flowers. King Conch and other great beings will also gather there, all of them bearing various offerings. The devas in the sky will all say, "Excellent!" The sound of this will be heard all the way to Akanishtha. Then the mansions will rise into the sky, spinning like potter's wheels. Like the moon surrounded by stars, the bodhisattva Maitreya and his consorts will fly off into space.

Accompanied by Mahabrahma, who will hold a white parasol one hundred thousand yojanas in diameter; Indra the devas' ruler, who will blow a conch; and many splendid and fortunate devis, Maitreya will travel to his awakening tree, which will be a naga tree. That tree will be one hundred twenty cubits in height. Its branches will cover a diameter equal to that. It will produce the most fragrant flowers. They will lie piled on the ground around the tree after they have fallen, emitting a delicious fragrance that will fill an area ten yojanas in diameter.

When Maitreya reaches the site of his awakening, all the land around it will be pleasant. Diverse birds will offer him their sweet calls. Maitreya will stay there for seven days, becoming a renunciate. The accessories of a renunciate will be offered to him by Mahabrahma. Maitreya's entire retinue will also become renunciates.

One day, the devi Moonface will offer Maitreya sweet fruit, which he will accept. That evening, he will sit down with crossed legs in front of the bodhi tree, facing east. He will immediately achieve unsurpassable wisdom. He will then remain seated in front of the tree for forty-nine days. Then Brahma will supplicate him to turn the dharmachakra. Accordingly, Maitreya will go to the Deer Park at Varanasi. Wherever he places his feet, lotuses will appear. Their petals will be thirty cubits in length, their lesser petals twenty-five cubits, their inner rings twenty cubits, and their centers sixteen cubits.

The light of that tathagata's body will surpass all other light, so that day and night will be indistinguishable from one another. One will only be able to tell day from night by the call of birds and the opening and closing of lotuses. The bhagavat buddha Maitreya will be eighty-eight cubits and one fist in height. From his feet to his knees, from his knees

to his navel, from his navel to his clavicle, and from his clavicle to the top of his head will each be twenty-two cubits. The distance from one of his shoulders to the other will be twenty-five cubits. His clavicle will be five cubits long on each side. The distance between his ears will be seven cubits. His eyes will each be five cubits wide. His eyebrows will each be five cubits long. There will be five cubits between his eyebrows. His nose will be seven cubits long. His upper and lower lips will each be ten cubits wide. His tongue will be five cubits wide. His ushnisha will be five cubits high. His face, like a mirror of gold, will be twenty-five cubits in width. His throat will be five cubits. Each of his two arms will be forty-two cubits long.

That peerless buddha, that tathagata, will turn the dharmachakra for the devas, and then the humans, of ten thousand worlds. Those wishing to see him then should now venerate the three jewels and engage as much as they can in the ten virtuous actions.

THE FOURTH CHAPTER: THE REGENT AJITA

THE PROTECTOR AKASHAGARBHA

I PROSTRATE TO THE BODHISATTVA MAHASATTVA
AKASHAGARBHA![91] I VENERATE YOU! I TAKE REFUGE IN YOU!

From the *Arya Akashagarbha Mahayana Sutra*

The bhagavat once stayed on Mount Khaladeya, accompanied by countless shravakas and bodhisattvas. At that time he predicted the tathagata Shrisamaya. Immediately thereafter a wish-fulfilling jewel appeared in the western sky, surrounded by millions of sapphires. The light of this jewel was so bright that it outshone all visible forms in these billion worlds. With the single exception of the tathagata's body, the bodies of all beings and the forms of the four elements disappeared in this light. Everything became a boundless expanse of space. No matter where you looked, all you could see was space, the resplendent body of the tathagata, and the light of those jewels. Your own body, those of others, and the light and form of the sun or moon were all invisible. Even the perception of your mind and its contents as "me" and "mine," and the perceptions of the six senses did not occur.

Other than those bodhisattvas on the tenth level who had achieved the heroic samadhi and were in their last life before

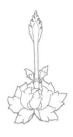

awakening, all the bodhisattvas, shravakas, devas, and others in that gathering became terrified. Unable to tell "here" from "there," they became agitated. Unable to see one another or anything else, they were too overcome to even ask themselves what was happening.

The bodhisattva Spike of Brahma bowed to the bhagavat and said, "This great miracle has bewildered this gathering. I pray that you reassure us. Surely this is a sign of the presence here of great bodhisattvas and heralds profound teaching!"

The buddha replied, "It is so." As soon as he said that, everyone in that gathering became able to see everything as before. Then the bhagavat stretched out his right hand and said, "The bodhisattva mahasattva Akashagarbha's samadhis are like the ocean. His bodhisattva training is like Mount Meru. His wisdom is like space. His diligence is like the wind. His patience is like a vajra. He is like the greatest victory banner among bodhisattvas, like a guide in leading all beings to nirvana, like a treasury of all virtues, like a vase of riches for all who suffer from poverty, like the sun for all who wander in darkness, like the moon for those who have lost their way, like Mount Meru for the fearful, like medicinal elixir for those tormented by the sickness of the kleshas, like a staff for those fallen from virtue, like a flower for those who weave garlands, like a mirror for those with vows, like clothing for those with modesty and a conscience, like a shelf from which one could climb to nirvana, like a boat for crossing to the other side of samsara, like a stairway to heaven, like a parasol shielding the reviled from abuse, like a lion defending those under attack, like water for those needing rain, like armor for those at war with maras, like opened eyes for those confused about the training, like the earth on which ripens all fruits of virtue, like medicine for the sick, like grain for the starving, like water crystal for the thirsty, like a bed for the exhausted, like a fire crystal for those with samadhi, like a chariot for those on the path to awakening, like a pool for those playing in a park, and like a garland for those cultivating the factors of awakening.[92]

"He is coming here.

"This son of family Akashagarbha is like the fruition of the paramitas, like a wish-fulfilling jewel for those on the ten levels, like a tree around which all those with the heroic samadhi gather, like a weapon that cuts through all bad views, and like a vajra that crushes all habitual kleshas. He is invincible to maras. Like the astrological calculations of the skilled, he unlocks wisdom. He is the abode of all buddhadharmas. He is like a mala for pratyekabuddhas, like robes for all shravakas, like eyes for the devas, and like a road for humans. He is the refuge of animals, a support for pretas, a protector for hell beings, and a fit vessel for the generosity of all beings. He is like a chariot for bodhisattvas, like a minister for all the buddhas of the three times, and like a gatekeeper of the city of dharma.

"This son of family Akashagarbha is adorned by all buddhadharmas including the eighteen unique attributes of buddhas. He has all the wisdom of a perfect buddha. This son of family is a holy object of worship for all beings other than the tathagata. Therefore all of you, welcome him! Venerate him! Serve him! You will acquire special qualities like his."

Everyone in that gathering arose and joined their palms, gazing expectantly in the direction from which the mahabodhisattva Akashagarbha was approaching. They all thought, "With what wondrous display of offerings shall we serve this son of family?"

Through the bodhisattva Akashagarbha's power this entire realm of Saha was transformed into a realm of equality, made entirely of the seven jewels. Its trees and other decorations were also made of the seven jewels. All suffering such as that

92. The seven factors of awakening are: recollection, discernment, diligence, joy, pliancy, equanimity, and samadhi.

of the three lower states and of sickness ceased. Everyone acquired food, clothing, jewelry, and all they needed. Every being became beautiful. Their wishes were all fulfilled. Their kleshas were pacified. They gained faith in the three jewels.

A jewel appeared in the hands of each member of that gathering. The light of these jewels illuminated this entire realm of Saha, which resounded with music. A great rain of diverse jewels, fabrics, ornaments, flowers, incense, garlands, and parasols fell. The road was covered with deva fabrics, flowers, and snakeheart sandalwood powder. To the road's right and left appeared mansions like the Palace of Victory, made from the seven jewels and filled with maidens like the wives of the ruler of the desire realm. All the maidens played cymbals with five attributes and danced gracefully.

Above the bhagavat's head appeared a parasol like Mahabrahma's, made of jewels and a hundred yojanas in diameter. It was decorated by webs and strings of jewels and pearls. The sounds of music beyond even that of devas issued from it. From all the grass, trees, flowers, and fruit came the sounds of melodious praises. Anyone who heard them became irreversible from the achievement of unsurpassable awakening.

Seeing this tremendous display, that entire gathering was amazed. They thought, "What seat shall we set out for such a holy being?" As they thought that, an enormous lotus flower with a diameter of two thousand cubits, composed of various jewels, appeared before the bhagavat. It was surrounded by millions of other lotus seats. Seated on the principal lotus with crossed legs was Akashagarbha. A brilliant jewel appeared above his head. The millions of mahabodhisattvas accompanying Akashagarbha — all of whom had achieved the heroic samadhi and were adorned by sapphires — appeared seated on their respective lotuses.

The bodhisattva Maitreya said then to the bodhisattva

Bhaishajyaraja, "All well-known bodhisattvas first prostrate to our teacher, and only then take their seats. This holy being, however, created this great display and then appeared already seated without prostrating to our teacher!"

Bhaishajyaraja replied, "This holy being dwells in the buddhadharmas. He does not dwell within any thought. He therefore does not see beings. Nevertheless, in order to ripen beings, he skillfully exhibits deeds such as this."

The bhagavat said then to the bodhisattva Bhaishajyaraja, "Excellent! Holy being, it is just as you said. All beings combined could not understand the experience, deeds, or liberation of any one stream-enterer. Therefore consider this: If all beings became stream-enterers, all of them combined could not understand the experience and so forth of any one once-returner. In the same way, once-returners do not understand the experience of nonreturners. Nonreturners do not understand the experience of arhats. Arhats do not understand the experience of pratyekabuddhas. Even if all beings became rhinoceros-like pratyekabuddhas, all of them combined could not understand the experience of a single bodhisattva who had achieved patience with unborn dharmas. Even if all beings became bodhisattvas with patience for unborn dharmas, all of them combined could not understand the experience, intentions, realization of absolute truth, or blessing of a single bodhisattva who had achieved discernment and the heroic samadhi.

"Countless kalpas have passed since this son of family, the mahabodhisattva Akashagarbha, achieved patience with unborn dharmas, discernment, and the heroic samadhi. Knowing the thoughts and dormant tendencies of my disciples, he has come here from the west for your benefit. He caught the attention of all beings by displaying a samadhi of boundless space unlike that of shravakas or pratyekabuddhas. Then in order to ripen innumerable beings, he revealed this

vast display of relative truth and samadhi. If this son of family revealed absolute truth, patience with unborn dharmas, the entire world including the devas would go mad! Everyone up to bodhisattvas on the eighth level would go mad. Therefore he cannot reveal the experience or attributes of absolute truth. Nevertheless, he dwells in its qualities.

"This son of family knows means. He dwells in all buddhadharmas. He is without doubt. His wisdom is independent of others. He is the greatest victory banner among bodhisattvas. He is like their king. This mahabodhisattva Akashagarbha shows all beings how to be reborn in higher states and reach liberation. He frees them from the mental illness of the kleshas. He heals the physical illnesses caused by the poison of the great elements. If someone polluted by incorrect views and ignorant of the path to higher states and liberation prostrates to Akashagarbha, offers him fragrant agaru incense, and prays to him, that person's past roots of virtue will be revealed to them in a way suited to their thinking and dormant tendencies. Akashagarbha will reveal them skillfully either while the person is awake or in dreams. This will quickly free the person from incorrect views, aspirations, objects of reliance, and so on. The behavior of their three gates, their aspirations, and their choice of spiritual friends will become correct. They will have a fine fragrance. They will be freed from kleshas and from all the karma that causes migration to lower states. They will gain control of their own mind and will discover the means to achieve patience with the profound.

"Also, if any being tormented by physical sickness, by mental distraction, by defective eyes or other sense organs, or by any physical impairment prays to Akashagarbha for relief, he will appear to them in dreams. He may take the form of a brahmin, or of Indra, or of Sarasvati, or of a minister of royal caste, or a physician, or either of the being's parents, or their son, or their daughter. In that form he will reveal to them medicine and other resources. By applying them, the being will be healed from all sickness.

"In the same way, if anyone who wants helpers, wealth, dependable resources, longevity, power, beauty, children, servants, wisdom, fame, holiness, family, qualities, gentle speech, harmony with others, freedom from wrongdoing, the virtue of recitation, learning, skill in crafts, solitude, meditation, or the six paramitas prays to Akashagarbha, he will teach them how to achieve them. He will fulfill their wishes.

"If those who wish to establish others in the paramitas, such as by transforming avaricious people into generous ones; or those wishing to establish other beings in perfect awakening, skillful means, the four immeasurables, or great compassion pray to the bodhisattva Akashagarbha, he will appear to them in a form appropriate to them and show them how to accomplish their aim. Through the means he has shown them they will, with little effort, irreversibly establish countless beings — those not involved in any vehicle and those involved in the shravakayana or pratyekabuddhayana — in the unsurpassable mahayana. They will be able to establish those beings in samadhi, retention, various aspects of patience, and even the ten levels. In that way Akashagarbha has inconceivable means, wisdom, and compassion.

"Son of family, there are some who could measure the extent of space. They could not, however, measure Akashagarbha's means, wisdom, compassion, samadhi, strength, or ripening of beings. His qualities are inconceivable. This son of family loves beings who are honest and upright; who have true devotion; who do not praise themselves or disparage others; who are without jealousy, avarice, and hypocrisy; and are benevolent. He will teach them means, wisdom, diligence, and discipline. They will be freed from suffering. They will generate unsurpassable bodhichitta. They will dedicate their virtue to awakening. They will be irreversible from the pursuit of

unsurpassable awakening. They will perfect the six paramitas with great enthusiasm and discipline. They will quickly achieve buddhahood. In this way, Akashagarbha's qualities are inconceivable. He ripens all beings."

Then the bodhisattva Maitreya asked the bhagavat, "Bhagavat, why does this son of family wear a great wish-fulfilling jewel on top of his head? He is more resplendent than other bodhisattvas."

The buddha replied, "Son of family, the bodhisattva Akashagarbha has great compassion. He lives to help beings. He frees them from great suffering. He awakens the dormant virtue of beings who have incurred root downfalls and would otherwise migrate to lower states. Akashagarbha heals those beings who have been abandoned by all the wise and who are without refuge or protector. He dispels the fog of bad views and frees beings from doubt. He shows them the path. He cleanses them of all their foul-smelling wrongdoing. He turns them away from bad karma. He places them in higher states and liberation. He closes the door to bad migrations for beings whose minds are immersed in intense desire; or disturbed by extreme anger, malice, or avarice; or so shrouded by thick stupidity that they are nihilistic — beings without fear of future lives, insatiably greedy for wealth and such things, and constantly engaged in the ten unvirtuous actions. He places them in higher states and liberation. This holy being is worthy of worship by all beings other than tathagatas, all in the world including devas.

"The bodhisattva Akashagarbha will appear in various forms to those who have incurred any of the five downfalls to which kings are prone, such as stealing the wealth of the three jewels; or the five to which ministers are prone; or the eight downfalls to which commoners and beginners are prone — anyone who has incurred any of the root downfalls of a bodhisattva — and to those who have incurred a root down-fall of a shravaka. Akashagarbha will teach them profound sutras. Those kings and the others, with broken hearts filled with regret and shame for their previous karma, will confess and abandon their wrongdoing. They will enthusiastically enter the path of virtue. Akashagarbha will thus place them in higher states and liberation.

"Therefore if those who wish to confess root downfalls burn fine incense such as agarwood or melilotus at dawn, call Akashagarbha by name, and pray to him, he will appear to them in dreams in a form appropriate to them. He will teach them both the means of arising from their downfalls and the skillful means of the mahayana. He will place them in sama-dhi, patience, retention, and even the levels. They will remain stably within the mahayana. They will be irreversible from the pursuit of unsurpassable awakening. They will develop unflagging diligence for the perfection of the six paramitas. Those beginner bodhisattvas will immediately achieve wis-dom, skillful means, and the samadhi of never forgetting bodhichitta. They will shortly achieve buddhahood. Because he lifts up those who have incurred downfalls and places them in unsurpassable awakening, Akashagarbha bears a wish-ful-filling jewel on his head as a sign of his extreme heroism.

"Son of family, beings who hear Akashagarbha's name, or cause images of him to be painted, or worship such an image, or serve it, or venerate it, or respect it, or make offerings to it, or prostrate to it, or offer their lives to it will not be killed by fire, water, weapons, or poison. They will die naturally; no human or nonhuman will be able to kill them. They will not die prematurely. They will not become invalids. They will not die from hunger or thirst. They will not be executed by rulers. They will incur no root downfalls during the rest of this life. At the time of death, as soon as their senses have ceased to function but before their consciousness leaves their bodies,

Akashagarbha will appear to them in whatever form they have imagined in their devotion, such as a brahmin or as Indra. He will teach them the four truths. Understanding them, they will be reborn in higher states. For those among them with faith in the buddha, Akashagarbha will appear as a buddha and teach them dharma. They will die in a state of joy, thinking of the buddha, and will be reborn in a pure buddha realm. To those with faith mainly in the dharma or the sangha, he will appear and teach accordingly.

"If those who wish to master various samadhis with their mind, or wish to read various teachings by the buddha or commentaries on them, or wish for recollection, or to enter the depths of the vast ocean of dharma, or enjoy its holy essence pray to Akashagarbha, their wishes will be fulfilled. If those who wish to be freed from sufferings such as illness, imprisonment, torture, execution, burning, drowning, poison, weapons, curses, attack by tigers or lions, robbery, fraud, separation from those they love, or encountering those unfriendly to them; or the impoverished who lack even dharma robes, alms, and sustenance pray to Akashagarbha with minds of love, call him by name, and make whatever offerings they can, he will appear before them in whatever form is appropriate and reassure them. He will free them from all their suffering. He will fulfill all their wishes. He will give them everything they need. If princes who wish to be enthroned as kings; or those who wish for greatness as brahmins or householders; or those who wish for greatness in crafts, learning, or meditation call Akashagarbha by name and pray to him, he will hear them with his divine ear and will teach them how to fulfill their wishes.

"Son of family, Akashagarbha has the quality of means. His intelligence is like a great ocean. It might be possible for someone to measure an ocean, drop by drop, or to measure the boundless reaches of space in every direction, but no one could

count the number of the mahabodhisattva Akashagarbha's diverse emanations in order to ripen beings. To some he appears as a buddha, but he can also appear to animals as an animal and to hell beings as a hell being. He emanates whatever form, such as that of a brahmin, will tame beings. To some beings his emanations appear in reality, to some in dreams, and to some as an object of cognition at the time of death. He cleanses beings of the karma of wrongdoing and frees them from bad migrations. He places them anywhere from higher states up to great awakening. Therefore because Akashagarbha has means, wisdom, and all the great qualities of buddhas, a wish-fulfilling jewel appears above his head."

After the buddha finished speaking, everyone in that gathering, awed, presented offerings to Akashagarbha. Akashagarbha presented all those offerings to the bhagavat buddha. He prostrated to the buddha and conversed with him about dharma. When Akashagarbha then proclaimed his dharani, countless devas and humans achieved samadhi, retention, diverse aspects of patience, and the wisdoms of the ten levels. Ten thousand beings achieved patience with unborn dharmas.

The bhagavat said to Akashagarbha, "You have the ability and compassion to teach many mahayana sutras to beings in countless worlds by displaying diverse forms, costumes, and behaviors in villages, towns, cities, valleys, counties, and royal palaces; to ripen beings; and to cause ignoble beings, everyone from ignoble royalty to ignoble renunciates, to give up wrongdoing and take up virtue."

From the *Sutra of Great Liberation*

The bodhisattva mahasattva Akashagarbha will, during the future kalpa called Pure Thousand, in the world realm called Luxurious, attain buddhahood as the tathagata arhat samyaksambuddha Pure Ornament. The mahabodhisattvas in that

world realm will practice only the mahayana. Any being who hears Akashagarbha's name, prostrates to him, and makes offerings will be born in that world realm, Luxurious. They will practice mahayana dharma there and achieve patience for unborn dharmas.

From the *Benefits of the Hundred and Eight Names of Akashagarbha*

Therefore all who wish for permanent happiness,
Rely always upon Akashagarbha —
The three worlds' protector, uniquely heroic
In rescuing beings — and upon his mantra.

THE FIFTH CHAPTER: THE PROTECTOR AKASHAGARBHA

THE BODHISATTVA KSHITIGARBHA

པ་འཆི་རྒྱལ་པོ

I PROSTRATE TO THE BODHISATTVA MAHASATTVA
KSHITIGARBHA!⁹³ I VENERATE YOU! I TAKE REFUGE IN YOU!

93. Kshitigarbha means "essence of earth."

From the *Kshitigarbhadasachakrasutra*

At one time the bhagavat resided on Mount Khaladeya — the abode of many rishis and sages — together with a sangha of bhikshus and an immeasurably great sangha of bodhisattvas. Immediately after the buddha taught the *Chandragarbha-sutra*, a vast cloud of fragrance appeared from the south. From the cloud fell rains of scented water, flowers, jewelry of divine origin, and fine fabrics, covering that whole mountain. From that rain issued diverse melodious sounds of dharma. Everyone present at that gathering found that their bodies had become adorned by their favorite fragrance and jewelry. Each of them discovered a wish-fulfilling jewel between the palms of their hands. Each of these jewels was producing a steady stream of other jewels. From all these jewels shone light rays of many colors, illuminating as many buddha realms in the ten directions as the Ganges' sand grains. In each of these realms could be seen their respective tathagatas attended by their immeasurable retinues. The light from these jewels also dispelled the suffering of sickness for all the beings

in all those realms. Any being about to be killed or imprisoned, or engaged in wrongdoing, or suffering from hunger or
thirst, or suffering through torture became freed from suffering as soon as the light struck them. They acquired all the
clothing, jewelry, and wealth that they wanted. They all abandoned the ten unvirtuous actions, and acquired whatever they
wished for. All of their suffering was pacified; they became
extremely happy.

As all of those realms became filled with the light of these jewels, everything unpleasant in those realms — such as clouds,
dust, wind, rainstorms, and inauspicious sounds — and everything dangerous or harmful within them disappeared, as did
all bad karma, inappropriate speech, and wrong thinking. The
ground in those realms became as smooth as the palm of a
hand and covered by everything that brings pleasure. All of
those realms became pleasantly temperate, without any suffering from heat or cold. While seeing all this, everyone in that
gathering also discovered that the earth element in their bodies was becoming heavier and heavier until they could no
longer support their own weight. They all began to wonder
what was causing these signs.

Indra, the ruler of devas, who was also called Stainless Birth,
was present at that gathering. He asked the bhagavat, "What
is causing all this?"

The bhagavat replied, "There is a bodhisattva mahasattva
called Kshitigarbha. He has ripened beings throughout countless kalpas during times of fivefold degeneracy in worlds without buddhas. He is coming to this world now, in the form of
a renunciate and accompanied by a large retinue of bodhisattvas, in order to prostrate and present offerings to me and
in order to view the mandala of my retinue. These miracles
are happening through his power. The mahabodhisattva
Kshitigarbha is adorned by immeasurable, innumerable,
inconceivable qualities. No one in the world — not even a

shravaka or pratyekabuddha — could appraise them. This bodhisattva is a treasure of all perfect qualities. He is a source of precious liberation. He purifies the vision of bodhisattvas. He guides beings to nirvana. Like a wish-fulfilling jewel, he fulfills hopes by raining down everything that is desired. He is like the island of jewels sought by many merchants, like a fertile field in which all roots of virtue can grow, like a vessel containing the bliss of liberation, like a good vase in being the source of all precious qualities, like the sun in that he provides light to all who seek virtue, like a beacon for the lost, like the moon in that he dispels torment by kleshas, like a mount for the lame, like a conveyance for those on a long journey, like a guide through the wilderness, like medicine for the insane, like a skilled physician for the gravely ill, like a staff and support for the aged, like a bed for the weary, like a bridge that spans the four rivers of suffering, and like a boat that conveys you across the water.

"Like the earth, he ripens the three types of roots of virtue and continuously gives forth the fruits of virtue. His generosity is as unceasing as the turning of a wheel. His morality is as stable as Mount Meru. His diligence is as indestructible as a vajra. His patience is as unshakable as the great earth. His meditation is as deep as a mine. His even placement is as beautiful as a flower garland. His wisdom is as vast and deep as a great ocean. Like space, he is free from attachment to anything. Like a flower in bloom, his fruition reveals the goodness of its cause. He is like a king of lions in his taming of tirthikas. He is like a naga or an elephant in his defeat of devaputramara. Like a divine sword, he cuts through all the kleshas' noise. Like the pratyekabuddhayana, he embodies sadness toward distractions. Like pure water, he washes away the stains of the kleshas. Like a tornado, he blows away the garbage of impurity. Like a sharp weapon, he cuts off access to affliction. Like a friend or family member, he protects from fear and anxiety. Like a trench or fortress, he protects against

attack. Like parents, he frees from all terror. Like a dense for-est, he shields the weak and timid. He is like a shady tree for those on a long summer journey, like cool water for those tor-mented by heat and thirst, like ripe grain for the hungry, like clothing for the naked, like a dense cloud for those menaced by heat, like a wish-fulfilling jewel for the poor, like a place of safety for the endangered, like rain for crops, and like a water-cleansing jewel for polluted water.

"As he protects the roots of virtue of many beings, he delights and satisfies those around him with his holy behavior. He encourages beings to be subdued and conscientious. He adorns others' accumulation of merit and wisdom. He is like a purgative in purging kleshas, like the experience of even placement in calming the agitation of others' minds, like a windmill in his unstoppable confidence, like the thought of beauty in his concentration, like Mount Meru in the stability of his patience, like a great ocean in the vastness and depth of his retention, and like space in the unobstructedness of his miraculous powers. He destroys obscuring habits like the hot sun melting ice. He is always engaged in meditation, the form-less states, and the perfect path. His omniscient wisdom is like an island of jewels; without trying to he is always turning the great dharmachakra. Son of family, the bodhisattva maha-sattva Kshitigarbha's qualities are immeasurable, countless, and unimaginable."

Immediately after the buddha finished praising him, the mahabodhisattva Kshitigarbha miraculously arrived from the south. Accompanied by a retinue of eight septillion bodhi-sattvas, he appeared before the bhagavat in the form of a renunciate. Kshitigarbha prostrated to the buddha's feet, praised him, presented offerings to him, and sat in front of him in order to hear dharma. The others in that gathering pre-sented offerings and praise to Kshitigarbha.

Present in that gathering was a mahabodhisattva called

Rational Questioner of Doubt. He bowed to the bhagavat and asked him, "Bhagavat, from where has this son of family come? How far from this realm does he live? How extensive are his qualities and roots of virtue? The bhagavat has praised him in many ways, and he has also praised the bhagavat's inconceivable ocean of qualities. As I have never seen him before and am amazed, I pray that the bhagavat explain these things."

The bhagavat replied, "Son of family, let it go! All the devas and humans in the world could not appraise the extent of this holy being's qualities and roots of virtue. If the tathagata were to explain the qualities and roots of virtue of this great being, all the devas and humans in the world would become bewildered. They would not believe it!"

The bodhisattva Rational Questioner of Doubt continued to insistently pray for an explanation. Finally the bhagavat said, "Listen well and remember! I will partially explain these things to you. This great being's qualities and roots of virtue are immeasurable and inconceivable. He remains at ease in a special type of heroic samadhi, and has fully realized what it is to be a tathagata. He has achieved a special type of patience with unborn dharmas and has mastered all buddhadharmas. He has achieved the patience of omniscient wisdom and has reached the other shore of omniscient wisdom. He remains within the samadhi called Majestic Lion's Victory Banner and has climbed the mountain of omniscient wisdom. He has defeated all aggression and tirthikas. In order to ripen all beings he inhabits all buddha realms. All buddha realms reflect this great being's state.

"For example, when in a particular realm Kshitigarbha enters the samadhi called Manifest Birth of Wisdom, that samadhi causes all the beings within that buddha realm to see the same things he does in his samadhi. Any buddha realm in which he is present becomes the reflection of his state at the time. When

he enters the samadhi called Immeasurable Wisdom, all the beings in that realm present immeasurable holy offerings to the bhagavat buddha of that realm. When Kshitigarbha enters the samadhi called Perfect Pure Wisdom, or the samadhi called Conscientious Wisdom, or the samadhi called Illumination of All Vehicles, or any other samadhi, all the beings within that realm enter that same state. Seeing the flaws in their usual behavior, they achieve purity of mind. Becoming extremely cautious in their behavior, they are freed from wrongdoing and thereby succeed in the achievement of their wishes. They attain the eye of skillful miracles and other supercognitions. They are freed from all misery, sadness, and depression. Freed from darkness, they actually see all the buddhas in the ten directions. Without wrong views, they take refuge in those buddhas. In their realm all the mountains, precipices, poison, predators, and all other defects disappear. The ground becomes even and adorned by many fine features. The kings of maras and their retinues become frightened and take refuge in the three jewels. All the beings in that realm are freed from fear of their future lives; they delight in dharma. All those beings acquire food and drink according to their wishes. They are strong and free from illness. They possess whatever seats, beds, clothing, and jewelry they desire, all of it pleasing. They are at ease in both body and mind. They are without enemies or restrictions. They are harmonious and joyful. They perfect the six paramitas. They have wisdom that is utterly joyous and unstoppable. Their faculties are complete and unimpaired. They are saddened by wrongdoing. Their minds are tranquil through their perfect engagement in the ten virtuous actions. They compassionately assist one another. They are free from war, sickness, and famine. All unpleasant sensations — such as unseasonable winds and rain — are absent there.

"In such ways, by entering various samadhis Kshitigarbha brings various benefits. When he enters the samadhi called

Ocean Lightning, all the ground in that buddha realm is transformed into various jewels and becomes free from imperfections. The realm comes to be adorned by jewel trees and countless other fine resources, ornaments, and musical instruments. Briefly stated, this son of family enters as many samadhis as the Ganges' sand grains every morning in order to ripen many beings. When he arises from them, he helps and ripens beings in every buddha realm in the ten directions, using whatever means necessary to tame them.

"This son of family has for countless kalpas ripened beings in worlds of fivefold degeneracy that are without tathagatas. In the future, when in some worlds the danger of war occurs and beings are tormented, this son of family will see it and enter samadhis in the morning that will dispel all danger and cause the beings in that world to love one another. Similarly, when the danger of sickness or famine arises, he will pacify those sufferings as well. This son of family is of immeasurable and inconceivable help to beings through his many samadhis. He brings them to happiness. Kshitigarbha made solemn and unbreakable promises in the presence of countless buddhas, as many bhagavats as the Ganges' sand grains, to protect all beings. He generated great compassion and unflagging diligence. These have increased steadily, so that he now tames a quintillion ordinary beings at every moment, freeing them from their respective suffering and fulfilling their individual wishes and hopes.

"If beings anywhere who are tormented by various desires pray one-pointedly to the bodhisattva Kshitigarbha, call him by name, and worship him with devotion, they will acquire whatever they desire, become free from suffering, and will either be born as devas in higher realms or achieve nirvana, depending on their condition. If those lacking food, drink, clothing, jewelry, or other things pray to him they will acquire whatever they desire and achieve states up to nirvana.

"If those separated from those they love; or those who have encountered hate-filled enemies; or those whose bodies and minds are tormented by illness; or those at war; or those who are imprisoned; or those who are being physically abused or are about to be killed; or the weak and powerless of body and mind; or those whose faculties are incomplete or impaired; or those struck by demons caused by insanity; or those whose bodies and minds are tormented by kleshas they cannot let go of, such as attachment or anger; or those who are terrified by dangers such as fire, water, and falling over precipices; or those menaced by aggressive snakes, predators, or any form of poison; or those who tremble and have impaired memory, struck by contagious illnesses caused by elemental spirits; or those who are attacked by yakshas, rakshasas, other nonhumans, humans, predators, wrathful beings, mantras, curses, or warfare — anyone who is tormented physically or mentally by any type of danger — call Kshitigarbha by name and worship him, they will soon be freed from their suffering. They will achieve the happiness for which they hope.

"If those who desire and hope for learning, motivation, morality, meditation, supercognition, wisdom, liberation, beauty or any of the five desirables, profit, wealth, fame, merit, craftsmanship, flowers, fruit, gardens, seats, mats, livestock, grain, medicine, travel, a home, servants, paints, rain, crops, warm weather, cool weather, fans, fire, conveyances, children, skill, goodness, honesty, or anything in the world or beyond it call the bodhisattva Kshitigarbha by name one-pointedly and worship him devotedly, they will be freed from the torment of their desire. All their hopes will be fulfilled through the awesome power of Kshitigarbha's holy samadhis. They will achieve either higher birth as devas or nirvana, depending on their condition.

"If those who plant in either fertile or infertile soil, whether they are diligent in farming or not, call Kshitigarbha by name

one-pointedly and worship him, they will reap good and fruitful crops. Why? Because of the power of the fervent aspirations made with great diligence by the son of family Kshitigarbha throughout countless kalpas in the presence of countless buddhas. In order to ripen beings, he always cares for the earth and its seeds. He always engages in the fulfillment of beings' wishes. Through this son of family's miraculous power, the grass, trees, and seedlings that grow on this great earth flourish and ripen with fruit. He makes them healthy, sweet, shiny, and fragrant.

"If any being engages in the ten unvirtuous actions because their three poisons are strong and acute, and thereafter calls Kshitigarbha by name, their kleshas will be pacified. They will turn away from the ten unvirtuous actions. They will engage in virtuous actions. Love, compassion, benevolence, and joy will be born in their minds.

"This son of family Kshitigarbha — through his holy qualities, his extreme diligence in samadhi, his power, and his majestic strength — can go to countless buddha realms in a single moment. In each of those realms, at every single instant, he frees as many beings as the Ganges' sand grains from suffering and brings them to bliss, even to the attainment of nirvana. This son of family's qualities, stable aspirations, and extremely diligent samadhis are inconceivable. In order to ripen beings, he appears in every world in the ten directions. In some he appears as Mahabrahma, the king of devas, and teaches dharma in that form to those best tamed by that appearance. In others he appears as Maheshvara, or as Master of Others' Emanations, the ruler of the desire realm. He can appear as a deva of any of the six desire deva realms, or as a buddha, a bodhisattva, a shravaka, a pratyeka-buddha, or a chakravartin. He can appear as someone of any of the four castes, such as royalty. He can appear as a man, a woman, a boy, or a girl. He can appear as a ghandharva,

an asura, a yaksha, or as any type of nonhuman being. He can appear as an animal, such as a lion, a horse, an elephant, or a bull. He can appear in any form, even that of a preta, a yama, a hell guardian, or a hell being. With such countless appearances, he teaches dharma to many beings in ways appropriate to each of them. He places them in irreversibility from the three vehicles.

"These are the inconceivable qualities of this son of family, this great being. He is a treasure of the greatest and best qualities. He is a source of all precious liberation. He is the pure eye of many bodhisattvas. He is the guide who leads beings to the city of nirvana. Without effort, through the qualities I have explained, he turns the great dharmachakra. It is like this: if a son of family were to one-pointedly take refuge in Maitreya, Manjushri, Avalokita, Samantabhadra, or any other bodhisattva mahasattva for one hundred times as many kalpas as the Ganges' sand grains, call their names, worship them devotedly, prostrate to them, and make aspirations for the fulfillment of their hopes; and someone else were to one-pointedly call the bodhisattva mahasattva Kshitigarbha by name for just an instant, a moment, a second — worshipping him devotedly and prostrating to him — the second person's hopes and aspirations would be more quickly fulfilled. Why? Because the mahabodhisattva Kshitigarbha fulfills the particular aspirations of individual beings in order to bring about the well-being and happiness of all beings. He is like a treasury of wish-fulfilling jewels. In order to ripen beings this great bodhisattva has long cultivated great stable aspirations, great compassion, and extreme diligence. He is superior to all other bodhisattvas. You should therefore worship him devotedly."

All the mahabodhisattvas gathered there from the ten directions, all the shravakas, all the devas, and all the others gathered there arose from their seats. They respectfully presented innumerable offerings such as precious flowers to the bodhisattva Kshitigarbha and praised him melodiously. Kshitigarbha presented all the divine offerings he received then to the bhagavat, saying,

"I present to the world's leader, whose qualities are
    so great,
The offerings of devas, nagas, yakshas, humans,
And the bodhisattvas of the ten directions.
I pray that you accept these, the best of offerings."

Kshitigarbha then prostrated at the bhagavat's feet. The bhagavat replied,

"With a stable mind and pure bodhichitta
You dispel the suffering of innumerable beings.
Like jewels, you bring joy.
Like a vajra, you cut through the web of doubt.

"With great compassion and diligence
You have presented holy offerings to the bhagavat.
Ocean of wisdom, you free beings from suffering.
Fearless, you've reached the other side of existence."

Then the mahabodhisattva Kshitigarbha arose from his seat and said to the bhagavat, "This is the great vidyamantra, the dharani of recollection, that I have heard from innumerable buddhas. I will recite it now in order to increase and render auspicious the mindfulness of the bhagavat's fourfold retinue, and in order to increase their health, well-being, beauty, strength, fame, roots of virtue, achievements of path and result, resources, disciples, and practice of the paramitas."

Kshitigarbha then recited that dharani of immeasurable benefit. Immediately, Mount Khaladeya shook and millions of divine musical instruments gave forth their sounds without anyone playing them. Immeasurable amounts of deva incense, flowers, and jewels fell like rain, amazing that large gathering.

Present at that gathering were eighteen thousand devis with mastery over the four elements, such as the devi Great Auspiciousness and the devi Great Glory. They all arose from their seats, prostrated at the bhagavat's feet, and said to him, "Bhagavat, this is wondrous! Sugata, we have mastery over the four elements. We do not, however, know the origin, state, or end of the four elements. We do not know how they arise and cease to be, or what supports and inhibits them. As this great being has achieved the most profound and subtle prajnaparamita, he wisely knows the origin, character, birth, cessation, supports, and inhibitors of the four elements.

"Like a wish-fulfilling jewel with many qualities that rains down various jewels in generosity to beings, this son of family rains down the various jewels of the factors of awakening, giving them to beings. Like an island of jewels filled with diverse jewels, this son of family is filled with the precious factors of awakening. Like the tree of the devas called Parichitra that is fragrant and beautiful with its flowers, this son of family is beautiful with the various precious buddhadharmas. Like a lion king who is not intimidated by or afraid of other animals, this son of family is never overwhelmed or intimidated by any being. Like the sun dispelling all of the world's darkness with its light, this son of family dispels all the darkness of bad views and ignorance. Like the moon revealing to all beings lost at night an easy road on which they can travel comfortably, this son of family reveals the perfect path of the three vehicles to all beings lost in the night of ignorance and wandering in the wilderness of samsara. He skillfully places them on the path to perfection appropriate to their condition. Like the great earth — the support for all seeds, trees, crops, and beings who have the earth element — this son of family supports and contains all the extraordinary features of the factors of awakening. Like Mount Meru — the king of mountains, which is composed of jewels, utterly stable, undiminished, and undamaged — this son of family has all the unique attributes of buddhahood, the undamaged resolve never to abandon any being, and the undiminished resolve to give all roots of virtue to beings. Like space, in which all beings live, this son of family is available to all beings. This son of family's qualities are innumerable and immeasurable."

Hearing these praises of the bodhisattva Kshitigarbha's boundless qualities, everyone present at that gathering was amazed. They worshipped and venerated him. They gazed upon the bodhisattva Kshitigarbha joyously with unblinking eyes and one-pointed minds. Then in order to clearly reiterate what had already been stated, the bhagavat said,

"The perfect being Kshitigarbha
    Has many wondrous qualities.
    Bearing the appearance of a renunciate,
    He has come here and prostrated to me, his teacher."

With that and other verses the buddha restated Kshitigarbha's qualities. He concluded,

"Even if we praised him and his qualities
    For many hundreds of kalpas,
    It would be very hard to capture them all.
    Therefore everyone, venerate him devotedly."

Then the mahabodhisattva Kshitigarbha asked the bhagavat questions about holy dharma, such as how to turn the dharmachakra with great compassion in worlds of fivefold degeneracy. The sugata replied by teaching the dharma of the ten great chakras, benefiting innumerable beings. The buddha entrusted that teaching to the bodhisattva Kshitigarbha and instructed him to protect all those who uphold that teaching from impairment of wealth, all harm, unvirtuous actions, disparagement, and six other evils — a total of ten. Kshitigarbha promised to do so.

THE SIXTH CHAPTER: THE BODHISATTVA KSHITIGARBHA

THE VICTORS' SON
SARVANIVARANAVISHKAMBHIN

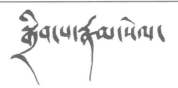

I PROSTRATE TO THE BODHISATTVA MAHASATTVA
SARVANIVARANAVISHKAMBHIN!⁹⁴
I VENERATE YOU! I TAKE REFUGE IN YOU!

The state of this mahabodhisattva is inconceivable.

94. Sarvanivaran-avishkambhin means "complete remover of all obscurations."

From the *Mahayana Sutra of the Council of Buddhas*

In the eastern world-realm called Ubiquitous Light, the buddha realm of the tathagata King of Existence, as many buddhas as the Ganges' sand grains gathered from the ten
directions to discuss various aspects of dharma. The youthful
Manjushri, thinking, "I shall go there," went from our realm,
Saha, to Ubiquitous Light in an instant. When he arrived, he
saw that to the right of the tathagata King of Existence was
his sister, Dispeller of Doubt. She was seated with crossed
legs, resting in the samadhi called Ubiquitous Stainless
Moonlight.

In order to demonstrate the inconceivable abilities of buddhas
and bodhisattvas, the tathagata King of Existence threw the
youthful Manjushri all the way to the peak of a distant mountain without Manjushri being aware of it. Once he became
aware of his surroundings, the youthful Manjushri exerted his

miraculous powers and went to countless buddha realms in the ten directions, seeking to return to the gathering from which he had been expelled. He was unable, however, to return to that gathering or even get one hair-tip's distance closer to it. Finally, he sat down where he was and rested in mindfulness free from mental engagement. He taught dharma there, causing twelve thousand devas to achieve patience with unborn dharmas.

Meanwhile, the buddhas' meeting had come to an end. The tathagata King of Existence emitted light from the palm of his right hand. This light summoned Manjushri. He returned to the realm Ubiquitous Light, prostrated to that tathagata, and said, "I was cast out of this gathering, but your sister was not. Her roots of virtue must be extraordinarily brilliant! When did she first generate bodhichitta? When did she achieve her present samadhi?"

That tathagata replied, "Manjushri, this sister of mine sees, through her samadhi, countless buddhas in the ten directions, hears dharma from them, and teaches that dharma to others. Nevertheless she is utterly free from even the slightest perception and from any mental engagement. Even if I were to describe her qualities for a kalpa, I would not exhaust them. Manjushri, rouse my sister from her samadhi and ask her about these things."

Intending to rouse her from her samadhi, Manjushri snapped his fingers. Failing to get her attention with the sound of an ordinary finger snap, he snapped his fingers so loudly that it was heard in every world in the ten directions. Still failing to rouse her, Manjushri caused all the cymbals in all these billion worlds to send forth their sounds. That having failed, he emanated innumerable cymbals, the sound of which filled worlds without end in the ten directions. That too having failed, he caused all the mountains in all those world realms to strike one another like hands clapping. The terrifying

sound this produced filled all those worlds but failed to rouse
Dispeller of Doubt from her samadhi.

Using all his miraculous strength, Manjushri then tried to pull
her by the hand. This caused countless realms below them to
shake, but failed to move her or disturb her samadhi by even
the width of a hair tip. Manjushri then tried to lift her. By
doing so he cast countless realms into the sky, but did not succeed in disturbing her. He then placed the entire environment
— the place where the tathagata's sister was sitting — in the
palm of his right hand, threw it all the way to the world of
Brahma, and then put it back where it had been originally.
This too had no effect on her. He next placed the tathagata's
sister in the palm of his right hand and went to as many buddha realms in every direction — east and the other nine — as
there are sand grains in the Ganges. In each of these realms he
caused the same sounds of cymbals and crashing mountains as
before, and sent down rains of flowers. When this too failed
to rouse the tathagata's sister from her samadhi, Manjushri
returned with her to the gathering in Ubiquitous Light.
Although Manjushri had failed to disturb Dispeller of Doubt,
the miracles he performed in all those realms in the ten directions ripened countless beings.

After his return, the youthful Manjushri said to the tathagata
King of Existence, "The state of bodhisattvas such as your sister is amazing!"

The tathagata replied, "Indeed, it is! The state of bodhisattvas
is inconceivable. To be precise, you could turn two billion-
world systems into a two-headed drum and beat it with drumsticks as long as the diameter of another billion-world system
for longer than a kalpa right in front of my sister, and she
would not even hear it. How could it disturb her?"

Manjushri asked him, "Who could rouse her from samadhi?"

The tathagata replied, "Only a tathagata or the bodhisattva

Sarvanivaranavishkambhin — no one else. Merely saying the name of this mahabodhisattva shakes the great earth six times. Saying his name even shakes realms other than those in which it is said!"

Manjushri asked, "Where is that mahabodhisattva now? Bring him here so that we can see him and watch him rouse your sister from her samadhi!"

Below that realm of Ubiquitous Light, past as many buddha realms as the Ganges' sand grains, was a world realm called Colorful Victory Banner. Sarvanivaranavishkambhin was there, in front of the tathagata called Roars Like Lions, Geese, and a Herd of Cattle. Summoned by light sent by the buddha King of Existence, Sarvanivaranavishkambhin and a retinue of five hundred thousand bodhisattvas traveled in an instant to Ubiquitous Light. They prostrated at the feet of the tathagata King of Existence, and then remained seated in the sky. They all entered a samadhi called Utter Renunciation of the Body, causing them to be invisible, and performed miracles such as sending down rains of flowers. When Manjushri and the others at that gathering asked why they could not see the bodies of Sarvanivaranavishkambhin and his retinue, the tathagata said, "It is through the power of their samadhi."

Manjushri thought, "I will accomplish such samadhi!"

Knowing Manjushri's thought, Sarvanivaranavishkambhin said, "This samadhi is not my only one. I can enter and arise from as many samadhis of invisibility as there are drops of water in a great ocean. You do not even know the names of these samadhis!"

Hearing this, Manjushri accomplished that samadhi — difficult for other bodhisattvas to achieve even through a quintillion kalpas of effort — in the time of a finger snap. Then Manjushri asked the tathagata, "Please allow us to see these bodhisattvas." The buddha commanded the mahabodhisattva Sarvanivaranavishkambhin and his retinue to reveal themselves, and they did so.

Manjushri then said to Sarvanivaranavishkambhin, "Please rouse the tathagata's sister from her samadhi."

Sarvanivaranavishkambhin replied, "I could rouse her from samadhi, but I request that the omniscient tathagata do so instead."

The tathagata King of Existence entered a samadhi called Rousing Others from Samadhi. By doing so he roused his sister and everyone else engaged in even placement in that world from their samadhis. Then Manjushri asked the tathagata's sister a number of questions such as, "When did you first generate bodhichitta?"

Her response to his questions, based on the inexpressible meaning, amazed everyone in that it demonstrated her confidence in teaching extremely profound dharma.

Manjushri then asked the tathagata, "Bhagavat, how long has it been since your sister first generated bodhichitta?"

The tathagata replied, "Manjushri, when you first generated bodhichitta, my sister had already been engaged in the deeds of a bodhisattva for ninety-nine sextillion multiplied by novemdecillion kalpas. She first generated bodhichitta in the presence of the tathagata Source of Solitude. The qualities and attributes of that buddha's realm could not be even partially described in as many kalpas as the Ganges' sand grains. At that time, when she first generated bodhichitta, my sister was a chakravartin called Silence. Do not think of my sister as a woman. As she has achieved the samadhi of magical illusion, she can emanate whatever sort of body she wants. My sister will achieve buddhahood as many kalpas from now as the

number of particles and leaves in a billion worlds multiplied by one hundred thousand novemdecillion. She will become the tathagata called Source of Ubiquitous Light. Her realm will be like that of the tathagata Ratnakara."

Then Sarvanivaranavishkambhin said, "The youthful Manjushri is still very active; he continues to conceptualize the past and the future."

Manjushri responded, "Son of family, it is true. I am very active. Since the dharmadhatu is inexhaustible, my deeds are inexhaustible."

The tathagata King of Existence interjected, "Manjushri, don't argue with Sarvanivaranavishkambhin. His confidence is inconceivable. You don't even know the names of his samadhis! If all the beings in these billion worlds were to become just like Manjushri, they would not know even the names of my sister's samadhis. All those beings together would still be incapable of even a hundred thousandth of her samadhi, miracles, or wisdom. If all the beings in these billion worlds were to become equal to my sister in samadhi and wisdom, they would not all together be capable of a hundred thousandth of the mahabodhisattva Sarvanivaranavishkambhin's samadhi, wisdom, strength, or miracles. My sister does not know even the names of Sarvanivaranavishkambhin's samadhis! If all beings came to equal Sarvanivaranavishkambhin in samadhi and wisdom, they would still, even all together, be incapable of understanding a single step taken by a tathagata. The wisdom of buddhas is inconceivable!

"It was my sister who first caused Manjushri to generate bodhichitta. She has caused the generation of bodhichitta by as many bodhisattvas similar to Manjushri in each of the ten directions as there are sand grains in the Ganges. It was Sarvanivaranavishkambhin who first caused my sister to generate bodhichitta. He has caused the generation of bodhi-

chitta by as many bodhisattvas similar to my sister in each of the ten directions as there are sand grains in the Ganges. Sarvanivaranavishkambhin also caused me to generate bodhichitta, long ago during the teaching of the tathagata Supreme Mountain Victory Banner. He has caused the generation of bodhichitta by as many tathagatas similar to me in each of the ten directions as there are sand grains in the Ganges. Many of those tathagatas are still alive, but countless numbers of them have already passed into parinirvana.

"Any woman who hears the name of my sister, Dispeller of Doubt; or the name of the bodhisattva Sarvanivarana-vishkambhin; or the name of the tathagata King of Existence, will be in her last ordinary body. She will quickly achieve unsurpassable awakening. After that life, she will be born in a world in which a buddha has appeared. She will be free from the eight unleisured states. She will recollect her previous lives. She will possess retention and the thirty-two marks of a great being. She will not inhabit a womb. This is because we have made the aspiration, 'May any woman who hears our names acquire these benefits.'"

From the *Ratnamegha Mahayanasutra*

Once, the bhagavat resided on Gaya Head Mountain along with all his vast retinue, including the sanghas of shravakas and bodhisattvas. From the crown of the bhagavat's head emerged a light ray called Radiance that filled all the worlds in the ten directions and then dissolved into the buddha's mouth. At that time there was a world realm to the east of ours called Lotuses, as many realms distant from our buddha realm as there are sand grains in the Ganges. In that realm the sugata Lotus Eyes taught dharma without even the names of the three vehicles; he taught them as one. All the beings in that realm were bodhisattvas irreversible from perfect awakening. In that realm also resided the bodhisattva mahasattva

Sarvanivaranavishkambhin. Merely hearing his name exhausts all of a being's obscurations.

Touched and alerted by the buddha's light ray, Sarvanivaranavishkambhin left his abode and entered the presence of the bhagavat Lotus Eyes. He asked that buddha, "Through whose power arose this delightful light-ray, soothing to both body and mind?"

Lotus Eyes replied, "Son of family, to our west is a world realm called Saha. In it resides a tathagata called Shakyamuni. Merely hearing his name causes beings to become irreversible from unsurpassable, perfect awakening. He sent forth this light."

Sarvanivaranavishkambhin requested, "Bhagavat, may I go to Saha in order to prostrate and present offerings to that tathagata?" Other bodhisattvas, alerted by the same light, made the same request.

The tathagata Lotus Eyes replied, "Children of family, if you know it to be the time to do so, then go. However, be careful in that world realm. Why? Because the beings in that realm have many kleshas. They do not even acknowledge their own fathers. They have many desires that conflict with dharma. They are negative. That tathagata teaches dharma among such beings."

The bodhisattvas said, "Bhagavat, in teaching dharma among such beings, that buddha has undertaken great austerity!"

The tathagata replied, "It is so. It is difficult for anyone in a world realm of such affliction to give rise to even a single thought of virtue. What is wondrous about the purity of beings living in pure worlds? It is far more wondrous when those in a world realm of affliction acquire faith for even the duration of a finger snap, or take refuge in the three jewels, or maintain morality, or generate bodhichitta through compassion and freedom from desire."

The bodhisattvas then went to the realm of Saha, bearing many offerings. Having arrived, the bodhisattva Sarvanivaranavishkambhin said to his companions, "My friends, the beings in this realm Saha are miserable! It therefore seems to me that we should perform miracles that will bring them the greatest joy."

All the bodhisattvas in his retinue agreed, saying, "Good!" So the mahabodhisattva Sarvanivaranavishkambhin performed a miracle. He emitted from his body a stainless, brilliant, pleasant light that caused great physical and mental pleasure. This great realm of a billion worlds was filled with that light and illuminated by it. As all the beings in the hells, all the animals, and all those in the worlds of yamas were struck by this light they were freed from all painful sensations and became happy. Freed from anger and malice, they regarded one another as their parents. Even the darkness between worlds, unlit by the sun or moon, was filled with the light's brilliance so that those born there could see one another. All the mountains, including the ring of mountains surrounding all billion worlds, were filled with light. There was not a single being anywhere, from the abodes of Brahma above to Avichi below, that was not lit up. That was the miracle Sarvanivaranavishkambhin performed.

The bodhisattvas accompanying him also performed miracles. They satisfied beings by providing everything they wanted, such as food, clothing, and wealth. All those with incomplete faculties acquired complete ones. The insane regained their senses. The miserable became happy. The pregnant gave birth comfortably.

Then Sarvanivaranavishkambhin and the other bodhisattvas approached Gaya Head Mountain. This entire realm of a

billion worlds became lit by a covering web of jewels. From vast clouds in the sky fell great rains of divine lotuses and other flowers, divine fruit, divine garlands, incense, powders, dharma robes, parasols, victory banners, and flags. All the beings these things touched became happy. All the ordinary trees and ground on Gaya Head Mountain disappeared. There appeared jewel trees, wish-fulfilling trees, flowering trees, fruit trees, sandalwood trees, and agarwood trees. That place became perfect in its appearance. From the sky came the sound of divine cymbals. The music of those cymbals contained the sound of stanzas of praise such as these:

"You were born in the great grove of Lumbini.
Peerless, you are never overpowered by kleshas.
You equal space. In order to pay you homage
We are gathering on this great mountain.

"You achieved perfect awakening in front of the
awakening tree.
Conquering Mara's forces, you became a buddha.
You are stainless and brilliant. In order to pay
you homage
We are gathering on this great mountain.

"You have realized that dharmas are like
Magical illusions, dreams, and water moons.
You are the best field of merit. In order to pay
you homage
We are gathering on this great mountain."

As soon as he heard these stanzas, the great Maudgalyayana arose from his seat. He bowed to the bhagavat with palms joined and asked him, "Bhagavat, who is causing these signs? I have never seen or heard their like before now!"

The buddha replied, "To the east of here, as many world realms distant as there are sand grains in the Ganges, is a world realm called Lotuses. In it resides the tathagata arhat samyaksambuddha Lotus Eyes. The bodhisattva mahasattva Sarvanivaranavishkambhin, accompanied by one hundred sextillion other bodhisattvas, has left the presence of that buddha and come here to this realm of Saha. These are signs of that."

As soon as the buddha said that, the mahabodhisattva Sarvanivaranavishkambhin and his retinue arrived in front of the bhagavat through the great miraculous power of bodhisattvas. They prostrated to the buddha and praised him with stanzas such as these:

"Famous, great in your wisdom,
  Great sage, great hero,
  You have escaped from the misery of existence.
  I prostrate to you who have escaped the kleshas.

"You are all-penetrating
  And always utterly brilliant.
  You are fully liberated from everything.
  I prostrate to the peerless.

"Like a mountain, you are unshakable.
  You are as deep and vast as an ocean.
  You are undisturbed by any tirthika.
  I prostrate to the king of dharma.

"When you turn the dharmachakra,
  Protector, you reveal
  Primordial tranquility,
  Unborn, natural nirvana."

The bodhisattvas then sat down in the centers of lotuses. The bodhisattva mahasattva Sarvanivaranavishkambhin soon arose from his seat, hung his shawl on one shoulder, planted his right knee on the center of his lotus, faced the bhagavat,

bowed to him with joined palms, and said, "Bhagavat, if you will permit me, I wish to ask the sambuddha a few questions."

The bhagavat replied, "Holy being, you always have the permission of all tathagatas. Ask the tathagata whatever questions you wish. My answers will please you."

Sarvanivaranavishkambhin asked, "Bhagavat, what is perfect generosity for a bodhisattva?" He asked him about all the paramitas up to perfect wisdom. He asked, "What are the bodhisattva levels like?" He asked about every aspect of the mahayana, including vastness, purity, and the manifest, perfect buddhahood of full awakening. The buddha answered each of Sarvanivaranavishkambhin's questions in detail with reference to the ten dharmas. As a result, innumerable beings were purified and ripened.

THE SEVENTH CHAPTER: THE VICTORS' SON
SARVANIVARANAVISHKAMBHIN

THE SUPREME ARYA SAMANTABHADRA

ཀུན་ཏུ་བཟང་པོ།

I PROSTRATE TO THE BODHISATTVA MAHASATTVA
SAMANTABHADRA![95] I VENERATE YOU! I TAKE REFUGE IN YOU!

From the *Avatamsakasutra*

95. Samantabhadra means "totally good" or "ubiquitously good

The state of the bodhisattva Samantabhadra is like an
unimaginably vast ocean. He has entered the ocean of the
tathagatas' qualities. He performs ten miraculous feats. With
the feat called Manifest Ultimate Accomplishment he purifies
all buddha realms and tames all beings. With the feat called
Access to All Qualities he enters the presence of all tathagatas.
With the feat called Ocean of Aspirations he fulfills the aspirations of every bodhisattva to pass from level to level. With
the feat called All-Pervasive he emanates innumerable replicas
of his body — as many as there are particles — and fills the
dharmadhatu with them. With the feat called Blessing
through Proclamation his name is proclaimed endlessly
throughout all realms. With the feat called Perfect Display he
displays within every smallest particle all the infinite deeds
and miracles of a bodhisattva. With the feat called
Appearance of Creation and Destruction he can display in a
single instant all the kalpas of past, present, and future. With
the feat called Display of Mutual Communication he can

cause bodhisattvas to experience the ocean of faculties of other bodhisattvas. With the feat called Blessing through Emanation he can fill the boundless dharmadhatu with emanations of his body. With the feat called Entry into Omniscience he reveals to bodhisattvas, through vast teaching, all the dharmas of other bodhisattvas.

The bodhisattva mahasattva Samantabhadra once appeared on a lion throne and lotus seat in the presence of the bhagavat Vairochana. Samantabhadra was immersed in the samadhi called Tathagata Vairochana, Essence of the Bodies of All Buddhas. He was immersed in a state of inconceivable qualities pervading all the dharmadhatu. Samantabhadra caused as many buddhas as there are particles in all realms to appear in each and every smallest particle throughout all the ocean of realms, throughout all space, throughout all the dharmadhatu. He appeared before each of those buddhas, resting evenly in samadhi. All the tathagatas of the infinite realms throughout the ten directions revealed their faces to Samantabhadra and said to him, "Son of family, it is good that you rest in such samadhi. Son of family, through the blessing of the buddha Vairochana's past aspirations, through the purity of your aspirations and deeds, and through being blessed by the boundless wisdom of all tathagatas, you have achieved the inconceivable power and state of a buddha." Saying that, they all placed their golden hands on the crown of Samantabhadra's head. Simultaneously, the same thing occurred in every realm within the ocean of innumerable realms.

As soon as the ocean of tathagatas placed their hands on the top of Samantabhadra's head, he arose from samadhi. He did so simultaneously in every particle in every world throughout the infinite ocean of realms. As soon as Samantabhadra arose from samadhi, all the other bodhisattvas surrounding him achieved qualities such as samadhi and retention equal in

number to the smallest particles in every world in the ocean of realms. Just as the bodhisattvas in our realm achieved these qualities, so did the ocean of bodhisattvas present within every smallest particle in each world in the ocean of realms. They achieved them through the power of the buddhas and through the samadhi of Samantabhadra. The entire ocean of realms throughout the ten directions shook. All those realms became decorated by jewels and filled with the sound of the ocean of dharma. Surrounding every one of the ocean of tathagatas fell a rain of golden victory banners adorned with true kings among jewels, and there arose clouds and rains of diverse great kings among jewels. From every pore on the body of every tathagata emerged light rays proclaiming stanzas like these:

"In every realm Samantabhadra
 Is present with beautiful mastery.
 In each one he displays miracles like these.
 His samadhi has no center or limit."

Then everyone in Vairochana's retinue joined their palms, gazed on Samantabhadra, and praised him. Through the buddhas' blessing, Samantabhadra looked upon the ocean of hopes of beings in every realm, the ocean of buddhadharmas, and the ocean of aspirations. He then taught dharma based on the infinite wisdom and qualities of buddhas to that assembly.

In the same sutra it is taught that once the bodhisattva All-Seeing asked the bhagavat Vairochana about the samadhis and liberation of bodhisattvas, about how to approach the state and deeds of Samantabhadra, about how to enter and arise from the samadhis and liberated states produced by aspirations, and about how to achieve diverse samadhis. In reply, the bhagavat said to the bodhisattva All-Seeing, "All-Seeing, your thought of asking the tathagata about the mandalas of all bodhisattvas of the past, present, and future, and about the

mandalas of all tathagatas, is excellent, excellent! All-Seeing, the bodhisattva Samantabhadra has the unimaginable miraculous abilities of a bodhisattva. He has diligently accomplished the powers of the best of bodhisattvas. His bodhisattva deeds are infinite. He is fully trained in the miracles and magical displays of bodhisattvas. He has diligently accomplished the aspirations of a bodhisattva. He is irreversibly a bodhisattva. He has cultivated infinite aspects of the paramitas. He correctly understands the immeasurably diverse objects of retention. He is inexhaustible, unstoppable, and pure. With great compassion — beyond discouragement — for all beings, his aspirations extend to the end of time. As Samantabhadra is here in this assembly, ask him your questions. He will teach you about samadhi and miracles."

Then all the bodhisattvas gathered there, as soon as they heard the bodhisattva Samantabhadra's name, achieved the inconceivable samadhis of bodhisattvas. They were blessed with minds free from attachment. They attained unimaginable wisdom. They experienced unassailable wisdom. They saw countless tathagatas. They achieved discernment. They understood the immeasurable power of tathagatas. They realized that their continuums and those of tathagatas were one. They understood how to enter the infinite three times. They gained splendid, inexhaustible merit. They understood how to perfect the wondrous ocean of miracles. All of them, with respect and awe, gazed upon the mandala of the tathagata. However, through the tathagata's blessing and through the great miraculous power of the bodhisattva Samantabhadra, they were unable to see Samantabhadra's body or his seat.

Then the bodhisattva All-Seeing asked the bhagavat, "Where is the bodhisattva Samantabhadra now?"

The bhagavat replied, "He's right here, in front of my feet. He hasn't moved."

Then the bodhisattva All-Seeing and all the bodhisattvas gathered there gazed upon the whole mandala of that assembly and said to the bhagavat, "Bhagavat, we can't even see Samantabhadra's seat!"

The bhagavat replied, "Children of family, it is indeed true that you can see neither Samantabhadra's body nor his seat. Why? Because the bodhisattva Samantabhadra rests in inexpressible profundity. He has entered the boundless expanse of wisdom. He has achieved the samadhi of a lion's poise. He has achieved the unsurpassable miraculous abilities of a buddha. He has accomplished the ten strengths of a tathagata and is pure in being free from all attachment. His body is the holy dharmadhatu. He rests in the blessings of all buddhas. He has gained the undifferentiated continuity of the wisdom of all buddhas of the past, present, and future. The bodhisattva Samantabhadra follows the discrete instants of the mind."

As soon as the bodhisattva All-Seeing heard from the tathagata of Samantabhadra's pure qualities, he entered one million novemdecillion bodhisattva samadhis. Wishing to see the bodhisattva Samantabhadra, All-Seeing searched for him carefully, prayed to him, and pondered him. Still, All-Seeing could not see Samantabhadra, and neither could any of the other bodhisattvas gathered there. Finally, All-Seeing again told the bhagavat of his inability to see Samantabhadra.

The bhagavat said, "You do not see Samantabhadra. Why? Because Samantabhadra is trained in the inconceivably miraculous state of a bodhisattva. If you cannot see in the letters of a magical spell the illusory forms created by that spell, how could you see or experience Samantabhadra's secret body, speech, or mind? The bodhisattva Samantabhadra's deeds are inconceivably profound. His mind is the boundless wisdom vajra. He rests in the endless and centerless dharmadhatu. He acts in every world realm without abiding in any of them. He

conforms to the bodies and forms of all beings. His state is unsurpassable dharma. He is perfectly and spontaneously accomplished in inexhaustible and unlimited miracles and the power of buddhas. He has realized the dharmadhatu. Son of family, gazing upon the bodhisattva Samantabhadra is meaningful. Seeing him is meaningful. Listening to him, hearing him, serving him, thinking of him, remembering him, worshipping him, examining him, searching for him, and aspiring to emulate him are meaningful."

Wishing to see Samantabhadra, the bodhisattva All-Seeing and all the bodhisattvas with him joined their palms and prostrated to the bhagavat and Samantabhadra while reciting words of homage.

Then the bhagavat said, "Children of family, prostrate and pray to the bodhisattva mahasattva Samantabhadra. Bring all space to mind and be blessed by the action of seeing everywhere. Considering Samantabhadra, be blessed by bringing the dharmadhatu to mind. By becoming free from attachment to anything, your aspirations will equal Samantabhadra's. Rest evenly in their nonduality. Be blessed by emanating your body in every world realm and by the nondifferentiation of your sense faculties. Cultivate the omnipresence of Samantabhadra's aspirations. If you do all this, you will see the bodhisattva Samantabhadra."

Then the bodhisattva All-Seeing and all the other bodhisattvas there bowed their heads, prostrated, and prayed to Samantabhadra. As soon as they did so, they all saw Samantabhadra seated on a lotus right in front of the tathagata. They simultaneously saw him appear from their own bodies, appear from each of the infinite number of world realms, appear before every buddha one after another, describe the activity of all buddhas in every world realm, display all the deeds of a bodhisattva, reveal the path to omniscient wisdom, display all the miraculous transformations of a bodhisattva,

describe the power of the greatest of bodhisattvas, and display throughout the three times innumerable tathagatas. They saw Samantabhadra perform all these miracles. Delighted, they prostrated to the bodhisattva Samantabhadra. Ten thousand clouds of offerings appeared, such as clouds of flowers emitting rains of diverse flowers and clouds of garlands emitting diverse garlands. Countless world realms shook six times. Musical instruments gave forth their sounds, and the melodies of the devas were heard. A great light filled the world. Beings became pure. Lower states ceased. Countless bodhisattvas began Samantabhadra's conduct, accomplished it, fulfilled their aspirations, and achieved the perfect awakening of buddhahood.

Then All-Seeing said to the bhagavat, "Bhagavat, the bodhisattva Samantabhadra performs the deeds of a truly great being. He is peerless, unceasing, and irreversible. He has realized equality. He cannot be stopped by anyone. He knows the sameness of all dharmas, the individual characteristics of all dharmas, and how to skillfully bless the minds of all beings. Samantabhadra has control over all dharmas. He has achieved samadhi and liberation."

The bhagavat replied, "It is so. Samantabhadra is pure in that his qualities are countless. He is adorned by peerless qualities. His qualities are immeasurable and precious. He is an ocean, a source of inconceivable qualities. His character has measureless qualities. He is a cloud of boundless qualities. His qualities are ceaselessly praised. His precious dharmas are inexhaustible. Samantabhadra's qualities are praised inexhaustibly by all buddhas."

Then the bhagavat said to Samantabhadra, "Teach the bodhisattva All-Seeing and all the other bodhisattvas gathered here about your deeds; about your ten samadhis of fulfilled aspirations; about your infinite, praiseworthy qualities; and about how a bodhisattva who achieves these is fit to be

called a buddha, a tathagata, a possessor of the ten strengths." As commanded by the tathagata, Samantabhadra taught that wondrous dharma to those gathered there.

The variety within beings' minds is endless. Although in absolute truth there is no birth, in relative truth there are infinite births. The bodhisattva Samantabhadra has realized an equally infinite number of aspects of dharma. The great rains caused by nagas are inexhaustible, even though each raindrop is the size of a barura berry. Each raindrop is new, yet the clouds never run out of rain. The bodhisattva Samantabhadra's samadhi, wisdom, access to buddhas, and miracles are equally inexhaustible, unceasing, and endless. Fire will burn as long as there is wood to feed it. The bodhisattva Samantabhadra will continue to appear as long as beings and the dharmadhatu remain. In these ways, Samantabhadra described his deeds.

Then the tathagata spoke to the bodhisattva King of Mind in verse:

"If Samantabhadra were praised for as many kalpas
As there are numberless particles,
His praises would not come to an end.

"There are countless Samantabhadras
Within the tip of every hair.
He is everywhere, in everything,
Throughout the dharmadhatu."

Then a quadrillion novemdecillion light rays called Perfect Courage emerged from the bhagavat's mouth. They illuminated all the countless world realms and then circled those world realms clockwise ten times. These light rays displayed the miracles of tathagatas, pacified lower states, overwhelmed maras, and filled all the mandalas of the retinues of buddhas. After filling all the countless world realms throughout the infinite

space of the dharmadhatu, the light rays returned, circled the mandala of gathered bodhisattvas clockwise, and finally dissolved into the bodhisattva Samantabhadra's mouth. As soon as that light touched Samantabhadra, the lion throne on which he was seated became a hundred thousand times more majestic. It became superior to all thrones other than the tathagata's lion throne.

Then in response to the request of the bodhisattva Glorious Descendant of the Tathagatas, Samantabhadra taught the wondrous dharma called Explaining the Tathagatas' Birth. He taught about the origin and birth of buddhas; the attributes of their bodies, speech, and minds; their deeds; their awakening; their turning of the dharmachakra; their parinirvana; and the virtue generated by seeing, hearing, or accompanying buddhas. While Samantabhadra was teaching all this, as many world realms as there are smallest particles in septillion world realms in each of the ten directions shook six times through the buddhas' power. Clouds of deva flowers, fabric, parasols, and victory banners gathered and sent down their respective rains. The great sound of all buddhas and bodhisattvas saying, "Excellent!" also descended as rain from the clouds. From a distance of as many world realms in each of the ten directions as there are smallest particles in eighty septillion world realms came as many bodhisattvas as there are smallest particles in eighty septillion buddha realms. All of these bodhisattvas bore the name Samantabhadra. They all rejoiced and praised Samantabhadra's teaching, saying, "In our respective realms we teach dharma with these very words!"

Through that teaching by Samantabhadra as many bodhisattvas as there are smallest particles in a hundred thousand buddha realms achieved all of the samadhis and supercognitions of a bodhisattva and received the prophecy that they would achieve perfect awakening in their next life. As many beings as there are smallest particles in a hundred thousand buddha realms generated perfect bodhichitta and received the prophecy of their future perfect buddhahood. In the future, all beings of the four continents will know and be tamed by this teaching, as will all the beings in all the world realms throughout the ten directions. This teaching was also praised by as many bodhisattvas — all named Samantabhadra — as there are smallest particles in septillion novemdecillion buddha realms.

Then amid that great gathering of bodhisattvas, the bodhisattva Samantabhadra entered the samadhi called Many Buddhas. As soon as he did so, all the worlds throughout the dharmadhatu shook six times, making beings in all those worlds aware of Samantabhadra's samadhi. He then arose from samadhi. Upon Samantabhadra's doing so, the mahabodhisattva Total Knowledge asked him more than two hundred questions, including questions about the causal correspondences of bodhisattvas, their wondrous perceptions, their deeds, and their parinirvana.[96] In response, the bodhisattva Samantabhadra taught, by means of tenfold exposition, the dharma called Perfect Cultivation of a Bodhisattva's Deeds. This caused countless world realms to shake and be filled with bright light. All the buddhas in the ten directions revealed their delighted faces to Samantabhadra and praised him greatly, saying, "Excellent!"

96. *Causal correspondence* refers to the causal relationship between the accumulation of merit by those on the path and their resultant physical and other qualities as buddhas and bodhisattvas.

Then Sudhana the merchant's son, who had achieved an inconceivable state like an ocean, like space, thirsted for the sight of the bodhisattva Samantabhadra. Sudhana sat there, gazing upon the tathagata's lion throne. Through the power of Sudhana's pure intentions, the blessings of all tathagatas, and Sudhana's harmony with the past virtues of the bodhisattva Samantabhadra, there occurred ten signs that Sudhana was about to see Samantabhadra. These included the purification of all buddha realms and their adornment by the ornamental sites of awakening; the eradication from all realms of unleisured states and bad migrations; the display of innumer-

able ornamental features and the purification of beings; and the appearance in every smallest particle in every realm of webs of light rays issuing from every tathagata. Sudhana saw ten such amazing, pervasive signs, and was then able to see the bodhisattva Samantabhadra. Sudhana felt that seeing Samantabhadra was like achieving omniscience. He saw that the bodhisattva Samantabhadra, in the tremendous power of his irreversible and inconceivable liberated state, was equal to all tathagatas; that he had realized the equality of the three times; that his state was inconceivable and impregnable; that his wisdom was boundless; that he embodied all bodhisattvas; that he surpassed all worlds; that he was followed by a vast mandala of followers; and that he was superior to others. Sudhana saw the bodhisattva Samantabhadra, surrounded by an ocean of bodhisattvas, seated on a lion throne and a great precious lotus in front of the bhagavat tathagata Vairochana.

Sudhana saw that from each pore on Samantabhadra's skin emerged light rays as numerous as the smallest particles in all world realms. They illuminated all the world realms throughout the dharmadhatu, pacifying beings' suffering. From the mandala of Samantabhadra's body emerged multicolored clouds of light as numerous as the smallest particles in all buddha realms, vastly increasing the joy and devotion of bodhisattvas. From Samantabhadra's head, shoulders, and pores emerged multicolored, radiant clouds emitting rains of fragrance that pervaded the mandalas of all tathagatas. From each of Samantabhadra's pores emerged clouds and rains of flowers, incense, bunting, colorful garlands, pearls, wish-fulfilling jewels, jewel trees, and the forms of the ruling devas of the form realm, the realm of Brahma, and the desire realm.

From his pores emerged clouds of spiritual leaders, reaching every pure and impure buddha realm; and clouds of buddhas surrounded by bodhisattvas, reaching every pure buddha realm. Samantabhadra emanated clouds of the bodies of all beings, clouds of bodhisattva bodies, and clouds of displays of

his own deeds. Each of these was as numerous as the smallest particles in all buddha realms. Each of them filled every realm throughout the dharmadhatu. They presented offerings and praises to all tathagatas, upheld their dharma, and ripened and liberated oceans of beings through various skillful means.

Seeing all this, Sudhana the merchant's son was delighted. He saw even more: He saw within the bodhisattva Samantabhadra's body, within each of his limbs, within every part of every one of his limbs, and within every pore on every part of his body, this entire realm of a billion worlds, from the mass of wind at its base to the form and formless realms at its peak. Sudhana saw the environment, its inhabitants, and time itself, like a reflected image within Samantabhadra. Sudhana saw not only this world realm but also all the world realms throughout the ten directions. He saw the coming of buddhas and their retinues of bodhisattvas. Sudhana saw within each of Samantabhadra's marks of a great being the entire history of this realm of Saha from its beginning, including the coming of every buddha and the appearance of every bodhisattva and ordinary being. He saw every buddha realm that will ever exist. He saw within each of Samantabhadra's marks and pores every world realm that has ever appeared or will ever appear in any of the ten directions, each appearing distinctly.

Sudhana saw that, just as Samantabhadra was seated before the tathagata Vairochana, he was seated before the tathagata Glorious Goodness in the eastern world-realm Glorious Lotus, and was similarly seated before every tathagata in every world realm in the ten directions. Sudhana saw that every smallest particle in every realm in the ten directions contained mandalas of buddhas, each as vast as the dharmadhatu. He saw that Samantabhadra was seated at ease on a lion throne and great lotus seat at the feet of every one of these tathagatas. Within each part of the body of each of these Samantabhadras appeared images of everything that has ever

happened or will ever happen anywhere. Sudhana saw every realm, every buddha, and every bodhisattva. He heard all the sounds of buddhas' voices, all the sounds made by beings, all the teachings given by all buddhas, all their dharmachakras, all the sounds of bodhisattvas bringing beings to perfection, and all the sounds of the deeds of all buddhas. Seeing and hearing Samantabhadra's miraculous display, Sudhana achieved the ten aspects of the paramita of primordial wisdom. He became able to fill all buddha realms with emanations of his own body in a single instant. He could simultaneously enter the presence of every tathagata, present offerings to them, and serve them. In a single instant, Sudhana directly and perfectly knew all of Samantabhadra's deeds.

Samantabhadra then placed his right hand on top of Sudhana's head. As soon as he did so, Sudhana entered as many samadhis as there are smallest particles in all buddha realms. In each of those samadhis he entered an ocean of previously unseen world realms as numerous as the smallest particles in all buddha realms. He encountered as many omniscient buddhas as fields of accumulation as there are smallest particles. He fully entered the dharma of each of them. He achieved omniscience, its path, its great power, and its superiority in the presence of each of them. As many oceans of aspiration, bodhisattva deeds, and radiant wisdoms of buddhahood as there are smallest particles in all buddha realms were revealed to him.

Just as the bodhisattva Samantabhadra in this world realm of Saha was seated in front of the tathagata Vairochana with his hand touching the top of Sudhana's head, in every world realm throughout the ten directions a Samantabhadra was seated in front of a tathagata. Within every smallest particle in each of those world realms were other world realms, and in each of those was a Samantabhadra seated in front of a tathagata. Each of these Samantabhadras was touching the

head of a Sudhana. Sudhana thus entered this great number of dharma gates.

Then the bodhisattva Samantabhadra said to Sudhana, "Son of family, you see my miraculous displays."

Sudhana replied, "Noble one, I do see them. Surely only a tathagata could count the number of your inconceivable miracles!"

Samantabhadra said, "Son of family, desiring omniscience I cultivated bodhichitta for as many kalpas as the smallest particles in countless buddha realms. During each of those kalpas I presented offerings to as many buddhas as the smallest particles in inexpressibly many buddha realms. I made that many aspirations. For the buddhadharma's sake I willingly gave away, during each of those kalpas, my head, limbs, body, and kingship as many times as the number of particles in all realms. I presented offerings that numerous to every one of that number of buddhas and upheld the holy dharma of all of them. During all those kalpas, I never gave rise to antipathy for any of those tathagatas' teachings. I never became angry. I never gave rise to a mind of self-fixation, self-cherishing, or dejection toward samsara. I gave rise to invincible bodhichitta and wisdom.

"Son of family, for the sake of perfection, ripening, and purification; and in order to guard holy dharma, I gave up my life so many times that even if I were to talk for an ocean of kalpas I would not finish telling you about them. For the sake of even a few words from those oceans of dharma, in order to protect all beings, and in order to perfect the buddhadharmas, I unhesitatingly gave up the throne and possessions of a chakravartin so many times that the telling of them would outlast an ocean of kalpas as numerous as the smallest particles in inexpressibly many buddha realms. Through the strength of my accumulation, roots of virtue, devotion, wis-

dom, compassion, training by spiritual friends, aspirations, diligence, supercognition, and understanding of all dharmas; and through the blessings of the tathagatas, I achieved a pure dharmakaya that does not change through time. My unsurpassable rupakaya, elevated above all the world, conforms to the wishes and ideas of all beings. I remain present in all buddha realms. I am everywhere. I display all miracles. I am able to please all beings.

"Son of family, my body is perfect. It is the result of countless oceans of kalpas of training. Its like is rarely seen in even septillion kalpas. Look upon it! Son of family, if I am unheard of by beings without virtue, what need is there to say that they do not see me? Any being who hears my name becomes irreversible from unsurpassable, perfect awakening. Any being who sees me, touches me, emulates me, sees me in a dream, or hears my name in a dream becomes irreversible from unsurpassable awakening. Beings who think of me for one day will be ripened. Beings who recollect me for seven days, a month, a year, a kalpa, or as many kalpas as the smallest particles in countless buddha realms will be ripened. Some beings are ripened by recollecting me for one life. Some are ripened by recollecting me for as many lives as the smallest particles in inexpressibly many buddha realms. Some are ripened by seeing the light rays I emit, some by seeing me cause realms to shake, some by seeing my form, and some by being delighted by me. Through as many diverse means as the smallest particles in all buddha realms I make beings irreversible from unsurpassable awakening. Son of family, anyone who hears of my pure buddha realm will be born in it. Anyone who sees my pure body will be born with a body like mine. Therefore son of family, look upon my pure body!"

Then Sudhana the merchant's son thought about the bodhisattva Samantabhadra's body. Sudhana saw within each of Samantabhadra's pores oceans of buddha realms. Within

them he saw countless oceans of buddhas with their retinues of bodhisattvas. The ground, shape, and features of these realms were diverse. Sudhana saw the environments of these realms, their clouds and skies, the birth of buddhas within them, and their diverse dharmachakras. Everything Sudhana saw within each of Samantabhadra's pores he saw within all his other pores, within each of his physical marks and signs, and within each of his limbs and digits. From each of these oceans of realms were emitted clouds of emanated buddhas as numerous as the smallest particles in all buddha realms, filling all ten directions and ripening beings into awakening.

Then through the bodhisattva Samantabhadra's instructions, Sudhana the merchant's son entered all of the worlds within the bodhisattva Samantabhadra's body and ripened beings. Reflecting on all this, Sudhana saw that all the brilliant wisdom and roots of virtue he had acquired through seeing and serving as many spiritual friends as the number of smallest particles of all buddha realms did not equal a hundredth, a thousandth, or even a hundred thousandth part of the virtue of seeing Samantabhadra. Starting with his initial generation of bodhichitta and up to his seeing Samantabhadra, Sudhana had passed through oceans of buddha realms. Nevertheless the number of buddha realms he entered within any one of Samantabhadra's pores was greater. In a single instant, Sudhana entered as many buddha realms as there are smallest particles in countless buddha realms. In every instant, Sudhana simultaneously entered as many buddha realms within every pore on Samantabhadra's body as there are smallest particles in countless buddha realms. The instants of mind during which Sudhana did so seemed to last, through Samantabhadra's blessing, until the end of time. Even though Sudhana entered oceans of world realms in this way, he did not reach the end of the oceans of realms within Samantabhadra's body. Sudhana did not exhaust the variety of the diverse realms' sizes, shapes, coming together, creation,

or destruction; the variety of buddhas who appeared within these realms with their retinues of bodhisattvas; the variety of beings, ways of ripening the diverse faculties of all these beings, or the variety of the profound miracles of bodhisattvas in these realms.

Sudhana remained within some of these realms without leaving them for a hundred kalpas, and within some for as many kalpas as the number of countless buddha realms. In each instant of mind Sudhana ripened the beings within countless realms. Finally, he equaled the deeds and oceans of aspirations of the bodhisattva Samantabhadra. He became the equal of all tathagatas. He equally filled all realms with his bodies. He equally filled all realms with the miraculous display of manifest buddhahood. Sudhana turned the dharmachakra equally within all realms. He achieved perfect individual knowledge; melodious speech; all aspects of euphony; the strengths, fearlessnesses, and deeds of buddhahood; great love; great compassion; and all the inconceivable miraculous displays of bodhisattvas.

Then the bodhisattva Samantabhadra melodiously recited in verse his aspiration to the deeds of ubiquitous goodness in order to describe their extent in time, throughout endless kalpas; and space, throughout as many world realms as the number of smallest particles in inexpressibly many buddha realms.

From the *Compassionate White Lotus Sutra*

The eighth of King Nemi's sons, Ahimsa, said to the tathagata Ratnagarbha, "Venerable bhagavat, I will engage in the deeds of a bodhisattva within a myriad of afflicted buddha realms until I can transform them all into pure realms like the buddha realm Stainless Fragrant Light that my seventh brother, the prince and bodhisattva Lion Incense, will create. Through my roots of virtue and pure intentions, may I remain

a bodhisattva until I fill all those realms with bodhisattvas immersed in the mahayana. May I engage in the deeds of a bodhisattva in afflicted buddha realms and thereby achieve the unsurpassable awakening of buddhahood. Bhagavat, I will engage in conduct beyond what any other bodhisattva has ever done! Bhagavat, for the last seven years I have remained in solitude contemplating the pure qualities of buddhas and bodhisattvas and the pure qualities of buddha realms. I have achieved twenty-one thousand bodhisattva samadhis, such as the samadhi called Radiant Display. Venerable bhagavat, these are my bodhisattva deeds.

"May I see all the bhagavat buddhas who reside in all the innumerable world realms throughout the ten directions, teaching dharma in order to ripen and help beings. May I also see and enter the buddha realm called Victory Banner Peak Bracelet, which perfectly transcends the three times and is filled with victors. Through samadhi, may I see as many bhagavat buddhas, surrounded by their retinues of bodhisattvas and shravakas, as the number of smallest particles. Through the power of samadhi may I be unlimited by location and prostrate to each of those buddhas with as many bodies as there are smallest particles in all buddha realms. May each of those bodies offer each of those buddhas the finest jewels, diverse flowers, incense, flower garlands, powders, ointments, and musical sounds. May I be able to remain in any one buddha realm for as many kalpas as the number of sand grains in an ocean. Through the samadhi of the Body's Destruction, may I be present in a single instant before as many buddhas as the number of smallest particles in all buddha realms. Through the samadhi called Origin of Qualities, may I praise each of those buddhas with as many unsurpassable praises as there are smallest particles in all buddha realms. Through the samadhi of Open Eyes may I see in every instant all buddha realms — each filled with buddhas — atop every particle. Through my samadhi free from kleshas may I see at every sin-

gle instant all the bodhisattvas of the past, present, and future within all buddha realms and all the features of those realms.

"Through my heroic samadhi may I enter the hells with the emanated body of a hell being, teach dharma to beings in the hells, inspiring them to seek perfect awakening and generate bodhichitta. May those beings, after their deaths, be reborn as humans where buddhas reside, hear dharma from them, and achieve irreversibility. May I similarly teach dharma to animals, pretas, yakshas, rakshasas, asuras, nagas, nonhumans, great serpents, carnivorous spirits, ghouls, rotten-bodied spirits, human outcasts, merchants, and prostitutes, placing them in irreversibility. May I emanate bodies like those of diverse beings, that are born however those beings are born, that experience pleasure and pain through whatever causes that type of being to experience pleasure and pain, and that exhibit attachment to whatever arts and work those beings are attached to. In those bodies may I display diligence in those arts and employments and speak those beings' languages. Pleasing them, may I teach them dharma, inspire them to seek unsurpassable awakening, and place them in irreversibility.

"Venerable bhagavat, I will continue the deeds of a bodhisattva until all the beings in a myriad of buddha realms in each of the ten directions have exhausted all of their karma and kleshas, until not even one being is oppressed by the four maras, until the continuums of all beings have been purified. Therefore may I make a myriad of buddha realms as pure as Array of Stainless Fragrant Light, the buddha realm of the tathagata Star King of Stainless Fragrant Light. In the same way, may my buddha realm and my retinue be just like those aspired to by the bodhisattva Lion Incense.

"Venerable bhagavat, if my hopes are going to be fulfilled, may all the suffering of all the beings in all the buddha realms throughout the ten directions be pacified now. May the minds of all beings become pliable and workable. May they see each

buddha in his own setting. May all those beings have and offer to those buddhas diverse jewels, flowers, incense, ointments, powders, parasols, victory banners, and flags. May all those beings then generate bodhichitta. Bhagavat, through the radiant display of my samadhi, may I see all this happen."

As soon as Ahimsa said those words, everything he had wished for occurred. He saw it happen. The bhagavat Ratnagarbha said, "Son of family, excellent, excellent! Son of family, you will create a myriad of pure buddha realms within the perimeter of your buddha realm. You will purify the continuums of countless beings. You will enthusiastically present countless offerings to countless buddhas. Son of family, may you therefore be known as Samantabhadra. Samantabhadra, after novemdecillion kalpas, as many as the number of sand grains in the Ganges River, at the beginning of another period of novemdecillion kalpas, you will achieve buddhahood. You will become the unsurpassable samyaksambuddha Ruling Peak Graceful Wisdom Vajra. This will occur in the world realm Qualities of Utterly Pure Wisdom Water, as many buddha realms to the north of our buddha realm as there are sand grains in sixty Ganges Rivers."

THE EIGHTH CHAPTER: THE SUPREME ARYA
SAMANTABHADRA

Feeling even slight admiration for these deeds of the eight mahabodhisattvas is the ground of immeasurable virtue. Based on admiration, we develop the aspiration to do what they have done. That wish is the root of the mahayana path. We also need to know that it is impossible to become a buddha without emulating the oceans of feats of bodhisattvas.

Through aspiration we correctly enter the path. Our faith in the mahayana path and its result become indestructibly strong. We gradually become equal to these children of the victors, the mahabodhisattvas. Finally, we will achieve omniscient wisdom.

For the sake of inspiration, I, Mipham Nampar Gyalwa, have collected these stories about the heart sons, the eight mahabodhisattvas, taking them from the precious treasury of the tathagata's perfect words. May all beings throughout space become equal to the eight bodhisattvas and possess all their qualities!

May I and all others become just like
The eight great heart-sons in their bodhichitta,
Deeds, aspirations, wisdom, love, capability,
And unsurpassable miracles of primordial wisdom.

Virtue! Mangalam!

Acknowledgments

We would like to thank Bardor Tulku Rinpoche for inspiring this translation, Khenpo Karthar Rinpoche for his foreword, Chökyong Radha for his calligraphies, Wendy Harding for her beautiful illustrations, Stephanie Colvey for the photograph of His Holiness Karmapa, and Sally Clay and Florence Wetzel for their fine editorial work.

Yeshe Gyamtso
Maureen McNicholas
Peter van Deurzen

Karma Triyana Dharmachakra

Karma Triyana Dharmachakra (KTD) is the North American seat of His Holiness the Gyalwang Karmapa, and under the spiritual guidance and protection of His Holiness Ogyen Trinley Dorje, the Seventeenth Gyalwang Karmapa, is devoted to the authentic representation of the Kagyu lineage of Tibetan Buddhism.

For information regarding KTD, including our current schedule, or for information regarding our affiliate centers, Karma Thegsum Choling (KTCs), located both in the United States and internationally, contact us using the information below. If you would like to make a donation to KTD, contact Development.

Karma Triyana Dharmachakra
335 Meads Mountain Road
Woodstock, NY, 12498 USA
845 679 5906 ext. 10
www.kagyu.org
Development: 845 679 5906 ext 38
development@kagyu.org
KTC Coordinator: 845 679 5701
ktc@kagyu.org

KTD Publications

Gathering the garlands of the gurus' precious teachings

KTD Publications, a part of Karma Triyana Dharmachakra, is a not-for-profit publisher established with the purpose of facilitating the projects and activities manifesting from His Holiness Karmapa's inspiration and blessings. We are dedicated to gathering the garlands of precious teachings and producing fine-quality books.

We invite you to join KTD Publications in facilitating the activities of His Holiness Karmapa and fulfilling the wishes of Khenpo Karthar Rinpoche and Bardor Tulku Rinpoche. If you would like to sponsor a book or make a donation to KTD Publications, please contact us using the information below. All contributions are tax deductible.

KTD Publications
335 Meads Mountain Road
Woodstock, NY 12498 USA
Telephone: 845 679 5906 ext. 37
maureen@ktdpublications.org
www.KTDPublications.org

Also from www.KTDPublications.org

Amrita of Eloquence: A Biography of Khenpo Karthar Rinpoche, by Lama Karma Drodül, translated by Yeshe Gyamtso, 2009

Thirty-Seven Practices of a Bodhisattva, Within Our Reach, by Ngülchu Thogme, Commentary by the 17th Karmapa, Ogyen Trinley Dorje, translated by Ringu Tulku Rinpoche, root text translated by Michele Martin A publication of *Densal* (Volume 19, Number 1)

The Quintessence of the Union of Mahamudra and Dzokchen, by Karma Chakme Rinpoche, commentary by Khenpo Karthar Rinpoche, translated by Yeshe Gyamtso, 2008

The Kagyu Monlam Book, the 17th Gyalwang Karmapa, Ogyen Trinley Dorje, English, Tibetan, transliteration, 2007

Karma Chakme's Mountain Dharma as Taught by Khenpo Karthar Rinpoche, Five-volume set: *Volume One*, 2005; *Volume Two*, 2006; *Volume Three*, 2008; *Volume Four*, 2009; and *Volume Five* [Tibetan text], 2009

Treasury of Eloquence: The Songs of Barway Dorje, translated by Yeshe Gyamtso, 2007

A Ceremony of Offering to the Gurus, the 17th Gyalwang Karmapa, Ogyen Trinley Dorje, India, 2006; USA, 2007

The Dalai Lama in Woodstock: Celebrating the United Nations International Day of Peace, full color photo book, 2007

Nyima Tashi: The Songs and Instructions of the First Traleg Kyabgön Rinpoche, translated by Yeshe Gyamtso, English and Tibetan, 2006

Chariot of the Fortunate: The Life of the First Yongey Mingyur Dorje, by Je Tukyi Dorje and Surmang Tendzin Rinpoche, translated by Yeshe Gyamtso, English and Tibetan, 2006

Bardo: Interval of Possibility, by Chokyi Wangchuk, commentary by Khenpo Karthar Rinpoche, translated by Yeshe Gyamtso, 2006

The Vajra Garland, The Lotus Garden: Treasure Biographies of Padmakara and Vairochana, by Jamgön Lodrö Taye, translated by Yeshe Gyamtso, 2005

Precious Essence: The Inner Autobiography of Terchen Barway Dorje, translated by Yeshe Gyamtso, 2005

MAY ALL BEINGS BE HAPPY